CHAUCERIAN PLAY

CHAUCERIAN PLAY

Comedy and Control
in the Canterbury Tales

LAURA KENDRICK

UNIVERSITY OF CALIFORNIA PRESS
BERKELEY   LOS ANGELES   LONDON

University of California Press
Berkeley and Los Angeles, California

University of California Press, Ltd.
London, England

© 1988 by
The Regents of the University of California

Library of Congress Cataloging-in-Publication Data

Kendrick, Laura.
  Chaucerian play: comedy and control in the Canterbury
tales / Laura Kendrick.
    p.   cm.
  Includes index.
  ISBN 0-520-06194-2 (alk. paper)
  1. Chaucer, Geoffrey, d. 1400. Canterbury tales.
2. Chaucer, Geoffrey, d. 1400—Humor, satire, etc.
3. Play in literature.   4. Comic, The, in literature.   I. Title.
PR1875.P55K46   1988   821'.1—dc19   87-20889

Printed in the United States of America

1 2 3 4 5 6 7 8 9

The Appendix appeared, in slightly different form, as "The
Troilus Frontispiece and the Dramatization of Chaucer's Troilus," The Chaucer Review 22, no. 2 (1987). Reprinted by per-
mission of the Pennsylvania State University Press.

for Gilles

Contents

Illustrations

Acknowledgments

I have rewritten this book several times over the course of several years and am most grateful to those who saw something of value in it in the first place and then bore with me while I changed virtually everything about the book except its title. These people are the late Donald Howard, who was my first Press reader, and Doris Kretschmer of the University of California Press. I am also grateful to Anne Middleton for strong encouragement with the manuscript at a crucially early date, as well as to Betsy Bowden, Susan Crane, Alfred David, Sheila Delany, Gilles Delavaud, Edwin M. Eigner, John H. Fisher, Leo Steinberg, John Warner, and Christian Zacher for criticizing and encouraging me with versions or pieces of *Chaucerian Play*. If it were possible, I would like here to discharge my debt of gratitude to the teachers whose interests have helped to shape my own: at Columbia, Joan Ferrante, Robert Hanning, W. T. H. Jackson, Meyer Schapiro; at the University of Illinois, Joseph Trahern and Leon Waldoff. The Rutgers Research Council has supported art-historical research and helped me to buy photographs and permissions necessary to my first chapter. Finally, I would like to thank Rose Vekony and Jane-Ellen Long for producing and copyediting this book with such care and efficiency.

The function of the poet still remains fixed in the play-sphere where it was born. Poiesis, in fact, is a play-function. It proceeds within the playground of the mind, in a world of its own which the mind creates for it. There things have a very different physiognomy from the one they wear in "ordinary life," and are bound by ties other than those of logic and causality. If a serious statement be defined as one that may be made in terms of waking life, poetry will never rise to the level of seriousness. It lies beyond seriousness, on that more primitive and original level where the child, the animal, the savage and the seer belong, in the region of dream, enchantment, ecstasy, laughter. To understand poetry we must be capable of donning the child's soul like a magic cloak and of forsaking man's wisdom for the child's.

Johan Huizinga, *Homo Ludens*

Laughter, Play, and Fiction

Baudelaire links man's sense of humor to the Fall: "the comic is one of the clearest signs of the devil in man and one of the numerous seeds contained in the symbolic apple."[1] Laughter is man's way of asserting his superiority or mastery in difficult situations, his way of dealing with the F/fall, that is, with his knowledge of his own imperfection, his ignorance and weakness. Laughter denies the reality or seriousness of whatever threatens to immobilize man's mind or body, whether this comes in the form of an aggressive gesture or word or in that of a seemingly unresolvable incongruity or challenging violation of conventions, such as a riddle or a grotesque drawing. Laughter is a metalinguistic sign, a framing "no" that reverses the meaning of all the signs within its bounds. In its assertion "this is not real," laughter is related to play of all sorts, including literary play or fiction, which denies everyday reality in order to replace it with a deliberately distorting mimesis. As Baudelaire observed, laughter is contradictory, acknowledging weakness by its very assertion of strength. Nevertheless, from a hard-line Christian ascetic viewpoint, laughter was worse than indecorous; it was subversive, egotistical, foolish. And so was fiction. Chaucer's Parson, quoting St. Paul, refuses the Host's request for a "fable," because fiction is pretense and lies and thus no better than chaff:

> "Thou getest fable noon ytoold for me,
> For Paul, that writeth unto Thymothee,
> Repreveth hem that weyven soothfastnesse
> And tellen fables and swich wrecchednesse.

Why sholde I sowen draf out of my fest,
When I may sowen whete, if that me lest?"
                                              (I 31–36) [2]

The Bible flatly discouraged laughter by associating it with a lack of wisdom or prudence. The fool raises his voice in laughter, but the wise man laughs silently, if at all ("Fatuus in risu exaltat vocem suam: vir autem sapiens vix tacite ridebit," Ecclesiastes 21:23). And it is only that archetypally "unaccommodated man," the fool, who denies God (Psalms 13:1, 52:1). [3]

Yet in spite of the Church's serious doctrinal approach, we find plenty of medieval Christians laughing—and not always when we might have expected them to laugh. Millard Meiss was surprised to find, for example, that "there is no trace of guilt, or persistent sadness, or asceticism in the entire work" of Boccaccio's *Decameron,* although it was written immediately after the Black Plague destroyed the fabric of Florentine society, as Boccaccio so vividly describes in his preface. [4] After such a chastening experience, why did Boccaccio laugh instead of writing a work that was even more devout than usual, a work to humble man and exalt God and the saints, such as contemporary artists were painting? Why did Chaucer end the "tragedy" of the immobilized lover, Troilus, by giving him one last laugh of superiority as he looks down after death at "this little spot of earth" and men's blind pursuit of their desires there? And why does Chaucer's writing move in the direction it does, toward the "comedy" of the *Canterbury Tales,* toward laughter? Is he just being devilish or "elvish"—or are we, to perceive humor where we should not—or is it more complicated than that? What are the mechanisms and meanings of medieval mirth, and, more especially, of Chaucer's literary play?

These are the questions I will explore in the present book, which will draw upon analyses of human behavior from modern psychological, psychoanalytic, and anthropological studies as well as upon historical interpretations of medieval culture and descriptions of medieval festive games. Perhaps the best attitude with which to read this book is a quizzical one involving some willing suspension of disbelief. By my incongruous analogies, drawing together phenomena usually treated by various academic disciplines, traditionally considered in different contextual frames, I intend to solve problems, not to provoke a throwing up of hands in self-defensive laughter at such disorienting, "grotesque" comparisons. The questions I am asking are important, even fundamental: what was medieval literature (of the sort that defined itself as fiction or play) for? What did its creators and performers and its audience do with it? What can we do with it? A child given a new toy asks, implicitly, these same questions. First the child explores the toy's given capacities (to roll, to beep . . .); then it explores further and invents capacities for which the toy was not intended (by stacking blocks on a toy car, for instance); finally the child *plays* with the car in a sort of compromise between ways it was made for and ways it was not, both making the toy peculiarly the child's own and accepting its given usages. Ought we not to do the same with Chaucer's literary texts? Indeed, I doubt that we could do otherwise, even if we wanted. But what we can do is become more conscious of the *re-creational* process we go through—and that medieval audiences, including authors re-creating texts, went through—in appropriating the new literary object.

Huizinga in *Homo Ludens;* Clifford Geertz in his study of cockfighting in Bali; Freud in his analysis of little Hans's game of "fort/ da," as well as in *Civilization and Its Discontents* and other writings; Melanie Klein, Jean Piaget, and other analysts of children's play;[5] Boccaccio, and, as we shall see, Chaucer, in the metacommentaries with which they framed their fictions—all understood, albeit in different terms, something of the meaningful *depths* of play and how man's creation and identification with unreal, fictional worlds helps him, not only to cope with the real world, but also to change himself and thereby, to some extent, the world. Play enables man to sublimate and channel his dangerous desires and to master his anxieties as he expresses these or sees them expressed in the safe, ordered "other world" of the game via transforming, controlling fictions comparable to Freud's idea of the dream-work or joke-work or, we might add, to art-work.[6] Virtually all types of play turn life temporarily into art. It is, indeed, not too much to claim, as Huizinga did, that culture arises from play, or that civilization rests on fiction.

The legacies of science have not always been comforting. One that we currently live with, the atomic bomb and the nuclear arms race, may produce as much general anxiety as the Black Death did in the late fourteenth century. We have invented fictions to help us deal with our feelings of powerlessness in the face of these weapons that could destroy the future of humanity, just as we have always invented fictions to help us deal with wars and natural catastrophes. As opposed to the legacies of science, those of art—the arts—have always been comforting, although we have not always understood how their consolation works or the degree to which it may protect us from or reconcile us to the very powers we fear. It is essential that artists go on producing art of all kinds, because we are more than ever in need of consolation. However, it is also important to understand how the consolation of different kinds of fictional structures—of play—works.

Chapter One

Reading for *Sentence* versus Reading for *Solas*

A Broadening Example

"An housbonde shal nat been inquisityf
Of Goddes pryvetee, nor of his wyf.
So he may fynde Goddes foyson there,
Of the remenant nedeth nat enquere."
(A 3163–66)

These lines from the "Miller's Prologue," which serve as a prefacing moral to his fabliau, used to seem dangerous to teach to under-
graduates. After I had explained the double meaning of *pryvetee* as
"secret intentions" or "private parts" (a euphemism for "sex organs") and pointed out what this meant in terms of a husband's
dealings with his wife—not to bother himself about whether he is
being cuckolded as long as he is getting enough sex—I would rush
on to the next lines before some perverse student had the chance to
pose the unseemly question I was trying to suppress of whether
the Miller was making a joke about God's genitals too: "An housbonde shal nat been inquisityf / Of *Goddes* pryvetee, nor of his
wif." The flimsy loincloth of *pryvetee* as euphemism seemed even
more lewd than the broken verbal taboo that gave Christine de
Pisan so much grief in *The Romance of the Rose:* Reason's outright
naming of the testicles of Saturn, father of the pagan gods.[1] Surely
Chaucer could not have intended that such a blasphemous innuendo raise its ugly head? Or could he?

What of the gigantically grotesque sign that hangs suspended over much of the action of the "Miller's Tale": two round containers and an oblong one, each big enough to hold a person, the "knedyng trogh," "tub," and "kymelyn" (A 3620–21) that the foolish carpenter hangs from the rafters of his house "in pryvetee" (3623)?[2] If the oblong trough were hung parallel to the ground, which it would have to be to serve as a boat, what would this trinity of containers look like from underneath? Might the carpenter's installation not look like the crude figure of huge male genitals in erection, a burlesque, carnivalesque version of "Goddes pryvetee," provisioned by the carpenter with "plenty" of bread and cheese and good ale?

Was I the only one to perceive such a blasphemous allusion? No, but not many scholars had mentioned it in print. There was Joseph Baird:

as a result of the ambiguity of *pryvetee* and contamination from the context, the "mysteries" of God leeringly invites the lewd, anthropomorphic "God's private parts."

Roy Peter Clark suggested more firmly the possibility of a deliberate innuendo:

Chaucer plays with the phrase "Goddes pryvetee." On one level the phrase means that Nicholas should not be concerned with astrological lore that seeks to detect the mysteries of God (God's private affairs). But the juxtaposition of *God* and *wife* in this sentence implies that the tale also concerns God's sex life (His private love affairs). So if the religious parody in the tale exalts the low-life characters of Oxford, it concomitantly humbles and despiritualizes God.

Paula Neuss, however, took away with one hand what she offered with the other:

We need not necessarily assume, incidentally, that the Miller intends any blasphemous reference to *God's* private parts (being so concerned with woman's), although this kind of pun is not without its parallels. In one of the most tender of mediaeval religious lyrics, *Amice Christi, Johannes,* occur the lines

> For thou were so clene a may
> The *prevites* of Hevene forsothe thou say
> Whan on Christes brest thou lay,
> Amice Christi, Johannes.[3]

Although I had some, not very reassuring, contemporary company in suspecting a subversively burlesque allusion to God's sex or his sex life in the proverbial-sounding introductory moral of the "Miller's Tale," my doubts about the possibility of a deliberate innuendo of this nature led to research on the historical contexts for interpretation of these lines, research motivated partly by inquisitiveness, partly by a desire to pass the buck. It would have been most satisfying to pass it to the author, but Chaucer explicitly refused it by voicing these words through the mouth of his churlish Miller persona and calling attention to this dodge:

> And therfore every gentil wight I preye,
> For Goddes love, demeth nat that I seye
> Of yvel entente, but for I moot reherce
> Hir tales alle, be they bettre or werse,
> Or elles falsen som of my mateere.
> And therfore, whoso list it nat yheere,
> Turne over the leef and chese another tale.
>
> (A 3171–77)

So be it. The burden of responsibility for the meaning of Chaucer's text would fall upon the reader, but I could shift blame too. Let the responsibility fall on the *medieval* interpreter, a species to which Chaucer-the-man belonged. In speaking of one I might almost be speaking of the other. The ambiguity of reference could be quite useful; the medieval interpreter is not exactly Chaucer, but is not exactly me either. Rather, the medieval interpreter is one of my personae, *not* me, as the Miller is *not* Chaucer. If Chaucer could play all the roles in his fiction and deny that he was playing them, I could play a similar game in interpreting—replaying—his fiction, imagining myself as "Chaucer" or the "medieval interpreter" or "the Miller" . . . anyone, of course, but the "real me." First, then, to play the "medieval interpreter" I had to prove that the context of medieval interpretation would have allowed or, even better, encouraged understanding of "Goddes pryvetee" not only as God's secrets but also as his private parts.

Medieval interpreters, I assume, behaved like us; they would understand the Miller's advice by contextualizing it, weaving it in their own minds into preexisting patterns of meaning: other written texts, sermons, drama and the visual arts, proverbial wisdom, religious and secular rituals and customs, and all the other patterns of signs, the designs that made up the fabric of medieval life. We call these patterns of meaning "historical" contexts because they survive for us mainly, though not solely, in the written texts of an earlier age. Investigation of historical contexts for interpretation would not, however, immediately allow me to shift the blame for the blasphemous innuendo to the medieval reader, because such investigation, by itself, does not pin down the variable of the individual interpreter's intentions—how he chooses to weave text and context(s) together and make sense of them. Although many of the larger interpretive contexts for a late-fourteenth-century English person would be the same, others would differ according to locality, social class, gender, age, and the like. The fabric of a miller's life and mind, for instance, would surely be different from a knight's, and so the two were likely, even without willing it, to put different emphases on their interpretations—of love, for example. But just as important as these socially determined differences of experience, and hence of understanding, are differences of individual choice, deliberate differences of intention. In the theoretical (but virtually impossible) situation that the contexts within which two medieval interpreters approached a text were exactly the same, one man might imagine a contrastive relation between text and context, the other a complementary relation; one, consonance; the other, dissonance.

Gentility—or its opposite, churlishness—is a matter of individual intention and not of social origin. Chaucer makes this point in his ballad on "Gentilesse" and again in the "Wife of Bath's Tale" (albeit through several superimposed personae).[4] He who thinks, speaks, and acts like a gentleman is one; he who thinks, speaks, and acts like a churl is a churl. Virtue directs the interpretations of the gentleman; vice, those of the churl. Right after "rehearsing" the Miller's proverb about "Goddes pryvetee," Chaucer defends himself by giving paramount importance to the reader's intentions, reminding us that gentle is as gentle reads:

> And therfore every gentil wight I preye,
> For Goddes love, demeth nat that I seye
> Of yvel entente . . .
>
> .   .   .   .
>
> Turne over the leef and chese another tale;
> For he shal fynde ynowe, grete and smale,

> Of storial thyng that toucheth gentillesse,
> And eek moralitee and hoolynesse.
> Blameth nat me if that ye chese amys.
> The Millere is a cherl; ye knowe wel this.
>
> . . . .
>
> Avyseth yow, and put me out of blame;
> And eek men shal nat maken ernest of game.
>
> (A 3171–86)

Gentle readers—that is, those bent on demonstrating their gentility by practicing St. Paul's (or St. Paul's school's)[5] dictum and
interpreting everything into moral or religious doctrine—should
not touch the "Miller's Tale," for they will find no morality and
holiness there, unless they "falsen" the "mateere" and make earnest out of game. This Chaucer commands them not to do ("men
shal nat maken ernest of game"), thereby suggesting that "gentils"
are prone to do precisely that.

    Clearly I could not pass the buck for perception of a joke about
God's private parts to "gentils," no matter how much the historical
contexts in which they interpreted "Goddes pryvetee" overlapped
that of "churls." Even if "gentils" did perceive the innuendo, they
would censor it in order to "take the morality," as good men
should, leaving the chaff of the sexual innuendo. They might read
the Miller's advice in one of several possible contexts that would
help to point a moral warning against the search for forbidden or
dangerous knowledge. For example, in the context of popular
wisdom, "gentil" medieval readers might understand the Miller's
proverb as a warning not to go looking for trouble (as B. J. Whiting
glossed it).[6] Why should what is kept secret mean trouble? Because
if it were lawful and harmless, it would not be kept hidden. This is
the logic of common sense. In the late fourteenth century, the
words *privetee, privy,* and *privily* did not yet have the positive, indi-
vidualistic connotations of our word *private.*[7] Instead, in most of
the contexts where it appears in Chaucer's texts and elsewhere, the
word *privy* and its forms signal malevolent intentions or individual
desires dangerous to others or to the common good. In the "Miller's
Tale," this holds true not only for the "sleigh and ful privee"
Nicholas (A 3201), who "prively" catches Alison "by the queynte"
(A 3276) and puts his own "ers" "pryvely" out the window (A
3802), but even for God. The hoked-up divine "pryvetee" (A

3558) that Nicholas reveals to Alison's gullible old husband is God's intention to break His promise and destroy the world a second time by water. A "gentil" medieval interpreter might also understand the Miller's proverb more specifically in terms of the Fall, which was precipitated in the plenty of paradise ("Goddes foyson") by husband Adam's excessive curiosity about God's secrets and his own wife's—after she first tasted the apple from the forbidden tree of knowledge and tempted him with it.[8]

A "gentil" medieval interpreter might also hear in the Miller's advice echoes of the warnings of contemporary mystics such as the anchoress Juliana of Norwich. The personal revelations of late medieval mystics (which do nothing so much as pry into God's secret meanings and intentions and the private life of the Holy Family) were hedged about with denials and warnings against curiosity such as the following by Juliana: "For I saw verely in our lordes menyng, the more we besy us to know hys prevytes in that or any other thyng, the ferthermore shalle we be from the knowyng."[9] Given the Miller's earlier characterization of his story as a "legende and a lyf / Bothe of a carpenter and of his wyf" (A 3141–42), the "gentil" medieval reader might perceive an allusion to the troubles of St. Joseph in the "husband who ought not to be inquisitive about God's secrets or those of his wife." Joseph's difficulties in surmounting his suspicions against his wife Mary—who kept God's secret until God himself revealed to Joseph in a dream that He had impregnated her—were treated at length in the *Protoevangelium of James* and interpreted in sermons, drama, and visual arts of the late medieval period, especially in works inspired by the revelations of mystics and the piety of mendicants.[10]

So much for "gentle," moralizing interpretations of "Goddes pryvetee." My only hope for shifting blame from my own shoulders to those of the medieval interpreter must lie with "churls" such as Chaucer's Miller. But if it is so hard to acknowledge a joke about God's private parts today, could even the most churlish of medieval churls do so? We know that medieval people joked about the devil's *pryvetee,* especially in a scatological sense. The devil himself does this at the end of the "Friar's Tale" when he promises the summoner, "Thou shalt with me to helle yet tonyght, / Where thou shalt knowen of oure privetee / Moore than a maister of dyvynytee" (D 1636–38). The Summoner on the pilgrimage im-

mediately elucidates this scatological innuendo and turns the tables
on his rival by painting a verbal picture of the place of friars in hell,
where they nest like a swarm of bees in the devil's anus (D 1689–
99). In the Middle Ages,the devil's *pryvetee* was not off limits as a
comic subject, but God's would seem to be another matter. The
Romans might make jokes of Jupiter's *amores* by miming them at
their spring Floralia games,[11] but was it not dangerous for medieval Christian "churls" to do that with God the Father? We know
what happened to Noah's son Ham for looking at the nakedness of
his Old Testament father: his lineage was cursed and enslaved.[12]
Were there any historical contexts that would enable or encourage
such profanation of the Holy of Holies? Did medieval writers discuss God's private parts or artists depict them? Was this as un-
thinkable to the medieval mind as to the modern one?

Leo Steinberg's *Sexuality of Christ* provided much-needed information: God the Father's private parts were as taboo in the late
fourteenth century as today; however, God the Son's were at this
very time suddenly being depicted and even stressed in visual art.[13]
This was as true in England, France, and Bohemia (Queen Anne's
homeland) as in northern Italy. The late-fourteenth-century de-
nudation of God the Son was a pan-European phenomenon. My
survey of medieval images of the Madonna and Child and the Holy
Family, based in part on Steinberg's pioneering study, showed that
"Goddes pryvetee" really was newly on display in the late fourteenth century, to both doctrinal and "solacious" intents.

The fixed iconography of the standard Byzantine Madonna and
Child long resisted humanizing changes; the type known as the
Throne of Wisdom was rigidly frontal, austere, commanding.
Gradually, over the course of the thirteenth century, Christ's body
shifts from this monumental frontal pose toward individualizing,
historicizing profile.[14] The Child's hemlines also go up, baring the
flesh of his lower body to verify his incarnation. First Christ's feet
(symbol of the flesh) are bared, with the Madonna sometimes
holding one foot in her hand (Fig. 1); then his legs are bared to the
knee (Fig. 2); then his garments begin to part to the groin (Fig. 3).

Nothing happens in such paintings without a doctrinal reason. In
one example from around 1280 (Fig. 4), the Child's spread legs, the
opening of the clasped garment almost to the groin, the Madonna's
hand drawing additional attention to the Child's hidden private

parts, which are implicitly in the visual center of the picture—all
suggest that the artist intended to offer a bodily equivalent to the
open scroll the Christ Child holds in one hand. St. Paul in Second
Corinthians says that the veil of the Old Testament is taken away
in Christ. That is, God's true meaning is revealed in the Incarnation; everything in the Old Testament may now be understood
with reference to Christ: "But their minds were blinded: for until
this day remaineth the same vail untaken away in the reading of the
old testament; which vail is done away in Christ. But even unto
this day, when Moses is read, the vail is upon their heart. Nevertheless, when it shall turn to the Lord, the vail shall be taken away"
(2 Cor. 14–16). In this late-thirteenth-century painting, while the
scroll in Christ's hand falls open, the clasped *text* of his garment
opens nearly to his phallus in the process of revealing a fleshly *pryvetee* that symbolizes God's hitherto hidden intentions, that "is"
the Word made flesh. This iconography is *highly serious.* Here we
see being formulated, in the late Middle Ages, a very powerful
myth of a central presence that fills, orients, and stabilizes language. This Italian master is fairly discreet, stopping short of total
fleshly revelation; other more prudish artists, even in the fourteenth century, modified their visual metaphors by placing an
open Bible in the fully clothed (Fig. 5) or otherwise entirely nude
Christ Child's lap (Fig. 6), using the Word inscribed in the Book
literally to conceal the fleshly embodiment of the Word, God's private intentions incarnate in the Child's private flesh.[15]

Readers who suspect that I am just being ingenious and that medieval artists (and those who commissioned their work) could not
possibly be playing seriously with analogies and using the *phallos*
to represent the *logos* (hundreds of years before Freudian analysis)
should consider the even more explicit formulations of later art,
such as the mid-fifteenth-century illumination, from the *Hours* of
Philip the Good, of Christ's presentation in the temple (Fig. 7).
Here is, as Leo Steinberg remarks, a veritable *ostentatio genitalium.*[16]
The fatherly, priestly hand frames and draws the audience's attention to the Child's private parts, which are entirely exposed with
the falling away of the long swaddling cloth that trails across the
altar, linking the scene of bodily exposure on one end of the altar
to the unclasped, open text of the Old Testament on the other.
One *pryvetee* here is clearly linked to the other. God's hidden

meaning is metaphorically revealed in Christ's revelation of his most private flesh.

In the first half of the fourteenth century, artists began to paint the Christ Child nude except for a sheer, gauzy fabric over his groin, a tissue that, as Steinberg pointed out, is often the lower part of the veil of the Madonna's head (Fig. 8).[17] The transparency of this veil covers—or discovers—the Child's private parts in an "expository" way (Fig. 9). In such paintings, the Christ Child no longer needs to hold a scroll symbolizing the Old Testament in his hand to remind us that he is the incarnate Word, that the text of his flesh is the key to understanding God's intentions. The transparent veil reveals the nude body behind it or falls away to discover God's *pryvetee* in a material, physical representation of the abstract sense of St. Paul's words.

By the late fourteenth century, especially in the north, in France and Bohemia, the Christ Child is often depicted without even a gossamer veil over his loins, as artists invented new ways of calling attention to the symbolic meaning of his nudity. One rather awkward technique to emphasize the Incarnation—it does not seem to have caught on—is the radiant halo surrounding the Child's groin area in late-fourteenth-century Lombard paintings and manuscript illuminations (Fig. 10). A more effective way of directing the viewer's attention to Christ's groin was to use the direction of the gaze of other viewers within the picture to direct ours, as in some late-fourteenth-century images of the Adoration of the Magi. A Lombard illumination from about 1390, for example, presents a kneeling old king kissing the Child's foot while gazing intently at the nude infant's private parts (Fig. 11). Bohemian paintings and manuscript illuminations of the 1360s and 1370s, while depicting a nude Christ Child, still use his foot (symbolic of the phallus, a kind of displaced penis, even in earlier Byzantine models) as the focal point of the picture: in a Madonna and Child painted before 1371, Christ's bare, upturned foot overlays Mary's own clothed *pryvetee* (Fig. 12); in an illumination of the Adoration of the Magi, a grey-bearded king kisses the nude Child's foot (Fig. 13).

This same Bohemian miniature from the 1360s attracts attention to the Child's genitals through the Madonna's shielding hand gesture. Her protective gesture is expository, like the gauzy veils previously discussed. The Child's upraised, outstretched arms and contorted physical position, coupled with the motherly shielding of his penis, suggest the painful fleshly punishments (Latin *poenas*) he will suffer for mankind, first in his *penis* at the Circumcision,[18] eventually stretched on the cross, with nails through hands and feet. Another Bohemian painting of Madonna and Child from about 1350 presents the same configuration (Fig. 14). Below a cruciform halo, the Child's limbs are stretched out by the way his mother holds him, calling attention to his penis with her protective gesture. At the end of the fourteenth century, and ever more blatantly for two centuries, the revelation of the Christ Child's penis in depictions of the Incarnation is a foreshadowing of the fleshly *poenas* he will undergo on the cross to redeem the flesh. This near-pun also motivates the protective gesture Steinberg notes of Christ's or the Madonna's hand over Christ's phallus in some images of the Deposition from the Cross, such as in a late-fourteenth-century French illumination where, in the artist's attempt to represent sequential motion, there are rather too many hands at Christ's groin (Fig. 15).[19] The full circle of Christ's passion is neatly summarized in a painting of the Holy Family from 1515–1520 (Fig. 16). Here the Madonna shields the Child's private parts, not with her hand, but with her rosary beads, the pendant cross of which exactly covers his penis. The knife on the cut orange beside his foot figures the first fleshly *poenas* of his submission to circumcision, and the cross over his penis signals the last. Renaissance painters go even further than late medieval ones in inventing ways to attract attention to Christ's genitals for doctrinal reasons.

The most fascinating question Steinberg's study raises is why we have not taken notice of such deliberate exposure of Christ's phallus when even the Madonna's index finger, like an embodied *nota* sign, points its *sentence* out to us (Fig. 17). We seem to have censored the exposure in our own minds, refused to see it. Nevertheless, the late medieval painters (and patrons) who started the vogue of Christ's nudity must have known what they were doing; an artist does not make Christ's penis—or his foot—the focal point of a picture by accident. I suspect that medieval spectators of all walks of life, when exposed to such exposure, must have noticed it, just as most modern men and women take note of suddenly rising hemlines or plunging necklines. To anyone who had grown up with the dreamlike symbolic displacements and disguises of Byzantine iconographic representations of the flesh, the new, more naturalistic, denuding representations of Christ must have been striking, if not shocking. I think it quite likely that medieval people noticed, as well, the exposure of the Madonna's breast when it had moved into closer relationship to her body and normal placement on that body in some fourteenth-century representations of the Madonna of Humility nursing, such as Lorenzetti's close-up painting with the Child in sharp profile (Fig. 18). To viewers who were used to seeing Mary's breast, if at all, in displaced and disguised Byzantine forms (such as the breast-shaped mountain symbolizing Mary in a thirteenth-century painted Nativity, Fig. 19) or in peripheral or odd positions and shapes on her body (Fig. 20), some of the more naturalistic depictions of the late fourteenth century must have seemed startling and provocative.

Ideally, "gentil" medieval viewers should handle such noteworthy nudity, such revelations of "Goddes pryvetee," not by actually covering it up (for slapping on a fig leaf, painting on an opaque loincloth, is really rather boorish), but by doing so figuratively; they should respond, not with curiosity about God's sex per se, as a material object, but by inquiring into the doctrinal meaning of such revelation. This is to say, "gentil" medieval interpreters would try to react to Mary's bare breast or Christ's bare genitals (much like modern Robertsonians) by searching for some Christian "morality" or "holiness" therein. In order to properly read the iconography of the Incarnation, one must search for the Word incarnated—materially represented—in the visual images of the flesh. One must treat the images almost like rebuses, as I have done in showing how the Madonna's expository "veil" represents "revelation" or how Christ's most secret flesh represents God's secret intentions. Because God's Word is embodied in Christ, gentle interpreters ought to understand Christ's material penis as a significant *word,* as a sign of the *poenas* or punishments he would suffer to redeem man. The problem, of course, is that not all interpreters were or wanted to be gentle; certainly Chaucer's Miller did not. Furthermore, as Mikhail Bakhtin has so forcefully reminded us, there were extraordinary times, such as feasts and Carnival, when, not "gentil" behavior, but, rather, its opposite was the order of the day: deliberately "churlish," sinful behavior, which included churlish—or goliardic—interpretation of sacred texts and rites, that is, debasing, materialistic parody or burlesque misappropriation of sacred signs aimed at rerooting them in the body, in the flesh.[20]

One of the oldest examples of goliard-style festive burlesque of sacred Christian texts is the Saturnalian *Cena Cypriani,* originally written in prose, versified in the ninth century and revised and dramatized many times thereafter.[21] The *Cena* is a medley that brings together Old and New Testament characters in the context of a contemporary wedding feast, each acting stereotypically: Pilate brings the finger bowls, Herodiade dances, Judas kisses everyone, and so forth. Chaucer's "Miller's Tale," told by a drunken churl, a "janglere and a goliardeys" (A 560), is another such deliberately perverse parody of familiar biblical episodes. I am not the first to point this out.[22] The plot involves a burlesque reenactment of Noah's flood with two tubs and a trough in place of an ark, all for the purpose of cuckoldry. The Song of Songs, as an allegory of Christ's love for Mary, and the Annunciation are also worked into the Miller's burlesque medley. Gabriel's comic embodiment in the "Miller's Tale" is the sweet young clerk, Nicholas, who claims to know God's secret will, who sings Gabriel's song of annunciation to Mary, "Angelus ad virginem," but whose annunciatory techniques and intentions are anything but angelic. Alison as Mary may be humble as a "piggesnye," but she is hardly chaste and virginal. Her second wooer is Absalom, the comic, pretty-boy embodiment of Christ as mystic bridegroom. Although Absalom characterizes himself as a "lamb yearning for the tit" and uses the language of the Song of Songs to urge his "bryd" to love, Alison, as opposed to the *sponsa,* by no means longs for the sweet "kiss of his mouth." Indeed, she profanes his kiss in the most vulgar way.

If the gentle interpreter tends to make earnest out of game by reading "up" for the *sentence,* a "churlish" interpreter or goliard, such as Chaucer's Miller, does just the opposite and makes game out of earnest by reading "down" for *solas,* which often involves putting the lowest possible interpretations on sacred images and texts. Given this burlesque intention, I would like to propose an image of the Nativity as a visual exemplar for the Miller's proverbial-sounding moral concerning husbands and "Goddes pryvetee."

Figures 1–21

1. Unknown master from Tressa, painting of Madonna and Child enthroned, thirteenth century. Siena, Museo dell' Opera del Duomo (photo courtesy of Enzo Carli).

2. Guido da Siena (?), panel painting of Madonna and Child enthroned, dated 1262. Siena, Pinacoteca Nazionale (photo by Grassi, Siena, supervised by B.A.S.–Siena).

3. Cimabue (?), painting of Madonna and Child enthroned, about 1300. Bologna, Church of Santa Maria dei Servi (photo by Alinari/Art Resource, New York).

4. Master of the Magdalen, painting of Madonna and Child, late
thirteenth century. London, Sotheby's, 24 March 1965 (photo courtesy of Department of Old Master Paintings, Sotheby's, London).

5. Nicolo di Pietro, painting of Madonna and Child, dated 1394. Venice, Galleria dell' Accademia (photo by Alinari/Art Resource, New York).

6. Hans von Judenburg, wooden statue of
Madonna and Child, about 1400–1410.
Private collection (photo by author).

7. Presentation in the Temple, from the *Hours* of Philip the Good, Duke of Burgundy, Flanders, Audenarde, 1454–1455. The Hague, Koninklijke Bibliotheek ms. 76 F 2, fol. 141v (photo courtesy of Koninklijke Bibliotheek, The Hague).

8. Lippo di Benevieni, painting of Madonna and Child, about
1330. Florence, Collection of Count Cosimo degli Alessandri (photo
courtesy of Leo Steinberg).

9. Nardo di Cione, painting of Madonna and Child with
four saints, about 1356. New York, New York Historical Society, Bryan Collection (photo by The New-York
Historical Society, New York).

10. Lombard illumination of Madonna and Child with donor, about 1385. Paris, Bibliothèque Nationale ms. lat. 757, fol. 109v (photo by Bibliothèque Nationale, Paris).

11. Lombard illumination of Adoration of the Magi, about 1390.
Modena, Biblioteca Estense ms. lat. 472 = α.R.7.3., fol. 230r (photo
by Roncaglia, Modena).

12. Bohemian, Czech Master, detail from votive panel painting of Madonna and Child, before 1371. Prague, National Gallery (photo courtesy of Dr. Ladislav Kesner, National Gallery, Prague).

13. Bohemian, the Adoration of the Magi, enlargement of the center of a historiated initial, about 1360–1370. Prague, Cathedral Library ms. Cim. VI, fol. 32 (photo by author).

14. Bohemian, Czech Master, Madonna and Child from Strahov, about 1350. Prague, National Gallery (photo courtesy of Dr. Ladislav Kesner, National Gallery, Prague).

15. French illumination, Entombment, *Petites Heures de Jean de Berry,* about 1380–1385. Paris, Bibliothèque Nationale ms. lat. 18014, fol. 94v (photo by Bibliothèque Nationale, Paris).

16. Master of the Death of the Virgin (usually identified with Joos van Cleve), the Holy Family, about 1515–1520. London, National Gallery (photo and reproduction courtesy of the Trustees, The National Gallery, London).

17. Bartolommeo di Giovanni, Madonna and Child, about 1490. Formerly Metropolitan Museum of Art, New York (photo courtesy of Sotheby's, New York).

18. Ambrogio Lorenzetti, Madonna and Child nursing,
about 1325. Siena, Museo dell' Opera del Duomo (photo
courtesy of Enzo Carli).

19. Master of St. Peter, Nativity, detail of altarpiece of St. Peter, about 1280. Siena, Pinacoteca Nazionale (photo by Grassi, Siena, supervised by B.A.S.-Siena).

20. Fresco, Veronese school, Madonna and Child nursing, beginning of thirteenth century. Verona, Castelvecchio Museum (photo by author).

21. East Anglian painted panel, Nativity, mid-fourteenth century. Paris, Cluny Museum (photo by Musées Nationaux, Paris).

I have already suggested that the gentle interpreter might find an allusion to Joseph and Mary in those lines, especially in the light of the Miller's earlier announcement that his tale will be a "legende and a lyf / Bothe of a carpenter and of his wyf" (A 3141–42). The medieval interpreter, either gentle or churlish, might call to mind and understand the Miller's advice in terms of a scene such as the mid-fourteenth-century East Anglian Nativity now in the Cluny Museum (Fig. 21).

The gentle interpreter should see in this painting a number of motifs symbolic of the Incarnation and the Nativity. The aged Joseph in his Jew's cap leans his arm on his tau stick and rests his head on his arm, closing his eyes to the scene on his right. The meaning of Joseph's behavior is that he represents the blindness of the Synagogue to the significance of Christ's Incarnation and the founding of the Church.[23] These are symbolized in ways conventional to medieval depictions of the Madonna and Child. There is the expository gossamer veil of revelation about the nude Christ's open thighs; he holds the Madonna's wrist, probably to symbolize his love for her as *sponsa* or Church; his cruciform halo, upraised arms, and contorted limbs foreshadow the Crucifixion; his miniature adult form, the frontality of his pose, and his forward gaze all encourage figurative interpretation.

If a learned interpreter would read the iconography in this "gentle" way, what would an unschooled, but still good-intentioned, viewer see in these same images? I suspect this viewer would see an image of Christ's humanity as evidenced by his need to suckle Mary's breast.[24] Further, such a viewer might see a tired old Joseph, or at least a discreet husband. Medieval contemplative texts often imagined Joseph turning away from the scene of the birth, not wanting to intrude on a woman's privacy. St. Bridget, for example, sees Joseph go outside so that he might not be present at the birth.[25] Pseudo-Bonaventure imagines Joseph seated beforehand and "downcast perhaps because he could not prepare what was necessary."[26] Such are the good-intentioned, but unlearned, humanizing interpretations of the iconography of earlier Byzantine Nativity scenes in which Joseph represents Synagogue.

Now we have come to the crucial question. What would someone with *bad* intentions—a churl, a "janglere and a goliardeys"

like Chaucer's Miller—see in our exemplary East Anglian Nativity
scene? How would he react to Joseph's closed eyes and weary pos-
ture and to the nudity of Mary's breast and of the infant Christ's
miniature-adult body? I suspect he might see Joseph as a van-
quished husband, a weary old man who already has more than
enough to face in his marriage with a pretty young thing and who
wisely closes his eyes to the scene of his cuckolding, which is happening right under his nose on the bed, where Mary and the nude
mannikin Christ engage in erotic suckling activity. Were he to
open his eyes, this Joseph would see "Goddes pryvetee" and his
wife's too—that is, their intimate love-play and their private parts,
Mary's exposed breast, Christ's gossamer-veiled, open thighs. He
would see Mary behaving as the Christ-God's wife instead of his
own: "An housbonde shal nat been inquisityf / Of Goddes pryvetee, nor of *his* wyf." Whose wife? The pronoun reference is
ambiguous.

Goliardic play involves just this kind of debasing interpretation
of sacred images and signs—even to the extent of taking the
Holy Family and "Goddes pryvetee" in vain. The Miller's simple-
sounding proverb is equivocal; we can deconstruct it in several different ways depending on the contexts we privilege. On the one
hand, it seems to offer orthodox patriarchal counsel—husbands
should have unquestioning faith in the ways of God—until we
come to the phrase "nor of his wyf." If we understand this to mean
the husband's wife, the Miller's moral lesson is anything but orthodox, for it puts women "on top," right up beside God. When
we think of the Miller's advice as an allusion to Joseph and Mary
and the Incarnation, and, even more specifically, when we think of
visual representations of the Nativity in which Christ and Mary
are depicted as *sponsus* and *sponsa,* the proverb turns on us again. It
suggests that God assumed human shape—like the philandering
Jove—in order to be privy with Mary, cuckolding her husband
(who should not be too inquisitive if he knows what is good for
him). Viewed from a slightly different angle, from the perspective
of the infant as God, the same Nativity scene represents the fulfillment of the Oedipal wish, the triumph of youthful desire over restrictive fatherly authority. Once again, if the bad old father knows
what is good for him, he will not interfere with the divine infant.
The infant God takes possession of his mother (Mary as Church);

he is the apple of her eye, excluding and replacing the old father (Joseph as Synagogue). In other images, the infant God is recognized king of all kings and worshipped by the aged Magi, who peer at his phallus as a thing of wonder.

Images of the "family romance" are the medium for Christian doctrine, which, by acts of sublimating exegesis, denies the primitive meaning and attraction of such images. Most of us have not consciously perceived the deliberate exposure of the Christ Child's penis in late medieval and Renaissance art; neither have we consciously perceived the primitive level of meaning, the motor of Oedipal wish-fulfillment, in many images from the same period of the Nativity, Holy Family, Adoration of the Magi, and Madonna and Child. Other texts, learned in the process of our schooling, have covered up the fundamental one. However, in the late Middle Ages, on festive occasions associated with seasonal change, and especially in the days leading up to and following the New Year, "youth" rebelled against the restrictions and censorship of age and authority and committed deliberately churlish, infantile, goliardic acts of interpretive parody or burlesque performance that, in effect, *desublimated the sacred texts and rites, unmasked the euphemisms, removed the verbal loincloths of exegesis, and exposed the revitalizing energy of infantile, egocentric desire.* In a seminal chapter on the "festive comedy" of the "Miller's Tale," Alfred David has understood this:

Much of the gaiety of the Miller's Tale comes from the inversion of . . . repressive attitudes. . . . One could go further and say that the fabliau opposes itself to the tendency of the medieval mind to see physical objects and everyday events as outward signs of an invisible higher reality— the exegetical [or sublimating] impulse. In the fabliau, attempts to get to the bottom of the mysteries of life usually backfire.[27]

The Miller's proverbial moral for husbands—implicitly casting the Reeve in the role of Joseph and understanding contemporary visual and verbal stories of Joseph and Mary in the basest possible manner[28]—is a fitting preface for the churlish, fabliau rendition of episodes of sacred history of the "Miller's Tale," which takes "humanistic" interpretive embodiment of religious texts and symbols to ridiculous lengths, making game out of earnest.

Chapter Two

The Spirit versus the Flesh
in Art and Interpretation

Paradoxically, one of the greatest modern theorists of play, Johan Huizinga, was also one of the most vocal scholars in expressing his disapproval of the mingling of sacred and profane—or the profanation of the sacred—in late medieval visual and verbal arts. For example, in his *Waning of the Middle Ages,* Huizinga deplored the cult of Saint Joseph, which depicted Mary's spouse as a clownish cuckold, perhaps in "reaction from the fervent cult of Mary."[1] Huizinga judged that such "familiarity with sacred things is, on the one hand, a sign of deep and ingenuous faith; on the other, it entails irreverence whenever mental contact with the infinite fails." And fail Huizinga thought it did, although evidently not for late medieval religious leaders such as Jean Gerson, who criticized statuettes of the Virgin that opened at the womb to display the Trinity for "the heresy of representing the Trinity as the fruit of Mary"— not for their coarseness. More common folk, however, were "in constant danger of losing sight of the distinction between things spiritual and things temporal." Huizinga judged that the "step from familiarity to irreverence" and "decadent impiety" was definitely taken whenever "religious terms are applied to erotic relations," as in his example of a painting of the Madonna with the features of the king's mistress. Furthermore, Huizinga seemed to recognize that such a combination of the sacred and the profane was not always good-intentioned or naive, but was sometimes playfully provocative or subversive: "The irreverence of daily religious practice was almost unbounded. Choristers, when chanting mass, did not scruple to sing the words of the profane songs that had served as a theme for the composition: *baisez-moi, rouges nez.*" Huizinga translates this phrase as "Kiss me, red noses," but its sense was probably more bawdy. Even without any telltale redness, noses represented penises in the folk imagination, as Bakhtin reminded us;[2] and the French word for "kiss," then and now, could mean "fuck." Huizinga's clean translation is a fig leaf.

Different scholars have handled their discomfiture at late medieval mixtures of the spirit and the flesh, the sacred and the profane, in different ways. Specifically with respect to Chaucer's *Canterbury Tales,* few scholars have silently "turned over the leaf" and averted their attention from temptation. This would be a true censorship, a total suppression or deletion of the offensive material. Most scholars have practiced, instead, some form of denial, a deliberately ineffective censorship (or censureship) that preserves in mind the very material it rejects. Virtually all negative statements work in this way. According to Noam Chomsky, there is no "no" in the deep structure of language. The true "no" is total deletion of words and phrases. The false "no" is the one we are familiar with, and it is a surface transformation, a mode of expression that modifies only the apparent meaning of the enunciation. In this respect, "no" works like laughter, which is another method of seemingly reversing the meaning of the signs within its bounds, a mode of equivocation that allows the laughing man, or the listener who identifies with him, to have the meaning of signs (whether words or gestures) both ways, one way on the surface and another way underneath.

Few critics have used such strong language in censuring Chaucer as Byron, who expressed outright disgust and condemned Chaucer's work as "obscene and contemptible."[3] However, many have made a show of averting their attention from obscenities, of choosing to "turn over the leaf." These have not accepted the apology of decorum or realism (that churls' words are appropriate in the mouths of churls) any more than did Dryden, who, like other translators, cut off the offending members by omitting them from Chaucer's corpus, but not without first calling our attention to what they were suppressing:

If anything of this Nature, or of Profaneness, be crept into these Poems, I am so far from defending it, that I disown it. . . . if a Man should have enquir'd of Boccace or of Chaucer, what need they had of introducing such Characters, where obscene Words were proper in their Mouths, but very undecent to be heard, I know not what answer they could have made: For that Reason, such Tales shall be left untold by me.[4]

Such censorship is done in the name of Christian decency and of protecting public morality, and it often presumes that the readers (with women and children foregrounded) are incapable of protecting themselves. The "infantile" eye will see that the emperor is wearing no clothes, whereas proper, sophisticated people will re-clothe him in their own minds.[5]

A long tradition of censorship in Chaucer criticism involves ignoring anything that does not seem sufficiently serious in Chaucer's writing, while demonstratively praising that which does. These censors often seem, however, to protest too much. Lydgate praised Chaucer for his didacticism, for "keping in substaunce / the sentence hool / with-oute variance, / voyding the chaf / sothly for to seyn. / Enlumynyng / the trewe piked greyn / be crafty writinge / of his sawes swete." For Hoccleve, Chaucer was the "mirour of fructuous entendement," of "fruitful understanding" (sententious rather than sinful). Caxton echoed Lydgate in praising Chaucer for writing "no voyde wordes / but alle hys mater is ful of hye and quycke sentence."[6] Such early readers, like many today, took Chaucer at his final word: "For oure book [the Bible] seith, 'Al that is writen is writen for oure doctrine,' and that is myn entente" (I 1083). Such reading for profit gives us the image of a serious Chaucer: an historical realist and sage dogmatist, a writer who used words to represent things, to describe vividly fourteenth-century life, to capture particular and eternal qualities of human character, to create fables containing moral truths or Christian, doctrinal lessons for the reader to discover and apply to his own life. He does these things, but there is another side to Chaucer that such criticism deliberately blinks out. As Absalom found out in the "Miller's Tale," the person who blinks at the wrong moment may live to regret it with crystal-clear hindsight.

Only very gradually have we become willing to acknowledge that Chaucer might play with language upon occasion, that he might take delight in the formal aspects of the tale, in "literature for its own sake," as a game of signification with no moral application, with no higher purpose than *solas*. At the end of the nineteenth century, Lounsbury pronounced Chaucer's writing to be free of "these verbal quibbles" and praised him for "restraint of expression that . . . is not only at all times and in all places free from literary vulgarity, [but] never loses the dignity that belongs, as well in letters as in life, to consummate high-breeding."[7] In the explanatory notes accompanying his 1957 edition of Chaucer's works, F. N. Robinson maintained that puns are relatively unusual in Chaucer, and perhaps even then unintentional.[8] The many Chaucerian puns discovered in the past two decades seem to have created uneasiness in the minds of some scholars, who would try to convince us, rather as May persuaded old January, that our sight is "glimpsing," that we misconceive and misjudge. In a major address at the 1984 Congress of the New Chaucer Society, Larry Benson warned against finding puns in contexts where none really exist, that is, against projecting our own erotic fantasies into Chaucer's innocent text, thereby debasing the master.[9]

Other scholars have tried to convince us to censor our own thoughts by arguing that our modern vision is faulty, that a medieval viewer or reader would find nothing sacrilegious in the image or the text; rather, he would discover there a Christian message, a good intention. This view is an orthodox Christian one, and D. W. Robertson, Jr., has been its most eloquent spokesman. He has argued in *A Preface to Chaucer* that Chaucer used "what we should call obscenity" to illustrate a moral point, so that his "obscenities" are philosophical, not funny:

The modern view that such materials represent a romantic assertion of the baser elements of human nature simply overlooks the fact that they were intended to be significant within the framework of Christian morality. Medieval writers were just as capable of a kind of philosophical obscenity as were later writers like Erasmus, Rabelais, Swift, and Sterne. The bare breasts of the mermaids so enticingly revealed on a capital at Sainte-Eutrope de Saintes, or on a roof boss at Exeter Cathedral, were designed not to produce dreams of the "breast of the nymph in the brake," but to suggest certain very Christian conclusions.[10]

If we see only the flesh in Chaucer's "obscenities," then our modern (or Romantic, viz., Byronic) eyesight is at fault. Augustine and other Christian authorities would have taken such erring vision as a sign of the reader's sinful, unregenerate state, of the Old Man. The good Christian should be able to pass from the obscenity to the morality, from the carnal perception to the intellectual understanding, from the flesh to the spiritual *sentence*. The trial of Christian interpretation requires this progressive self-censorship, which begins with an admission of the "glimpsing" imperfection of sensory perception and a refusal to believe what is literally before one's eyes. From this orthodox Christian point of view common in the late Middle Ages and the Renaissance, representation of the flesh in devotional images could, with some guidance and reinforcement from the pulpit, exercise the individual's capacity for self-censorship, form the habit of searching for the moral *sentence,* and thereby internalize the authority of Christian morality.

Nevertheless, I doubt that such representations of the flesh in devotional images or in the fictions of literature always had the intended didactic, uplifting effect. As Leo Steinberg noted, the "revelation" of the Christ Child's phallus in some paintings resembles coy striptease, as the Child or the Virgin pulls up or drops his clothing or diaphanous veil in just the right spot at just the right moment.[11] To many untaught fourteenth-century eyes, and to some religious conservatives as well, the didactic display of the Christ Child's penis and the Virgin's breast must have seemed like indecent or erotic exposure of "Goddes pryvetee." In spite of what we like to call the alterity of the Middle Ages, it is hard to believe that no medieval individuals were aroused by the display of sexual parts, especially when such bare depictions of Virgin and Child were just beginning to come into fashion. It is even harder to believe that no medieval individuals responded with pleasure to the infantile fantasies elaborated under the guise of art in paintings of the Madonna and Child, the Madonna Nursing, the Holy Family, the Adoration of the Magi.[12] The new nudity of late medieval religious art and the stimulation in some genres of infantile, especially Oedipal, wishes may have been, ideally, a way of encouraging the viewer to censor his own carnality and to exercise moral restraint, but it was also, even more fundamentally, a play for the viewers' attention. Medieval preachers also played for their listeners' attention by using the sensuality of the literal level of meaning of the Song of Songs to talk about divine love or by incorporating into their vernacular sermons "serious" puns such as the one on *vierge*

(Virgin) and *verge* ("wand" or "penis" or, figuratively, typologically, "tree of Jesse").

We may be reminded of the techniques of modern advertising by Gregory the Great's explanation, in beginning the commentary on the Song of Songs usually attributed to him, of how carnal language attracts the listener's attention:

> in this book love is expressed as if in carnal language, so that the mind, stimulated by words it is accustomed to, may be aroused from its torpor, and through words concerned with a love which is below, may be excited to a love which is above. In this book are mentioned kisses, breasts, cheeks, and thighs. Nor is the Sacred description to be ridiculed on that account, but the greater mercy of God is to be considered; for when He names the members of the body and thus calls to love, it should be noted how wonderfully and mercifully we are treated. For in order that our hearts may be inflamed with sacred love, He extends His words even to wicked love.[13]

Michel Zink has remarked that some medieval preachers seem to have taken pleasure in the "intellectual game of turning around the [secular] text and in the unexpected allegorical interpretation," in "reducing *vanitas ad veritatem*." Thus one preacher from Amiens used the refrain of a secular love song, with its conventional erotic undertones, "Bone est la dolor dont ge atent douchour / Et soulas et joie" ("Good is the suffering from which I expect sweetness / and pleasure and joy"), to point out the relationship between penance and paradise.[14] The more stubbornly carnal the text, the greater pleasure the preacher took in reversing its meaning with his gloss. Indeed, in reading vernacular sermons and imagining their oral performance, one can sometimes catch glimpses of a preacher playing games with his audience.

As an instance of syllogistic reasoning in vernacular sermons, Zink paraphrases the following sequence from a thirteenth-century sermon, which, as he notes, is periodically punctuated with the exhortations "don't be stupid" or "listen and understand":

> The body of Christ gives *la vie* to him who receives it. God, is he not *vie*? Yes. Is there anything better than eternal *vie* in joy without end? No. God is *vie*: everything that is God is thus *vie*. The flesh of God, is it not God?

Yes. And whoever receives it, does he not receive *vie?* Yes, it is even eternal *vie* that he has within him if he receives it in a worthy way.[15]

The preacher's warnings, "Or m'atendez e entendez," "Mais entendez, ne soiez mie bestes," may be necessary because of the novelty of syllogisms, as Zink suggests, but they also call attention to the possibility, for the listener, of misunderstanding *vie* (life) as *vit* (penis) in several contexts of this argument. In effect, the preacher is playing a sort of peekaboo, both suggesting the carnal interpretation and insisting that the listener subordinate it to a higher meaning. By alternately teasing and prodding his audience, the preacher makes the implicit point that the Christ Child's *vit* represents the eternal *vie* Christ made possible for men through his Incarnation, by assuming the flesh, the phallus.

Zink also remarks that etymological wordplay based on Latin *virgo* and *virga* or Old French *vierge* and *verge* is common in thirteenth-century sermons and that it is consecrated by the Church for the Office of the Virgin at Easter and justified by Hugh of Saint Victor in a chapter entitled "Quod multiplici ratione Maria dicatur virga, et Christus flos ejus."[16] To the medieval listener, explanations of why the Virgin should be called "wand" (or "penis") may have verged upon the ludicrous, even though the purpose of the pun is serious, to bring together Old and New Testaments through typological allusions. Thus we see young vines climbing up aged trees—or other references to the Tree of Jesse—in the background in pictorial representations of the Virgin and Child wherein the Child's penis is prominently exposed, peered at, or even pointed to by the Virgin or his grandmother.[17] Pure-minded people should have no great difficulty with such serious puns or devotional images of the *Vierge / verge* but should surmount their initial carnal attraction with a doctrinally serious, typological interpretation.

But why should the Christian preacher or artist or writer run such risks of being misunderstood by appealing to the flesh, to carnal sensation, in these ways, only to block or cover it over in the end? Why should the artist whose message is spiritual resort to such manipulations? Gregory the Great's admission is more forthright than most: carnal imagery stimulates, attracts the audience's attention, gets energy flowing that may then be diverted and redirected toward God. Indeed, no art can appeal primarily to the intellect, for it must be mediated by the senses; paradoxically, that art which appeals most strongly to the senses may finally be most challenging to the intellect, which seeks to control the emotional response. Good art is always a dangerous game. Augustine and other theologians rationalized the carnal imagery of the Bible on the grounds that the hunt for the "true" meaning beneath the carnal surface figures (the quest for control) was pleasurable and, further, that the effort of the interpretive search fixed the hidden truth in the interpreter's mind once he had discovered it. In his explanation of how to allegorize and thus arrive at a doctrinally safe interpretation of an apparently dangerously immoral biblical text such as the Song of Songs, Augustine also admits that it is pleasurable to understand doctrine through carnal figures, such as the figure of the saints as teeth biting off and chewing up sinners:

> For example, it may be said that there are holy and perfect men with whose lives and customs as an exemplar the Church of Christ is able to destroy all sorts of superstitions in those who come to it and to incorporate them into itself, men of good faith, true servants of God, who, putting aside the burden of the world, come to the holy laver of baptism and, ascending thence, conceive through the Holy Spirit and produce the fruit of a twofold love of God and their neighbor. But why is it, I ask, that if anyone says this he delights his hearers less than if he had said the same thing in expounding that place in the Canticle of Canticles where it is said of the Church, as she is being praised as a beautiful woman, "Thy teeth are as flocks of sheep, that are shorn, which come up from the washing, all with twins, and there is none barren among them"? Does one learn anything else besides that which he learns when he hears the same thought expressed in plain words without this similitude? *Nevertheless, in a strange way, I contemplate the saints more pleasantly when I envisage them as the teeth of the Church cutting off men from their errors and transferring them to her body after their hardness has been softened as if by being bitten and chewed.*[18]

What is fascinating about this example is that Augustine has, in effect, created two new texts out of the literal level of the line from the Song of Songs, which compares a beautiful woman's teeth to shorn sheep coming up from the wash, each bearing twins, none sterile. The imagery of the original passage suggests fecundity and wealth. Augustine, however, has created a downright cannibalistic

secondary text from this, making the teeth bite and chew people—
only to block this aggressive fantasy at a higher level by insisting
that the biting teeth signify saints softening up sinners for their
own good. Perhaps the nature of his pleasure in contemplating
such figurative expressions of Christian doctrine escaped even the
introspective Augustine, and that is why he never returned to the
question, as he suggested he would do later in *On Christian Doctrine*. Augustine manipulates his texts, but they also manipulate
him. He uses the positive connotations of the saints to suspend the
threatening image of the biting teeth (which is his own creation,
although he seems to attribute it to the literal level of the text of
Canticles). As he reads it, the passage from Canticles is not about
biting teeth, but about the beneficial action of saints on sinners.
His denial of the "literal" level(s) of meaning through allegorization works rather like a continuous series of negations with substitutions. These denials and metaphoric substitutions control or
neutralize the threat of the carnal imagery (which he himself has,
in part, invented) and thus enable him to take a subdued, covert,
sublimated pleasure in the fantasies such imagery stimulates.

One might propose Augustine's exegetical practice as a model
of the mechanisms of Christian exegesis, albeit in a different sense
than Robertson has done. What the Christian interpreter does is
control the threateningly immoral, arousing aspects of the literal
level of a fiction by creating a second text or allegory that is supposed to convey the "true" moral message of the first text. The
second text is, so to speak, a sublimation of the first; it feeds upon
the arousing aspects of the first text but tames and transforms
them in a way that is acceptable to the Church, that is consonant
with Christian doctrine. Some of the most famous preachers, such
as Bernard of Clairvaux, and no doubt also their audiences seem to
have derived much pleasure from such sublimation: the Song of
Songs is the most rewritten—glossed, allegorized—text of the
whole Bible. The source of this interpretive pleasure lies (and this
is what Augustine could not admit) not solely in the controlling
transformations or art-work of constructing the secondary text or
allegory, but also in preserving, by such legitimization, the arousing, carnal images of the original text. In other words, part of the
pleasure of Christian exegesis lies in finding ways *not* to have to
give up the original sin entirely. Covert pleasures are often more

pleasurable than overt ones. Just as the clothed, partially censored body can be more erotic than the entirely nude body, so the allegorization of an immoral text, which denies ineffectively, covers incompletely, can preserve and even heighten the forbidden pleasure of the original text.

Christian exegetes are not the only ones who treat texts in this way; nearly all scholars do. As we see with contemporary interpretations of the "Miller's Tale," even medievalists who concentrate on biblical parody and burlesque try to recover a tatter, at least, of serious *sentence* from this obscene tale by concluding that the imitation implicitly reaffirms Christian doctrine. (This is true, as we will see, not in the sense these Chaucerians suggest, but instead in the psychological sense that any playful parody—even an imitation motivated by rebellious or derisive intent—involves some identification with, some accommodation to, the "other" that the impersonator temporarily, playfully replaces.) Robert Kaske concludes his exegesis of the "riotous" parody of the Song of Songs in the "Miller's Tale" on a moral note. He judges that the total effect of the reminiscences of Canticles "will be not to turn the *Miller's Tale* into a kind of covert sermon put together from the unlikeliest of available materials, but instead to give the tale itself what I would describe as a 'moral edge'—an implicit orientation toward a controlling set of values"; Kaske sees the "Miller's Tale" as "part of a governing moral theme in the *Canterbury Tales.*" James Wimsatt concludes that Chaucer was not "an impious comedian, an apostate, or a liberated spirit in a shackled age," but, rather, that "the biblical echoes show up Absolon, Alisoun, and Nicholas, January, May, and Damian as monstrous creatures who are ultimately funny in the same way as the grotesque beings who inhabit Hieronymus Bosch's 'Paradise of Worldly Delights' are funny." Beryl Rowland ends her article on the Miller's blasphemy on a note similar to Kaske's: "It is a humour which, if it makes no overt distinction between the sacred and the profane, nevertheless seems to offer another perspective. The Annunciation, perennially enacted, was too miraculous to be forgotten. Through the parody, the ephemeral world of trivial lust and vulgar jest is set against the cosmic and timeless background of divine ordinance." Even Roy Peter Clark terminates his exegesis of the Miller's Christmas games seriously: "Through acts of copulation and sodomy committed in the Oxford fabliau, we are reminded that by the Incarnation, God has indeed exalted the human body and human nature. . . . As poet, [Chaucer] can accept credit for infusing his greatest comic tale with symbolism that suggests the principal doctrines of the Christian faith." [19]

To end on a serious moral note sets the previous forbidden pleasures of the text right again, or at least appears to do so. This is the strategy of many a medieval writer of fabliaux, wherein the meta-commentary of a little moral *sentence* feebly attempts to cover over much *solas*. The basic device of artistic fictions—and of their criticism—seems to be a combination of denial and substitution or transformation whose purpose is to allow the interpreter to have it both ways, to express and savor the forbidden desire while controlling it through a kind of sublimation. Both art and criticism are partially censoring orders that enable expression. Literary scholars and critics are accomplices to the cover-up of art, but, like Augustine in his allegorization of biting teeth as saints, critics often reveal by their glossatory texts precisely the pleasures they explicitly seek to conceal. Thus, for example, Larry Benson's 1984 Chaucer Congress paper warning Chaucerians against projecting their own erotic fantasies on Chaucer's *queyntes* and against finding other vulgar puns where none were intended had the effect of an extended denegation, of deliberately ineffective censorship or censureship; Benson's denials enabled him, to everyone's amusement, to dwell at length on bawdy words. In much the same fashion, the thirteenth-century preacher kept warning his audience "not to be stupid" (not to misunderstand) as he strung out a series of *vies* in a context that could also support the punning sense of *vit*. Even in this book, I might be said to be doing the same thing, under cover of scholarship—which does not make it any less scholarly, only more duplicitous.

The *sentence* or doctrine of art, whether expressed outright by its creator or by its re-creator, the critic, is likely to be a cover-up designed to partially censor and at the same time to enable the appreciation of the forbidden pleasures of the text. It is here that Roland Barthes does not give conventional (as opposed to deconstructive) criticism its due, but stops short of exposing one of its important underlying motives. [20] To read for *sentence* enables, not prevents, a covert appreciation of *solas*. Nor, for that matter, does writing for *sentence,* for the perfectly turned, authoritative-sounding phrase, for the epigram (of which Barthes is a great master), preclude the expression of desire. We need not believe that the medieval and Renaissance readers who inserted all the *nota* signs in the margins of manuscripts beside nuggets of "wisdom"—or the authors who expressed them in the first place—were any more sober-minded than we are. For example, the manuscript of the *Canterbury Tales* copied in the fifteenth century by Duxworth for Count John of Angoulême (Paris, B. N. anglais 39) intercalates in bolder black letters eight Latin proverbs in the "Man of Law's Tale" and nine scriptural texts and one Latin proverb in the "Wife of Bath's Prologue."[21] It seems that the copyist, perhaps directed by the Count, was a particularly sententious reader to go hunting out and pointing up the proverbial *auctoritas* behind lines in the Man of Law's tale of the trials of Constance and to supply the very scriptural texts the Wife of Bath alludes to, in the fragments she requires, to support her argument. Just as the Wife of Bath uses Scripture to authorize—that is, to mask—and at the same time to express her erotic and aggressive desires, so the copyist's intercalations of scriptural *auctoritas* may authorize his own pleasure in the Wife's provocative text.

Different individuals and audiences will, of course, have different levels of need to control arousing or threatening elements of fiction. From the multiple framing moralizations, often strained, of the tales of John Gower's *Confessio amantis,* it seems that "the moral Gower" had greater need than Chaucer did to control or disguise the meanings of his fictions. Among Chaucer's fictional characters there are also differences in this respect; for instance, the Miller ends his bawdy fabliau with no moralizing *sentence,* whereas the Reeve begins his with preaching that is a pastiche of proverbial wisdom, and he ends his fabliau with a moral:

> Lo, swich it is a millere to be fals!
> And therfore this proverbe is seyd ful sooth,
> "Hym thar nat wene wel that yvele dooth."
> A gylour shal hymself bigyled be.
>
> (A 4318–21)

Different versions of a fabliau show that the same fictional content may be given different metafictional moralizations, some more

adamantly censorious than others, sometimes introducing, sometimes concluding the fiction, sometimes framing it at both ends.
Even though the fifteenth-century Italian Renaissance scholar Poggio Bracciolini called his Latin *Facetiae* trifles not to be taken seriously, his French translators, such as Guillaume Tardif at the end
of the fifteenth century, concluded many of them with a moral,
often quite tangential.[22] Many a medieval fabliau expressing a load
of forbidden desires begins and ends in this way, first announcing
that it is just a joke, a little rhyme for fun, but concluding with the
moral lesson, no matter how lame, that may be learned from it.
The tendency to take fiction seriously in the end—especially for
those of us who earn our livings explicating it—is overwhelming
and, at the same time, deceptive.[23]

   If the function of serious exegesis was—and is—to cooperate
with the censoring artifices of fiction, to mask and prolong the
forbidden pleasures of the text by further sublimating and authorizing them, the function of the "unserious" or facetious mimesis
and interpretation of medieval goliardic and jongleuresque play
was to *desublimate*—to discover and exaggerate erotic or aggressive or other forbidden desires covertly expressed through the
words or gestures of authoritative and often ritualized texts. This
unmasking of the "true face" of the text required the interpreter
himself to assume a mask that excused his words and actions, usually an obviously irresponsible (low or subservient) persona—the
fool, the naive rustic or churl, the infant, the wife, Golias. By putting the mask over his own face, either literally or by means of
grimaces and other contortions and excessively abnormal or in-
verted kinds of behavior such as wearing his clothing inside out or
his breeches on his head or female garb, the facetious interpreter
licensed his own outrageous behavior. His "foolish" persona announced that the interpreter was not taking himself or his public
image seriously for the time and space of the interpretive game,
which usually occurred on a festive occasion devoted to such play,
a ludic time that permitted everyone in the society to play roles
different from his or her status in everyday life. In addition to his
literal or figurative mask, the facetious interpreter's laughter protected him by denying serious intent. What enabled his rebellious
and revitalizing discovery of forbidden desires, his undoing of the
censoring artifices of the authoritative, ritualized text, were these

metatextual, contextual denials of reality or seriousness: festive time, laughter, and the foolish persona that was patently *not himself*. Before discussing in more detail Chaucer's versions of medieval goliardic and jongleuresque interpretive play, we need to examine some of the basic pretenses of the "serious" fictions that such comic play periodically unmasked and deconstructed.

Chapter Three

Power and Play

The Consolations of Fiction I

Let us begin this chapter with an incongruous comparison between the mechanisms and meanings of a two-and-a-half-year-old boy's presleep monologue and the first story of Boccaccio's *Decameron*. First the monologue, as tape-recorded and transcribed by its analyst, Ruth Hirsh Weir, the child's mother:

Don't touch Mommy Daddy's desk.
I should
He say so (2 ×)
Daddy's desk and Mommy's desk.
Don't go on the desk.
Don't take Daddy's glasses
Don't take it off
Don't take the glasses off
Daddy's wearing glasses
Daddy's always
Dadada
Leave it
Daddy's glasses (*some whispering, banging, squealing*)
Doggie, Mommy, cookie (2 ×) (*unintelligible low volume with much banging, hitting of the microphone, squealing*)
Mike (15 ×) (*hitting of microphone, squealing*)
SLEEP[1]

Such monologues, which occur shortly before sleep, after the child has been put to bed alone in the dark, are among every person's first sustained fictions. At a later stage of mental development, they become internalized, unvoiced speech. Weir has pointed out that her son's presleep monologues are really dialogues or plays in which the child repeats the words and assumes the roles of parents and others he knows. Concerning the example quoted above, Weir explains, "the things he has been forbidden to do during the day preoccupy him at the moment of sleep. There are two very strict rules in the household: nothing on the parents' desks is to be touched, nor taken for play. . . . The other absolute, never to be tampered with, are eye-glasses which both parents wear."[2] In this instance some of the child's aggressive feelings against his parents for restricting him during the day (and putting him to bed) are taken out in the nonverbal actions of banging and squealing, but his verbalized role-playing is an even more effective way of controlling in his imagination a situation over which he has no control in reality. His parents have used the negative on him during the day, and now, in an assertion of his own will in play, he rectifies the imbalance by taking over the parental role and practicing their "don't." In his presleep monologues the child works through the problems and frustrations of his day by playing *all* the roles, the powerful parental ones as well as his own weaker one. There is often considerable wish-fulfillment evident in these monologues. Although Daddy has just walked out and shut the door, the child may talk to Daddy as if he were still there and play Daddy to respond, prolonging his father's presence in imagination.

In his preface to Weir's study, Roman Jakobson underlines another striking aspect of these presleep monologues: how "the lowering of the cognitive, referential function . . . brings to the fore all the other language functions." For Jakobson, "the predominantly metalingual concern of the somnolent child with language itself comes as a great surprise."[3] Children seem to be "practicing" language in their presleep monologues. On the one hand, they play the parent to correct their own grammar and usage; on the other hand, they break rules deliberately (as poets do) in order to play with paradigmatic and syntagmatic substitutions of sounds and words and phrases. In this play world of the child's own creation, linguistic reference does not matter; no one "really" hears; nothing will "really" come of it (even though the child may play the parent to correct or respond); signifiers can be treated as signifieds with impunity; sounds can be treated as objects to manipulate for the pleasure of it, for the pleasure of making new combinations, the pleasure of mastery. The two-and-a-half-year-old who has just been put to bed against his will and been made to feel how little control over the world he really has plays roles and plays with language in order to regain a sense of control. According to Jean Piaget, play is a deliberate denial of what we perceive to be reality. In play the child assimilates the world, controls it by making it in imagination what he wants it to be.[4] Although play inevitably involves much mimesis, it also involves deliberate distortion of what is imitated, in order to satisfy the child's desires—especially thwarted desires for power, which parents or circumstances do not allow him to satisfy.

Like the child in his vocalized presleep monologues, the writer of fiction plays all the roles and gains a sense of control over real-life situations—or gives himself and his audiences the temporary assurance of doing so—by replaying or imitating life in fiction, but life changed in various ways to suit his desires. Boccaccio's use of fiction in his *Decameron*[5] or Chaucer's "Nun's Priest's Tale" (from the Nun's Priest's point of view) are examples of abreactive play that satisfies a desire for control frustrated in reality. After describing in his prologue how plague victims, abandoned even by their closest relatives, died alone and were dumped unceremoniously into mass graves without any religious rites, Boccaccio writes a first story of "consolation" that expresses and fictionally fulfills the thinly disguised desire of the individual to be able to control his own death and future reputation—even to force God's hand in the matter.

The hero of the first story, Ser Cepperello, is a dying man and an incorrigible sinner whose hosts fear they will suffer reprisals from the local people if the truth about Ser Cepperello's sins comes out in his last confession and he is refused Christian burial. Ser Cepperello, however, takes care of the problem. As a notary, he is used to bearing false witness and making up false contracts, so without the slightest remorse he lies to the friar during his last confession. Much impressed by the goodness of "Ciappelletto" ("Chaplet," as he is miscalled by the locals), the friar gives him absolution, gets him buried in the friars' chapel, and preaches such a fine funeral sermon on his virtues that the local people begin praying to him to intercede for them, and the reputation of *Saint* Ciappelletto's miracles spreads far and wide. Not only does this foxy notary trick the Burgundians in the end (into believing in his sanctity), but he also tricks God into honoring a fraudulent contract. Even beyond the grave, Ser Ciappelletto is able to work wonders, because God, whether he saved the sinner or not, must respect the people's sincere faith in their saint.

For the reader who identifies with the hero, this comic fiction takes the fear out of death. It is a fiction of mastery for the powerless: for Boccaccio, with his memories of death during the plague; for his fictional travelers and storytellers, who are trying to keep their health by escaping into the pastoral world and the world of fiction; and for Boccaccio's readers, whom he designates in his foreword as melancholy women who are in love and can do nothing about it because they are "forced to follow the whims, fancies and dictates of their fathers, mothers, brothers and husbands," spending "most of their time cooped up within the narrow confines of their rooms" (p. 46). For such readers, these stories may offer escape from conscience and the burdens of moral rectitude as well. What a relief to imagine life from Ser Ciappelletto's perspective for a few moments, with no horrible consequences but, on the contrary, sainthood in the end!

Although the concluding moral of the "Nun's Priest's Tale"— keep your eyes open and your mouth shut—is good advice for courtiers and royal servants (like Chaucer) and for people in subservient positions (such as the Nun's Priest, one of three priests accompanying the Prioress [A 164]), the very action of telling this story belies its *sentence*. As Chaucer scholars have recognized, the "Nun's Priest's Tale" is a fiction of power, chiefly over females, told by a fictional character whom we might suppose to experience considerable sexual frustration, for his service to a group of nuns is restricted to the spiritual domain. By means of the fiction he tells, the Nun's Priest temporarily reverses the real order of things in his milieu, not only by putting the barnyard world on top of the human one, but also by giving his major play persona, the gorgeous cock Chauntecleer—who sings his "hours" so canonically and punctually in a voice even "murier than the murie organ / On messe-dayes" (B^2 4040–48)—the role of "omnipotent" ruler over a harem of hens headed by the courtly, Prioress-like Pertelote. Chauntecleer is not only greatly enamored of the chief hen, but, more important, he is constantly proving his prowess on her. He puts Pertelote down intellectually in a debate on the meaning of dreams that gives him occasion to parade male kinds of wisdom and authority, including his Latin, and he puts her down physically by "feathering" her constantly. Chauntecleer's triumph extends even over destiny and death. That he is caught by the fox proves he was right about the meaning of his dream, and yet he does not suffer the consequences: he tricks even the fox into releasing him.

The "Nun's Priest's Tale" may not have been very consoling to the Prioress, or, for that matter, to the Wife of Bath, or to late-fourteenth-century women, yet fictive and historical women were prevented from protesting, just as we are, by all the blatant artifices and comic incongruities of the "Nun's Priest's Tale"—from its beast-fable genre, to the narrator's outlandish rhetorical amplifications, to his metafictional interventions such as "Thise been the cokkes wordes, and nat myne" (B^2 4455). These function like the Freudian notion of joke-work, which disguises and sanctions enjoyment of the aggressive or erotic desires expressed by the joke.[6] The exaggerated artifices of the "Nun's Priest's Tale" insist: "This is just play, this is not real, this is fiction," thereby enabling the teller to get on with his covert, imaginary self-aggrandizement. Harry Bailly, saddled with a shrewish, domineering wife, according to his own—perhaps facetious—testimony (E 2427–34), evidently identified with the heroic cock and appreciated the tale enormously, and so have a great many other interpreters for whom the "Nun's Priest's Tale" is one of Chaucer's best.

Boccaccio begins the *Decameron* with the reflection, "To take pity on people in distress is a human quality which every man and woman should possess, but it is especially requisite in those who have once needed comfort and have found it in others." Boccaccio regards his fictions, even the comic ones, as very serious business because of the consolation they can give to readers (and writers). A reality full of unsatisfied and unsatisfiable desires, figured in Boccaccio's preface by his own desire for the unattainable lady, would be insupportable without the relief of unreality, without the freedom of imagining life from other viewpoints that compensate our own unsatisfactory one or make us forget it temporarily or relativize it. A collection of stories, some comic, some serious or even tragic, can be very consoling, because the process of identification with a series of different characters working through different conflicts—as in the *Thousand and One Nights,* the *Decameron,* the *Canterbury Tales,* or the portable "library" of many a medieval manuscript collection of poetic fictions—gradually relativizes our own perspective, giving us distance on it.

The fictional replaying of a fearful situation or conflict not only enables the powerless to gain some measure of reassuring, albeit imaginary, control, but may also reinforce the power of the feared authority. In playing the powerful roles as well as the weak ones, the player identifies with authority. We may identify with the "aggressor" in self-protection, to reduce our anxieties. Let us consider a concrete example: young children in a hospital under physiological and psychological stress. Psychologists have found that it is extremely beneficial to these children's mental health if they act out their fears in play, assuming the roles of the doctors and nurses who have such power over them and give them pain. One study summarizes: "Through expressing disorganized emotions, repeating painful experiences, and reversing roles, play assists the child in mastery." [7] Such abreactive play involving repetition with role reversal also helps the child to accept and internalize authority's point of view, that is, the parents', doctors', and nurses' view that this painful experience is for the child's own good.

It is precisely this kind of abreactive play that Millard Meiss discovered in the visual art of Florence and Siena in the years following the Black Plague and that Huizinga remarked in late medieval northern art in various forms: morbid depictions of human skeletons and skulls, crucifixions, Ecce Homo portraits, gruesome martyrdoms of saints, and death dances. [8] This is the art of Chaucer's "Pardoner's Tale," of the anxiety-enhancing fictional sermon exemplum of the three young sinners in time of plague who, in the course of (prophylactic?) sensual indulgence and merrymaking, gather up their courage to confront "this false traytour Deeth" and slay him—only to die gruesome deaths themselves by poisoning and murdering one another over the treasure they discover. The inhabitants of plague-stricken Europe, with the Church telling them that God was administering this affliction for the good of their souls, were in a physically and mentally stressful situation comparable to that of children in a hospital. The act of re-creating death in the visual and verbal representations of late medieval art was a way of controlling fear of it, for the artist had the upper hand over the imaginary space and time of the painting or the narrative. Furthermore, many of the conventions of artistic representation, which act as an announcement of art's fictional status, help to contain the fear that is aroused, in both artist and audience, by such mimesis of death. The exercise of looking at life from the perspective of death, identifying with death, presumably decreases fear of it. This kind of abreactive play aimed at mastering anxieties was encouraged by churchmen in sermons, religious literature, and paintings in the later Middle Ages, in part because such art reinforced the Church's power and authority.[9] The purpose of the Pardoner's exemplum, after all, was to extract money and goods from people whose anxieties he had aroused about their own powerlessness in the face of death. Through his fiction, in the role of controlling and intervening narrator, the Pardoner demonstrates his ability to control the figure of Death; to the extent that his audience identifies with the Pardoner's superior power—and the Church's—to control what they fear, they give.

According to Meiss's analysis, post-plague painting in Florence and Siena emphatically exalted the Trinity, Christ, and the saints in ways that twelfth- and thirteenth-century art had done, but which had been abandoned in the early fourteenth century in favor of more realistic and humanistic trends of representation, epitomized in Giotto's art. Post-plague paintings regressed by representing deities in frontal poses, floating on air, hierarchically positioned, having no visual contact with other figures. Even the Madonna of Humility was no longer represented seated on the ground, but suspended above it on a cushion. Post-plague painters literally increased the distance between God and man, exalting God and demeaning man, and thus encouraged viewers to identify in their imaginations with deific figures in order to master their own fear and feelings of powerlessness. One might even argue that such self-chastising abreactive play is fundamental to the Christian religious cult. The medieval flagellants were not the only ones who played both torturer and tortured; in imagination, every maker or viewer of a Crucifixion scene did the same, and so did every priest who performed mass in recollection and re-creation of Christ's self-sacrifice.

This kind of pious artistic abreaction, which masters anxiety by exalting and identifying with the powers that be, Meiss was surprised *not* to find in the literary fictions of Boccaccio's *Decameron*. Boccaccio was not writing under the patronage of the Church; consequently, he was more free to use forms of play that involved imaginary rebellion and denial of authority in order to alleviate the psychological suffering of late-fourteenth-century people. One of the devices Boccaccio could and did use, for example, was the power of laughter to subvert and reverse the conventional meaning of signs, as does Chaucer's Host in the aggressive *jape* with which he "quits" the Pardoner's manipulative, anxiety-enhancing exemplum (C 946–55).

How much medieval people may have *consciously* understood about the therapeutic possibilities of play or fiction is difficult to determine. In his excellent study of medieval theories on this subject, Glending Olson has shown that medieval physicians and theologians were aware of the good effects, hence the practical usefulness, of reading or listening to fictions, as well as of various other sorts of entertainments, in order to combat illness or to restore physical strength after much work.[10] The key idea of medieval medical thinking was that good health required balance in every respect; anything that gave pleasure could rectify the imbalance created by anxiety, sadness, and other debilitating emotions or *accidentia animae*. Likewise, the strain of ordinary physical and mental labor needed to be relieved or balanced by relaxing pursuits, one of which might be the pleasure of listening to fictions. What was true for the individual body was true for the social body as well. Thus the healthy state for an individual or a society would involve an alternation between states of tension and relaxation, work and play, waking and sleeping (or dreaming), reality and unreality, everyday life and festivity, Lent and Carnival. Joy opposed and combatted, thus balancing, sorrow. This much was observable. Because it was the effect that counted, there is very little medieval theorizing about exactly how it is that amusements amuse, consolations console, or fictions give pleasure.

Theologians tended to attribute the pleasure of the medieval fictional text to its style, surface ornament, or artifices of narration, in other words, to those conventions of artistic representation that call attention to language itself. They did not go far in analyzing how these "superficial" stylistic effects produced pleasure, because this would be to give in to the senses, to sin, to let oneself be diverted from seeking the true, spiritual meaning beneath the surface ornament. Although medieval commentators often observe that literature diverts men's attention from their troubles, there is little evidence that the scholarly authorities understood that the satisfaction of listening to fictions might reside in the diversionary *expression* (rather than the forgetting) of troubles, that is, in the expression, through the transformations and disguises—the diversions—of fiction, of anxieties and desires that are ordinarily repressed in medieval society.

For example, Boninus Mombritius, in a late-fifteenth-century treatise on how to cope with the plague, recommends Boccaccio's "book of the hundred tales" along with other books of "pleasure and delight" in order to "dispel destructive accidents of the soul."[11] These destructive *accidentia animae* were debilitating emotions. Mombritius's advice suggests that he is still thinking in terms of psychomachia or combat (pleasure driving out sorrow) rather than in terms of the diversion of harmful emotions through fictional outlets such as literature, hunting, love debate, or chivalry (all those medieval "play" activities that we would include under the psychoanalytic category of sublimation, which is related to the Aristotelian idea of catharsis, or purification through purgation of emotions). Likewise, the *Tacuinum sanitatis*'s prescription of stories to provoke anger (and thereby body heat) for people with cold hearts might work,[12] but not for the reasons the medieval physicians gave. If the cold-hearted man was suffering from depression due to repressed anger and guilt feelings, then the story to fire him with anger might give him temporary release. The story might restore his "imbalance," not by putting combative anger into him to heat up his body but, rather, by letting pent-up anger out in a controlled way through his identification with fictional characters and situations.

Medieval writers and performers of fictions for entertainment may intuitively have understood far better than did theologians and physicians how fiction worked to give pleasure and keep people healthy. With his *Decameron,* Boccaccio offers a secular, humanistic alternative to the pious abreactive fictions of other post-plague artists. At the same time, the *Decameron* offers a more controlled and reasonable (because imaginary) alternative to the real rebellion against law and authority that was another prevalent reaction to the plague, as Boccaccio describes in his prologue. Laughter, feasting, jesting, and sexual license were anxious responses meant either to promote a prophylactic joy that people believed might protect them against death, or to annihilate death by denying its seriousness and even its reality with a laugh. Boccaccio describes people dying alone while their closest relatives spent their time in mirth, feasting, and jesting: "more often than not bereavement was the signal for laughter and witticisms and general jollification—the art of which the women, having for the most part suppressed their feminine concern for the salvation of the souls of the dead, had learned to perfection" (p. 55). Olson rightly assesses what Boccaccio was doing with fiction: "the richest morality of the *Decameron* . . . lies not so much in any particular assertions of value within the fictions [any *sentence*] as in the implications of their structure: that in the face of chaos and disintegration it is possible for people to reassert civilization, to conduct their lives in an orderly manner, and to reaffirm the stability and worth of such secular virtues as polite discourse, wit, and even recreational pleasure."[13] The purpose of Boccaccio's literary play is mastery, and that is the object of Chaucer's fictions as well.

Like Boccaccio, Chaucer thought of the good of fiction in terms of consolation. His *Canterbury Tales,* with their framing action and commentary, provide a model for the equilibration by means of fictions and laughter of the badly disrupted late-fourteenth-century English social body, as represented by a group of pilgrims drawn from different estates and professions. However, before conceiving this grand project, which was to use all the resources of fiction and humor, Chaucer had long been writing fiction for consolatory purposes, to comfort either himself or a patron (such as John of Gaunt in the *Book of the Duchess*) or a group of people (such as frustrated "lovers" in *Troilus and Criseyde*). Indeed, much of Chaucer's early writing seems to fall into the category of abreactive fiction of the pathetic sort that evokes fears and anxieties and enables both author and audience to gain some measure of self-mastery and control over these anxieties through the formal conventions of the fictional genre, through distancing metacommentary, and through identification, not only with the suffering character, but also with the higher, punitive power. Such self-protective identification with authority involves an open belittling of the self and the things of this world. The English translations Chaucer ascribes to himself in the prologue to his *Legend of Good Women* (G 413–18) as works of "holynesse" or "besynesse"—Boethius's *Consolation of Philosophy*, Pope Innocent III's *De contemptu mundi* ("Of the Wreched Engendrynge of Mankynde"), a life of St. Cecilia (recycled as the "Second Nun's Tale"), and Origen "upon the Maudeleyne" (on St. Mary Magdalen)—all are fictions that console by helping to master anxiety in the face of death or powerlessness.

Not surprisingly, this sort of consolatory literature and visual art was in great demand during the years following the great plague of 1348–1350 and its periodic recurrences later in the fourteenth century, a generally difficult time of economic depression, intermittent warfare between England and France, schism in the Church, social unrest, and political instability in England.[14] Although he learned to use it in more subtle ways in his later works, Chaucer never gave up writing (or rewriting) this kind of pathetic, abreactive fiction, which, like tragedy, usually features some version of the killing or punishment of the "child" figure by the "father" (or bad mother) figure. Let us consider for a moment the "Man of Law's Tale" of the trials of Constance from Chaucer's *Canterbury Tales*. The Roman emperor's beautiful young daughter, Constance, is married off and sent away to live with the sultan of Syria, who has converted to Christianity in order to possess her. The narrator points up, as seriously as if he were describing her death or the Last Judgment, the heroine's anxiety at this separation from her kin and at her own powerlessness:

> The day is comen of hir departynge;
> I seye, the woful day fatal is come,
> That ther may be no lenger tariynge,
> But forthward they hem dressen, alle and some.
> Custance, that was with sorwe al overcome,
> Ful pale arist, and dresseth hire to wende;
> For wel she seeth ther is noon oother ende.

Allas, what wonder is it thogh she wepte,
That shal be sent to strange nacioun
Fro freendes that so tendrely hire kepte,
And to be bounden under subjeccioun
Of oon, she knoweth nat his condicioun?
Housbondes been alle goode, and han ben yoore;
That knowen wyves; I dar sey yow na moore.
(B¹ 260-73)

Constance's parting speech increases the pathos of her situation:

"Fader," she seyde, "thy wrecched child Custance,
Thy yonge doghter fostred up so softe,

. . . .
. . . hire recomandeth ofte
Unto youre grace, for I shal to Surrye,
Ne shal I nevere seen yow moore with ye.

"Allas, unto the Barbre nacioun
I moste anoon, syn that it is youre wille."
(B¹ 274-82)

Finally the narrator intervenes (B¹ 288-94) to amplify the significance of Constance's departure by comparing the sorrow at her leaving to the emotional response provoked by the fall of Troy or Thebes or the sack of Rome by Hannibal (epic comparisons that Chaucer will use again in a comic vein in the "Nun's Priest's Tale" to describe the sorrow in the chickenyard at Chauntecleer's capture by the fox [B² 3355-65]).

Over and over again the "Man of Law's Tale" replays frightening situations in order to comfort us. Although Constance faces death several times, she does not die. She survives a massacre at her wedding banquet, an accusation of murder that would carry the death penalty, an attempted rape, and being several times set adrift in a tiny boat at sea, symbol of man's situation in the world, of his powerlessness to control his destiny. Constance is a "child" persecuted or sacrificed by evil parental figures, especially by wicked mothers-in-law. We see her first being sent away to Syria by her father; later, she mothers a child whose father's mother, unbeknownst to the father himself, in her jealousy forges a letter commanding the exile of both Constance and her infant. The religious analogies the narrator invokes are the Passion and images of the Madonna holding the Child in a way that foreshadows the Pietà. As Constance lulls her child in her arms prior to being set adrift in her boat once again, she compares her situation to that of the Virgin, whose sorrows included the spectacle of her child's crucifixion (by bad judges, but ultimately in accordance with the will of God the Father):

> "Mooder," quod she, "and mayde bright, Marie,
> Sooth is that thurgh wommanes eggement
> Mankynde was lorn, and damned ay to dye,
> For which thy child was on a croys yrent.
> Thy blisful eyen sawe al his torment;
> Thanne is ther no comparison bitwene
> Thy wo and any wo man may sustene.
>
> "Thow sawe thy child yslayn bifore thyne yen,
> And yet now lyveth my litel child, parfay!
> . . . .
> "O litel child, allas! What is thy gilt,
> That nevere wroghtest synne as yet, pardee?
> Why wil thyn harde fader han thee spilt?"
> (B¹ 841–49, 855–57)

Such comparisons suggest that Constance's suffering at the "bad" parental figures' hands—like Mary's, like Christ's—is salutary, because it is really all in the control of a benevolent Father, who may at times appear to be bad or use bad people as instruments, but who will make everything turn out right in the end, who only makes people suffer for the good of their souls. In her weakness, in order to get through her troubles, Constance identifies with Mary and God. Medieval people who had suffered or feared to suffer sudden reversals of fortune due to events beyond their control—plagues, wars, political upsets—could empathize and identify with Constance and, in reading or listening to her story, imagine fearful situations analogous to, privately symbolic of, yet reassuringly different from, those they experienced in life. As they reenacted Constance's tribulations in their own imaginations, medieval people could play all the roles, not only that of the powerless "child" heroine, but also that of the wicked worldly persecutor, that of the heavenly "father," and, perhaps most important, that of the manipulative narrator (a capable alter ego) who plays a very active role in this tale.

The pathos of the "Man of Law's Tale," that is, our empathetic identification with Constance and her suffering, is very carefully controlled, in part by the regular interruption of the story's action by narratorial interventions that provide a proverbial analogy, allude to other literary texts, or point up a *sentence*—sometimes even a distancingly ironic one such as "Housbondes been alle goode, and han ben yoore" (B¹ 272). The effect of such interruptions is to call attention to the controlling role of the narrator, to remind us that the text is a fictional construct, to pull us back periodically from our empathy with suffering characters. Everything that calls attention to the linguistic matter and to the formal structure of the tale—such as its carefully patterned, rhymed stanzas; braking rhetorical dilations; repetitive plot structure—also works to remind us that it is "in play" ("illusion"), thus making our identification with a suffering heroine tolerable, because we know that all the terrible things that happen in the story are really under the author's control, and under ours too, in an even more fundamental way, for we have but to close the book or shut our eyes or walk out of the performance to end these fictional experiences.

The consolation of the "Clerk's Tale" of patient Griselda—so antipathetic to most modern readers, so much appreciated in post-plague Europe—works in much the same way. Griselda's trials evoke and allow readers to work through anxieties about powerlessness and loss of loved ones. Without the slightest rebellion against the punitive father figure, her husband and lord, the Marquis of Saluzzo, Griselda gives up first her infant daughter, then her infant son, to what she is made to believe is their certain death. Indeed, Griselda's self-mastery (her self-protection by identification with the man who has power over her, first her father, then her husband and lord) is complete. Walter makes her promise to obey him in everything without complaining "by word ne frownyng contenance," but she goes even farther in subjecting herself to her husband than he asks; she promises to let his very will be her own, never to disagree with him in act or *thought*:

> Wondrynge upon this word, quakynge for drede,
> She seyde, "Lord, undigne and unworthy
> Am I to thilke honour that ye me beede,

> But as ye wole youreself, right so wol I.
> And heere I swere that nevere willyngly,
> In werk ne thoght, I nyl yow disobeye,
> For to be deed, though me were looth to deye."
>
> (E 358–64)

Furthermore, she keeps her promise and even cheerfully approves (1032–36) Walter's decision to replace her by a younger, nobler, and more beautiful wife (in fact, her daughter, whom she believes dead).

The story of Griselda is an abreactive fiction of total accommodation to the laws and will of the figurative father, who may stand for the progenitor, husband, political ruler, or God. In life, especially if demanded of us in situations that allow us no illusions of control, such total accommodation is generally painful, because it involves suppression of our own desires. We would find it painful, for example, to be in Griselda's position, confronted with the accommodation her husband and lord demanded of her: that she give up her children to be murdered, that she totally suppress her motherly desire to protect her infants. Most accommodations are softened somewhat by our identification with the powerful "other"—the parent, the husband, the government—that blocks the satisfaction of our desires. This imagined identification often takes place in the context of play or ritual, that is, within a fictional world of our own creation or consent, within a game that gives the player the illusion of control necessary for him to make the identification and to give up his own desires—or, rather, to find a vicarious satisfaction in suppressing them and mastering himself, in imagining the pleasure of the (now internalized) authority figure in mastering him. Identification involves role-playing; by becoming *more than one,* by fictionalizing experience, we are able to adapt to painful exterior realities and rules. Within the fiction of the "Clerk's Tale" there is a familiar fiction, a ritual of accommodation and status elevation, that enables Griselda to identify with her husband, to make his will her own. This is the rite of passage of marriage whereby she begins a new life: first she is stripped of her old clothes; then she is dressed from head to toe in new clothes symbolic of her new identity. Griselda's marriage festivities are not described in detail; nevertheless, the extended holiday of a medieval wedding was a fictive time (like the modern honeymoon) that marked and encouraged the accommodation of the new wife to her new identity, that is, her husband's.

Literary fictions can work in much the same way as—indeed, can serve as simulacra for—a society's venerable rites of passage, which take the threat out of and thus facilitate people's accommodation to novel and difficult situations. A fiction such as the "Clerk's Tale" provides a safe framework within which we may identify with patient Griselda and vicariously experience her persecution by her husband, all the while knowing, with Walter, from his perspective, that he is merely testing Griselda and that, far from having their children murdered, he is sending them to be fostered and instructed in proper fashion in his sister's household. Narrative interventions criticizing Walter for giving in to his desire to test his wife's loyalty work to assure us, even before we reach the pathetic climax, that this is a mere testing, that the "father's" intentions are not truly malevolent:

> He hadde assayed hire ynogh bifore,
> And foond hire evere good; what neded it
> Hire for to tempte, and alwey moore and moore,
> Though som men preise it for a subtil wit?
> But as for me, I seye that yvele it sit
> To assaye a wyf whan that it is no nede,
> And putten hire in angwyssh and in drede.
>
> (E 456–62)

Such narratorial interventions remind us that the narrator is in control of the story, just as do his efforts at formal perfection and closure, his interlacing rhyme schemes organizing the verses into stanzas grouped into longer narrative sections.

The private symbolic referents of Griselda's and Constance's trials may be different for each reader or listener; these would depend on the kinds of reversals each interpreter had experienced or feared in life. However, in his moralization of the story, the Clerk defines one universal referent for Griselda's trials: she represents the faithful Christian, imitator of Christ, being tested by God, who is figured by Griselda's husband Walter:

> For sith a womman was so pacient
> Unto a mortal man, wel moore us oghte
> Receyven al in gree that God us sent;

For greet skile is he preeve that he wroghte.
But he ne tempteth no man that he boghte,
As seith Seint Jame, if ye his pistel rede;
He preeveth folk al day, it is no drede.

(E 1149–55)

The Man of Law also concludes his tale by moralizing Constance's experience, pointing out the mutability of this world and of whatever pleasures we may find in it, and turning to heaven in the end with a prayer:

Who lyved euere in swich delit o day
That hym ne moeved outher conscience,
Or ire, or talent, or som kynnes affray,
Envye, or pride, or passion, or offence?
I ne seye but for this ende this sentence,
That litel while in joye or in plesance
Lasteth the blisse of Alla with Custance.

. . . .

Now Jhesu Crist, that of his myght may sende
Joye after wo, governe us in his grace,
And kepe us alle that been in this place! Amen.

(B¹ 1135–62)

The purpose of pathetic, abreactive fictions such as the "Clerk's Tale" and the "Man of Law's Tale"—or, for that matter, the "Prioress's Tale," "The Knight's Tale," or the *Book of the Duchess*—is to work through anxieties by repeatedly replaying fearful situations (with their private, symbolic referents), thus gradually leading the reader to accommodate himself to a difficult reality such as a sudden reversal of fortunes or a death (his own or that of a loved one), in short, to lead the reader to accept his own inability to control his life. This eventual acceptance, however, is based on illusion. The interpreter's accommodation to reality takes place within a safe, fictional world where his private reality is represented indirectly, figuratively, by the experiences of fictional characters. The reader may identify most strongly with the suffering hero or heroine, but he also experiences the perspective of the controlling narrator and of fictional characters who have control over the hero or heroine. The reader's acceptance of a harsh reality—the hero's powerlessness, representing the reader's own—is made possible by compensating illusions of power that the passive reader or listener, like the passive or immobilized hero, achieves through identification with the competent, controlling narrator and other powerful figures— in the story of Griselda, for example, with Walter and God.

To be effective, pathetic abreactive fictions must be repetitive, episodic. They cannot console if they are too brief, which is one reason why the "Physician's Tale" (of a father's murder of his beautiful young daughter in order to protect her from defilement by a false judge) leaves the Host feeling so angry and sorrowful (C 287–317). Likewise, the Monk's series of thumbnail tragedies, "da casibus virorum illustrium," provokes more anxiety than it assuages, causing the Knight and the Host to halt the relentless progression of decline:

> "Hoo!" quod the Knyght, "good sire, namoore of this!
> That ye han seyd is right ynough, ywis,
> And muchel moore; for litel hevynesse
> Is right ynough to muche folk, I gesse.
> I seye for me, it is a greet disese,
> Whereas men han been in greet welthe and ese,
> To heeren of hire sodeyn fal, allas! . . . "
>
> . . . .
>
> "Ye," quod oure Hooste, "by Seint Poules belle!
> Ye seye right sooth; this Monk he clappeth lowde.
> He spak how Fortune covered with a clowde
> I noot nevere what; and als of a tragedie
> Right now ye herde, and pardee, no remedie
> It is for to biwaille ne compleyne
> That that is doon, and als it is a peyne,
> As ye han seyd, to heere of hevynesse.
> "Sire Monk, namoore of this, so God yow blesse!
> Youre tale anoyeth al this compaignye.
> Swich talkyng is nat worth a boterflye,
> For therinne is ther no desport ne game."
>
> (B² 3957–81)

The Monk's highly abbreviated, tightly controlled stories of the falls of famous men may satisfy the need to repeat fearful experiences to master them, but the mastery in these stories is almost exclusively the narrator's. It is a formal, rhetorical mastery. The Monk does not give us time to identify with the suffering hero and

thus to work through anxieties, nor does his abbreviation allow
for the comforting, wish-fulfilling detours of more effective abreactive fiction (which presents escapes from death, raising of the
humble to high positions, return and reunion with loved ones believed dead). Like the Knight's life of chivalry and crusading as described in the "General Prologue," the "Knight's Tale" offers
youth a lesson in sublimating desire and aggression into socially
acceptable, utopian forms of ludic or ritualistic endeavor, such as
the pageantry of Theseus's tournament, that support the existing
social and political hierarchies. The Knight interrupts the Monk's
relentless tragedies, before he has the chance to tell the hundred
such he claims to know (B² 3162), because the Monk's exempla
offer no illusions, no substitute satisfactions.

Fiction must do two things: it must imitate public order or morality, and it must satisfy selfish individual desires. These two
functions—in Piaget's terms, accommodation and assimilation—
are by nature contradictory. Fiction is a paradoxical structure, a
means of having it both ways, of conforming and rebelling, submitting and mastering at the same time, of being two or more.
Some fictions, which we might call pathetic or tragic, emphasize
submission and accommodation to exterior orders at the expense
of the satisfaction of individual desires for power or control; other
fictions, which we might call ironic or comic, focus on the satisfaction of individual desires for power at the expense of public
order or morality. Nevertheless, in both kinds of fiction, the apparent "expense" is generally compensated or paid back in some
covert way, usually by means of symbolic transformations and
substitutions. We have already seen that, in the case of pathetic fictions in which the "child" passively accepts the punishments of the
"father," this accommodation on the part of the powerless figure
is enabled or compensated by an identification with, an imaginary
becoming and *replacing* of, the authority figure. Griselda in the
"Clerk's Tale," for example, not only "becomes" Walter by conforming her will to his, but she nearly replaces him in his people's
affections (E 407–41). Pathetic fictions tend toward a moralizing
sentence on the necessity of accommodation, such as the Clerk's
conclusion:

> And suffreth us, as for oure excercise,
> With sharpe scourges of adversitee

Ful ofte to be bete in sondry wise;
Nat for to knowe oure wyl, for certes he,
Er we were born, knew al oure freletee;
And for oure beste is al his governaunce.
Lat us thanne lyve in vertuous suffraunce.

(E 1156–62)

This *sentence* about submission is expressed from a position of power (both the narrator's and God's) with which we have gradually come to identify. The moral *sentence* of pathetic fiction does not so much mask as covertly realize the desire for self-aggrandizement.

Fiction is play, and play, as Piaget defined it, deliberately distorts what is perceived to be real (or lawful or moral) in order to satisfy illicit or impossible individual desires. We have seen that the consolation or self-satisfaction of fictions of the pathetic or tragic sort lies, not only in an Aristotelian purgation of emotions, as commonly recognized today, but also in a covert illusion of power that comes from identifying with, from oneself "becoming" the powerful parental figure or "father," replacing him, rendering him redundant. Thus we see Griselda, in effect, triumph over Walter by "mastering herself," by conforming her will entirely to his. We might even say that she wins the implicit contest with God, as Christ did through his Crucifixion, as all faithful Christians do. Although such pathetic fictions offer a covert, imaginary satisfaction of the individual's desire for power, this kind of play basically reinforces the status quo, which is why it was encouraged in many forms by medieval authorities.[15] The pleasure of the text in ironic, comic fictions, as we shall see, involves rather more rebellious satisfactions of egotistical desires, although even these are usually masked or accommodated to public morality, however superficially, by censorious metacommentaries, controlling artistic frames, and laughing denials.

Chapter Four

Dangerous Desires and Play

The Consolations of Fiction II

Artists themselves are probably the ones who best understand the meanings of their art-work—afterward, if they analyze their finished texts. However, artists are not likely to understand the deeper meanings of their own works *during* the process of creation when, using the forms and conventions of their chosen artistic medium and genre, they are struggling for control. Igor Stravinsky has said, for instance, that expression has never been the purpose of art. Rather, its purpose—the individual artist's purpose—is to impose order and unity on the multiplicity and confusion of feelings. Stravinsky is, of course, speaking of the *conscious* purpose of artistic creation, which seems to require, in effect, an attitude that "this is play." The artist imposes rules (or plays by rules and conventions of his genre and medium of expression) in order to gain mastery within the bounds of an unreal, fictional world, whether it be that of the symphony, the sonnet, or the painting of Madonna and Child. Stravinsky claims that, if his music seems to express something, this is an illusion (here used in the sense of delusion); yet elsewhere Stravinsky admits: "When we suddenly recognize our emotions, they are already cold, like lava."[1]

The fictions of art are expressive on an individual and often on a social level, but the desires and anxieties art expresses can only be released to be transformed and dealt with under the assurance of a controlling framework. On the one hand, the act of making the artistic artifact involves a denial of the real world; it involves the free and liberating step of entering into a play world that apparently constitutes itself against the real world,[2] a game world in which the language of representation imitates and yet functions somewhat differently from the way language functions in the real world. We do not hear our neighbors naturally speaking rhymed verse. To enter into a work of art, both for the artist and for the recreating interpreter, involves an act of negation of the real world, but this negation does not annihilate reality. The combination of negation and affirmation in the structure of artistic play resembles that of the denegation, which patently affirms the opposite of what the person really means.[3] Play does the reverse, denying in order to affirm. When we decide to make or to interpret a work of art, we say "no" to our immediate surroundings, to external reality, and this "no" and willing entry into a fictional world enable the artist to express and the interpreter to appreciate otherwise inadmissibly dangerous desires. By our willing denial of a representational intention behind the language of art—by trying to turn off the world, to cut art off from external reality, thus making it safe, a game we play according to its own rules—we gain the illusion of control necessary to turn on our own *interior* realities, to imagine, to dream.

After our initial willing entry into the game of art, there is a second controlling framework of negation that continually reminds us that what we are experiencing is "not real," "doesn't mean anything," is "not serious"—in short, is "not life," but something else. This second controlling framework includes all the conventions of artistic representation, the rules, so to speak, of the particular artistic game, which serve to distinguish the language of art from ordinary language and thus to deny that art refers to anything outside itself.[4] That Chaucer wrote almost all of the *Canterbury Tales* in rhymed verse emphasizes the fictional nature of the representation. People do not ordinarily speak in poetry or embellish their speech with rhetorical amplifications; nor do they relate ordinary events artfully, to emphasize parallels and create suspense; nor do they usually speak through fictitious personae; nor do they engage in commentaries on their own speaking style. The conventions of artistic representation differ from or greatly exaggerate those of ordinary representation in a way that calls attention to language itself, and this self-referentiality of artistic representation tends to create the comforting impression that the world of art is closed off from the real world that lies outside art's ludic boundaries.

It is understandable why artists in their commentaries should try to prolong the framing "not" of fiction beyond the act of creation. To publicly explain the deep personal meanings of their artistic play, if they have analyzed and understood these, may not be in their own interest, and they may not be aware of the more general social malaises that affect them as individuals and thus find expression, disguised to various degrees, in their art.[5] When artists do explain the meanings of their work—its connections to the real exterior and interior worlds—their rational explanation or *sentence* often seems to us terribly unsatisfactory, even diversionary, masking. The same is often true, for the same reasons, of scholarly and critical interpretations of the meanings of works of art.

Boccaccio's rationale for the first tale of the *Decameron,* expressed through the persona of Panfilo, is a good example of a masking moral *sentence*. Panfilo announces that his tale will be about one of God's miracles, a special act of grace:

I propose to begin by telling you of one of His marvellous works, so that, when we have heard it out, our hopes will rest in Him as in something immutable, and we shall forever praise His name. It is obvious that since all temporal things are transient and mortal, so they are filled and surrounded by troubles, trials and tribulations, and fraught with infinite dangers which we, who live with them and are part of them, could without a shadow of a doubt neither endure, nor defend ourselves against, if God's special grace did not lend us strength and discernment. Nor should we suppose that His grace descends upon and within us through any merit of our own, for it is set in motion by His own loving kindness, and is obtained by the pleas of people who like ourselves were mortal, and who, by firmly doing His pleasure whilst they were in this life, have now joined Him in eternal blessedness.

(pp. 68–69)

The moral with which Boccaccio begins and ends this tale explains it as an exemplum of God's power. The tale is supposed to work like contemporary post-plague paintings to magnify God and demean man and to express man's extreme dependence on God's mercy. Such a moral *sentence,* which encourages identification with God and the saints in self-protection, is one way of dealing with anxiety about death and powerlessness, but the fiction of the sinful Ser Cepperello's achievement of sainthood offers a different kind of consolation: a rebellious fantasy of man's own power over the manner of his death and of his ability to get what he wants from his fellow men and from God too. Taken together, the meta-fictional moral *sentence* and the fiction itself reproduce the structure of a denegation. The *sentence* is a morally "correct" affirmation that denies and thereby enables expression of the dangerous desire of the fiction. Our pleasure in this rebellious fantasy is covert; it is masked and controlled by a moral interpretation that assures us the fiction means just the opposite.

The more dangerous and openly expressed (nude of symbolic transformations) the desires expressed by the fiction and the closer its language to that of everyday representation (the less the artistic techniques and conventions call attention to themselves as such), the more boldly the artist must intervene on a metafictional level to point out the status of the art object as unreal. He may intervene by calling attention to those artistic techniques he does use—or by apologizing for those he is not using, which achieves the same purpose—or by giving the fiction a masking moral *sentence,* or by openly belittling his fiction and encouraging the audience to laugh at it and not to take it seriously. All such introductory metafictional denials enable the expression of forbidden desires in the ensuing fiction.

The medieval fabliau, a genre in which Chaucer excelled, so flagrantly satisfied erotic and aggressive desires and flouted authority that it had special needs for denying devices, some of the most powerful of which were metatextual or contextual. Of these negating frames, the most important has not been preserved in the manuscripts of the French fabliau collections, although Chaucer tries to suggest it in his *Canterbury Tales.* This frame is comic performance and reception, smiles and laughter that deny a dangerous, aggressive, "serious" intention on the part of the fabliau's teller or of those who identify with its characters, no matter how punitive the fictive dethronement of the "father," no matter how indecent the exposure of the fabliau's ribald language.

In order to understand how laughter may work as a metaverbal frame to change the meaning of all the signs, whether actions or words, within its bounds, we might think of the childhood game of tickling, wherein the parent or adult signals with smiles and laughter and comic expressions the benevolent intention behind his aggressive tickle attack. The child uses the same smiles and laughter to show that he understands or that he has chosen to interpret as nonthreatening these potentially dangerous intrusions into his personal space by a stronger person than himself. As we see here, laughter as the response of the immobilized or weaker person may deny a threat from the outside, just as, on the part of an aggressive, stronger person, laughter may be an assertion that his own signs do not mean what they appear to. For the weak, passive, or subservient person (and this might include the audience of a fiction as well as any other social group), laughter may be an assimilating assertion of self, an attempt to take control of the situation and, in the case that it denies a seriously intended threat from an authority figure who is not laughing, such laughter may be rebellious. On the other hand, for someone in a position of power and authority (which might include the author of a fiction, its teller, or members of the audience who identify with these or with the fictive aggressor), laughter can also be a way of denying and ineffectively censoring aggressive desires, thus enabling their expression and enjoyment, a way of equivocating, of having it both ways.

As we shall see later at greater length, Chaucer's Host, temporary ruler of the group of Canterbury pilgrims, time and again uses laughter to deny his aggression in comic deflations and mocking exposures of other pilgrims, generally at the moment when he puts them on the spot by requesting a tale. The Host insists on the protective cover of play, which should enable him to tell "the truth" without making anyone angry: "'But yet I pray thee, be nat wroth for game; / A man may seye ful sooth in game and pley'" (A 4354–55). However, the fiction of "just play" occasionally fails and pilgrims do get angry over the Host's tendentious *japes,* which injure their public image and self-esteem.

Chaucer's fictionalization of the storytelling situation enables us to see fabliau tellers using metatextual denying devices. The Miller, for instance, first takes care to announce that he is drunk and therefore not responsible for what he will say:

> "Now herkneth," quod the Millere, "alle and some!
> But first I make a protestacioun
> That I am dronke; I knowe it by my soun.

And therfore if that I mysspeke or seye,
Wyte it the ale of Southwerk, I you preye."
(A 3136–40)

Like the laughing person, the drunk person is defenseless, and this self-incapacitation prevents us from taking his threats seriously. When the Reeve protests because he perceives himself to be the butt of the Miller's fictional cuckolding of a carpenter, the Miller uses other denying devices. He insists on the difference between proverbs and tales—artfully organized language—and life; and he argues that an interpreter is free to make of his fiction whatever he wants, that a married man, like the Miller himself, is perfectly free to see the cuckolded husband of the tale as someone other than himself:

. . . "Leve brother Osewold,
Who hath no wyf, he is no cokewold.
But I sey nat therfore that thou art oon;
Ther been ful goode wyves many oon,
And evere a thousand goode ayeyns oon badde.
That knowestow wel thyself, but if thou madde.
Why artow angry with my tale now?
I have a wyf, pardee, as wel as thow;
Yet nolde I, for the oxen in my plogh,
Take upon me moore than ynogh,
As demen of myself that I were oon;
I wol bileve wel that I am noon."
(A 3151–62)

In spite of the Miller's denials, the Reeve is peeved and announces that the motivation for his own fabliau is revenge. He will set the Miller's "hood," just as the Miller has set a carpenter's "cap," by using force against force, churls' terms against churls' terms, fabliau against fabliau. The Reeve peels back the fiction of "just play" before he tells a fabliau that mocks and derides the Miller through the character of the cuckolded fabliau husband, whom he describes initially in the image of the Miller. Because of their metafictional frames, Chaucer's fabliaux are not just rebellious against authority in general (in ways to be discussed later), but they also deflate the pride of particular pilgrims who have earlier presumed to set themselves up by putting others down. The Cook calls the Reeve's fabliau a "jape of malice in the derk" (A 4338) and an-

nounces his own fabliau also as a tendentious joke, a "litel jape."
For the Host's "playfully" disparaging comments about the Cook's
pies and, implicitly, his stories, the Cook promises to get even
later by telling a _jape_ against the Host:

> ". . . 'sooth pley, quaad pley,' as the Flemyng seith.
> And therfore, Herry Bailly, by thy feith,
> Be thou nat wrooth, er we departen heer,
> Though that my tale be of an hostileer.
> But nathelees I wol nat telle it yit;
> But er we parte, ywis, thou shalt be quit."
>
> (A 4357–62)

The rules of the game permit only fictive revenges for fictive injuries. The player who gets angry is a spoilsport and suceeds only in
making his own fall into a reality. The way to counter the mocking
debasement of a rival's fabliau is to laugh it off and then tell a
fabliau featuring one's rival in the role of scapegoat. In this situation, the laughter of the butt saves his esteem by announcing one
of two things (neither of which may be true): either that "the shoe
does not fit," that he does not perceive himself in or identify with
the fabliau's scapegoat, but instead with the winners; or that he
does identify with the scapegoat, but only partially, for "he" com-
prises more than one self, and his superior self, invulnerable,
is capable of laughing along with everyone else at the inferior
self mocked in the fabliau's fiction. This may be the relationship
Chaucer intended to depict between the Merchant and the cuckolded husband in his tale. Not only is the "Merchant's Tale" a
riposte to the Clerk's tale of an exemplary wife (which has already
been deconstructed by the Clerk himself in his burlesque lyric envoy), but it may be the Merchant's way of putting himself on top
by telling a joke on "himself" (that is, on his inferior or former
self, as represented by the newly married, soon-to-be-cuckolded
January).

In addition to these kinds of contextual and metafictional denying devices, the medieval French fabliaux—and, even more so,
Chaucer's elaborate English versions—displayed poetic and narrative artifices that announced, from within the fabliau fiction,
"this is play." The rustics featured in many fabliaux did not signal
to courtly and high bourgeois audiences realism or a serious at-

tempt at representation, but, instead, artifice, fiction. For low bourgeois or popular medieval audiences, the main characters of certain fabliau plots were changed from rustics to nobles to emphasize the fiction. (Likewise today, the audience of the television series *Dallas* is not, for the most part, rich people; and peasants have never been the ones who got pleasure out of playing shepherds.) One man's reality is another man's fiction. The situations of medieval fabliaux were meant to seem artificial, not real. As for their language, the fabliaux were usually written in rhymed couplets, and the rhymes were sometimes quite rich and ingenious, calling attention to themselves and turning the signifier into the signified, the object of the story into play with language itself. The effect of such artifice is to create an unreal space and time and thereby enable the expression and appreciation of the fabliau's fulfillment of rebellious and forbidden desires.

In the medieval fabliau, in spite of all the strictures of age and authority, youthful—indeed, largely infantile—desires are satisfied in one way or another. These forbidden desires are of various sorts, and different aspects of the same fabliau may address different desires. One that I will discuss later is the desire to break the rules of proper speech, not only with respect to polite diction (avoiding dirty or rustic words), but also with respect to clarity of expression and singularity of intention (avoiding ambiguity and double entendre). Nevertheless, it would probably be fair to say that the chief desire expressed and fulfilled through the fictional action of medieval fabliaux was some version of the Oedipal fantasy: the cuckolding of the old husband by the younger man, aided by the desirous wife, who is not satisfied with her husband's sexual abilities. Like the mimed plays of Atellan farce centuries earlier, medieval fabliaux involved a basic Oedipal triangle of characters—father figure, son figure, and the desired and desiring female (wife/mother) figure. These characters might be doubled or supplemented by peripheral characters to modify in some way the fundamental comic action of dethroning and deriding the father figure.

All of Chaucer's fabliaux present variations on the Oedipal conflict. In the "Miller's Tale" we might say that the young boarder, Nicholas, contends not only with a jealous father figure in his host, the old carpenter, but also with a younger brother in Absalom, who is after (indeed yearning "as dooth a lamb after the tete" [A 3704] for) the same love object as Nicholas, the carpenter's wife Alison. The "Reeve's Tale" gives both the figurative sons satisfaction by providing the jealous father of the story, the miller, with both a wife and a daughter to protect from the young clerics whom he shelters for the night in his own bedroom. Both women in this tale chose "son" over "father/husband," the wife by preferring the younger man's lovemaking (A 4230), the daughter by switching loyalties to reveal to her lover her father's treachery and to give back the stolen grain (A 4240–46). In the "Merchant's Tale," old January is cuckolded in his own pleasure garden by his young squire, Damian, who has got in by counterfeiting January's "key"; and in the "Shipman's Tale," the thirty-year-old "yonge monk"—that Ur–Don Juan, "Daun John" (B² 1233)—claims relation to the older merchant in order to gain closer "aqueyntaunce" with his wife and eventually to cuckold him under his own roof.

There is comparatively little overt physical aggression by the son figure against the father figure in Chaucer's fabliaux; instead, filial aggression is disguised or transformed, generally by displacing it to other characters. The miller's wife in the "Reeve's Tale" is the one who knocks him out with a blow to the head; in the "Miller's Tale" the naive husband hanging in his kneading trough in the rafters both actively and passively participates in the comic "mechanism":[6] he cuts the rope, which precipitates his fall, which fractures his arm and brings, along with Nicholas's howling, all the neighbors in to mock his foolishness. Having set himself up in a gigantic male genital configuration at Nicholas's instigation, the carpenter, upon the cry of "water," cuts loose one member of the hanging trinity in an act that we may perceive, although he would not be in a position to do so, as a figure for self-castration. Only in the "Reeve's Tale" does the father figure know he has been cuckolded. January in the "Merchant's Tale" is glimpsingly conscious of the wrong done him by his squire and his wife, but he is easily persuaded otherwise, and the merchant and carpenter in the "Shipman's" and "Miller's" tales never even suspect that they have been dethroned and dishonored. But this is often the case in medieval fabliaux, where the fun comes from the deception, from our understanding of the "true" sense of the signs (spelling his cuckolding) that the husband is blind to or takes in a different sense.

The verbal duping of the father may have the symbolic effect of a cuckolding, as, for instance, in the fabliau of "La Saineresse" ("The Lady Leech"),[7] in which a husband who has boasted that no woman can deceive him is duped and cuckolded by his wife: she has her lover enter the house in the guise of a female leech, who then proceeds to "treat" her in the privacy of her bedroom. Afterward, the wife uses the vocabulary of leechcraft to give her husband a figurative account of her lovemaking (and his cuckolding) under his very nose. The husband, of course, does not suspect a thing:

> Par .iii. rebinées me prist,
> Et à chascune fois m'assist
> Sor mes rains deux de ses peçons,
> Et me feroit uns cops si lons;
> Toute me sui fet martirier,
> Et si ne poi onques sainier.
> Granz cops me feroit et sovent;
> Morte fusse, mon escient,
> S'un trop bon oingnement ne fust.
> Qui de tel oingnement éust,
> Jà ne fust mès de mal grevée.
> Et, quant m'ot tant demartelée,
> Si m'a après ointes mes plaies
> Qui moult par erent granz et laies,
> Tant que je fui toute guerie.
> Tel oingnement ne haz-je mie,
> Et il ne fet pas à haïr,
> Et si ne vous en quier mentir;
> L'oingnement issoit d'un tuiel,
> Et si descendoit d'un forel
> D'une pel moult noire et hideuse,
> Mais moult par estoit savoreuse."
> Dist li borgois: "Ma bèle amie,
> A poi ne fustes mal baillie;
> Bon oingnement avez éu."
> Cil ne s'est pas apercéu
> De la borde qu'ele conta.
>   (MR, vol. 1, pp. 291–92)

Three times s/he[8] repeated the procedure, / and each time placed / on my thighs two lancets / and gave me such a hard blow / that I was virtually martyred by it, / and still I couldn't bleed. / S/he gave me great blows and often. / I would have died, I believe, / if it hadn't been for a wonderful ointment. / Whoever has some of this ointment / no longer feels any pain. / And when s/he had pounded me so much, / afterwards s/he anointed my wounds, / which were by then great and ugly, / with the result that I was completely cured. / That ointment I surely don't dislike, / and it doesn't do anything hateful, / and I'm not trying to deceive you. / This ointment came out of a pipe, / and this hung down from a case / with a very black, ugly cover, / but it was savory in every way." / The bourgeois [husband] said, "My dear, / although you were a bit roughly handled, / you got a good ointment." / He did not perceive / the trick in what she recounted.

The wife's little "allegory" of lovemaking, her elaboration of a masking, partially censoring fiction of medical treatment, enables her to enjoy her lover in spite of her jealous husband and the social and religious sanctions against such illicit pleasures. Our vicarious pleasure in the fulfillment of forbidden erotic desires and in the foiling of authority—in the "father's" cuckolding—are made possible by the double denial of the two fictional frames: first by all the generic artifices of the fabliau, second by the wife's fictionalizing of the fabliau action.

When a lascivious, middle-aged priest represents a higher, "fatherly" authority in medieval French fabliaux, the action may focus less on fulfillment of erotic desire (taking his woman, cuckolding the father) than on physical aggression and revenge (that is, on the actual bodily punishment or castration of the father figure). For example, in the fabliau of "The Crucified Priest" ("Du Prestre crucefié," MR, vol. 1, pp. 194–97) the cuckolded husband, who is a carver of religious statues, especially crucifixes, sets off to market with a crucifix on his back, but he does not "carry his cross" for long. He returns rapidly to interrupt his wife making love with the priest, who hides in the carver's workroom. To escape detection, the priest stretches himself out naked against a cross in simulation of a statue of Christ. The husband, after a leisurely dinner, sharpens his knife and goes into his workroom, where he notes the well-hung Christ and rectifies his previous error of making a crucified Christ with obvious sex organs; in short, he castrates the flawed image of Christ (the rival priest):

"Dame," dist-il, vilainement,
"Ai en cest ymage mespris:
J'estoie yvres, ce m'est avis,
Quant je ceste chose i lessai;
Alumez, si l'amenderai."
Li prestres ne s'osa mouvoir;
Ei ice vous di-je por voir
Que vit et coilles li trencha,
Que onques riens ne li lessa
Que il n'ait tout outre trenchié.
(MR, vol. 1, p. 196)

"Lady," he said rudely, / "I did a bad job on this statue. / I was drunk, I think, / when I left this thing. / Light up, and I'll fix it." / The priest did not dare to move. / And I say this truly, / that he cut off the cock and balls / so that he left him nothing / that he had not entirely cut off.

Gautier Le Leu wrote two expanded variations on this plot involving the crucifixion/castration of the priest by the angry husband: "De Connebert" (MR, vol. 5, pp. 160–70) and "Du Prestre Teint" or "The Dyed Priest" (MR, vol. 6, pp. 8–23).[9] In the former version the cuckolded husband, a blacksmith, gathers his male relatives together in a parliament to decide how to be revenged upon the priest who dishonors them all. This "epic" council is rendered comic by the low characters, subject matter, and language, which is brought down even further by subversively vulgar puns. One man offers to kill the priest, but the husband responds that he has no desire to take the priest's "vie" (punning on *vit*), only his balls:

". . . Je n'ai envie
Qu'i perde ja par moi la vie,
Mais se gel puis ceianz tenir
Ne à l'aler ne au venir,
Je li voldrai coper les cous,
Par cui je sui Elnol et cous.
Por Deu, amis, or en pansez
Si q'an façois mes volantez."
(MR, vol. 5, pp. 163–64)

"I don't desire / that he should lose, because of me, his life, / but if I could catch him here, / either going or coming, / I would like to cut off

his balls, / because of which I am an Arnoul and a cuckold. / For God's
sake, friend, now consider / how you can accomplish my wishes."

The plan they elaborate forces the trapped priest to cut off his own
testicles, nailed in five places to a wooden stump, to escape being
burned to death. He saves his life (and his *vit*), but it will henceforth be a chaste one: "'Vos ne batroiz jamais crepon, / Ainz man-
roiz vie de chapon'" (p. 169); "'You will never again pound the
flesh, / but you will henceforth lead the life [or, bear the cock] of a
capon.'" Gautier provides himself and his interpreters with alibis
by means of his rather more elaborate than usual wit or joke-work
(his clever rhymes, his puns, and his burlesques of the Crucifixion and of the epic parliament), along with his moral *sentence*
against priestly philandering (for priests should truly be imitators
of Christ). By means of such equivocation, he preserves a certain
ambiguity of intention, which enables us to enjoy this vicious fantasy of revenge against an inhibiting authority figure.

The twelfth-century Latin fully dialogued play of *Babio,* which,
for its content, Edmond Faral considered to be a fabliau just as
much as later vernacular ones,[10] also features the cuckolding and
castration of the father figure by the son figure. In this case, the
young servant, Fodius, in complicity with the wife, Petula, cuck-
olds the married priest, Babio, who is a miser and a coward, a
foolish old pedant who "babbles" away, all sophistry and self-
aggrandizing classical allusions, all words and no action. The
names of the characters in this play are all comically significant.
When Babio accuses Fodius of adultery with Petula, Fodius gets
off the hook by means of a simple ruse of grammar. He swears
that he is not fucking Petula, meaning at that very moment: "Iuro
sacras per aras, non *fodit* hanc *Fodius*" (p. 44, line 272). When
Babio does not catch the equivocation and takes *fŏdit* for the past-
tense *fōdit,* Fodius escapes, rejoicing in his own ingenuity and
mocking the stupidity of Babio, "Beef-tongue," who cannot even
distinguish between the sounds *bu* and *ba:* "Scit neque *bu* neque *ba*
Babio lingua bovis" (p. 44, line 276). In the climactic scene of this
hilarious comedy, which must have been enormously appreciated
by young clerics under the discipline of their masters, Fodius
jumps out of bed with Petula to catch Babio spying outside the
bedroom; Fodius pretends not to recognize Babio, accuses him of

being a robber, and castrates him (p. 54, lines 451–52).
promptly decides to leave the couple in peace and become a
and the play ends with Babio repeating the old proverb, the truth
of which the play has just demonstrated: never trust your wife,
child, or dependent.[11]

On the level of their plots, Chaucer's fabliaux, as I have already
suggested, tend to focus on the satisfaction of forbidden erotic desires (the "son" cuckolding the "father" or the wife cuckolding her
husband) rather than on the satisfaction of the "child's" illicitly aggressive, physically punitive desires against the "father." The
"Summoner's Tale" is the exception to this generalization, and
even in this tale the aggression of the fart is symbolically more deflating than it is physically harmful. Nevertheless, in the French
fabliau version, "Li Dis de la vescie à prestre" ("The Tale of the
Priest's Bladder," MR, vol. 3, pp. 106–17), the insult is much
tamer: the dying man pestered by friars for a legacy leaves them
his bladder. In the French version, the dying man is a priest and
has no wife for the friars to be too intimate with, whereas in the
"Summoner's Tale" Chaucer suggests an Oedipal triangle:

> The frere ariseth up ful curteisly,
> And hire embraceth in his armes narwe,
> And kiste hire sweete, and chirketh as a sparwe
> With his lyppes: "Dame," quod he, "right weel,
> As he that is youre servant every deel,
> Thanked be God, that yow yaf soule and lyf!
> Yet saugh I nat this day so fair a wyf
> In al the chirche, God so save me!"
> "Ye, God amende defautes, sire," quod she.
>   (D 1802–10)

The friar assumes an authoritative attitude, as if he were not only
spiritual father or "master," as he is addressed by Thomas and his
wife (D 1781, 1800, 1836), but also master of the house; when he
arrives he immediately drives the cat off the bench (D 1775) and
orders just what he wants for dinner (D 1838–41). The friar's ha-
rangue warning Thomas against anger and asking for a penitential
gift brings his spiritual son, for so he calls Thomas (D 1996), to the
brink of explosion (D 2121). The sick man has been immobilized
long enough. His revenge both demonstrates Thomas's power (by

tricking the friar into handling Thomas's anus and by the magnitude of his fart) and puts the friar down (literally, as he bends over awkwardly groping about Thomas's "pipe" ["tuwel," D 2148] and symbolically, through the friar's nose, which takes the brunt of the insult). Thomas's fart is a symbolic castration of the friar, a deflation of his masculine pride, and that is how the friar takes it. The anger of which Thomas relieves himself through the vengeful fart now inspires the friar. The problem of dividing the "gift" or "fartingsworth" in twelve, as the friar has promised to do in sharing it with his convent, is resolved in a way that multiplies the insult and puts the noses of his fellow friars on the line—or, rather, neatly lined up around the circle of a cartwheel, in a burlesque of contemporary representations of the descent of the Holy Spirit at Pentecost, when Christ's disciples were inspired with the power of the Word.[12] This resolution raises derision of paternal authority to a new high.

Some of the best medieval fabliaux mock and dethrone the "father" on several levels simultaneously. As I have suggested, the fictional action may feature the cuckolding or castration (the latter usually symbolic) of the most authoritative character or "father" by the "child" (usually either "son" or wife). An analogous cuckolding or castration may occur on the level of language when an illicit connotation dethrones an authoritative denotation, when an infantile or rustic or foolish interpretation overthrows a proper, conventional, authoritative one.[13] The conflict featured in many fabliaux is a conflict of intention, of understanding; in this conflict the "childish" understanding displaces the authoritative, "adult" one, turning it into a misunderstanding. This is what happens, for example, in the previously discussed fabliau of the "Lady Leech" in the wife's euphemistic account of her lovemaking. The husband is attentive solely to the denotation of his wife's words as determined by their supposedly medical context, which she has constructed to mislead him. Because we know that a male lover lies beneath the disguise of the lady leech, illicit connotations arise in the wife's speech to form a second, erotic discourse that effectively displaces and dethrones the first—apparent, proper—meaning. The effect is that of an extended obscene pun.

In a number of fabliaux the dethronement of the authority figure is entirely linguistic, with the ruler being shown to be incapable of controlling or legislating meaning, of imposing his interpretation on a word, a phrase, a sign. This is the case in the fabliau of "Le Roi d'Angleterre et le jongleur d'Ely" ("The King of England and the Jongleur from Ely," MR, vol. 2, pp. 242–56), in which the king questions the jongleur about his identity and, instead of getting conventional responses to his questions in the form of names, receives responses from the jongleur that avoid naming and define by relationship or else bring out possible puns and other types of double entendres in the king's words and idioms by assuming an entirely different context for understanding them than the king had intended. To the king's first question, "Who is your lord?" the jongleur replies, "The husband of my lady." This continues: "How are you called?" "The same as the one who brought me up.". . . "Where is your town?" "Around the church." "Where is the church?" "In the town of Ely." "Where is Ely located?" "On the water." "How is the water called?" "You don't have to call water; it always comes of its own accord." The jongleur's overly literal interpretations of the king's conventional idioms create *équivoques,* ambiguities that overthrow the authority of the king's words.

The most clever series of such twisted idioms occurs in a situation of horse trading. After offering to buy the jongleur's horse, the king questions him on its qualities, and the jongleur defeats the king's intentions by understanding each of the king's horsetrading idioms as though it referred to human accomplishments: "Does he not know how to draw ('trere')?" "He knows nothing of the bow or crossbow.". . . "Does he amble ('emble') well?" "He has never been taken at stealing.". . . "Now tell me, is he healthy ('seinz')?" "He's no saint ('seintz'), of that I'm certain." To the king's command that he answer correctly ("à droit") what land he is from ("De quele terre estez vus?"), the jongleur replies, once again, "à rebours" (against the grain, the wrong way):

> —Sire, estez vus tywlers ou potters
> Qe si folement demaundez?
> Purquoi demandez de quele tere?
> Volez vus de moi potz fere?
> (MR, vol. 2, p. 247)

"Lord, are you a tile maker or a potter / that you ask me such a silly question? / Why ask me what earth I'm made of? / Do you want to make pots out of me?"

The deflating lesson the jongleur then proceeds to teach the king, at some length, is that people will interpret in the way that suits them, especially to build themselves up at another's expense: "Car nulle rien ne purroi fere / Qe um ne trovera le countrere"; "For I can do nothing / that someone else won't interpret the wrong way" (MR, vol. 2, p. 255). This subversive fabliau's concluding, rectifying moral, expressed in Latin, is that the best rule to follow is the Golden Mean: "Medium tenuere beati."

The fabliau of "La Male Honte," by Guillaume le Normand, also dethrones the ruler by means of wordplay. A peasant named Honte dies and sends a friend to the king of England to deliver to the king the "male" (bag) containing the peasant's worldly fortune, which is the king's by right when one of his peasants dies without an heir. The conflict of intention in this tale arises when the peasant, in his crude manner, announces to the king that he has brought him "la male Honte," meaning Honte's bag. The king, however, does not perceive that "honte" is a name; he automatically thinks, given the appearance of the speaker, that the peasant's phrase is a shameful malediction aimed at undermining his own power (and potency). In his anger, the king has the peasant thrown out of court and beaten. The peasant does not understand why he is being treated so roughly, but he is determined to keep his promise to his dead friend, so he makes his announcement two more times, each time to the king's increasing astonishment and outrage, until finally a counselor advises the king that he is in the wrong not to inquire what the "male Honte" is, whereupon the peasant explains, and the king rewards him by giving him Honte's bag. The joke is not on the peasant but on the king, for vulgar understanding and jumping to conclusions. When the peasant returns home, he broadcasts the story of the king's misunderstanding, to the king's real shame this time:

> Ce dit Guillaumes en son conte
> Que li vilains en a portée
> La male Honte en sa contrée.
> Si l'a as Anglois departie;
> Encor en ont il grant partie;
> Sanz la male ont il assez honte,
> Et chascun jor lor croist et monte.
> Par mauvais seignor et par lasche
> Les a honte mis en s'ataiche [or "sa taiche"].[14]

So says Guillaume in his tale, / that the peasant carried / Honte's bag back to his land. / Yet he shared it with the English. / They still have a big part of it: / without the bag, they got plenty of shame, / and every day it grows and increases. / Because of a no-good, cowardly lord, / Shame has put them in her hat ribbon [or, her purse].

The fabliau of "La Male Honte" is a rebellious one with political undertones that uses a rustic, childish figure to mock authority.

As I have already suggested, illicit intention or understanding (the improper, unconventional joining of words with the "wrong" context) is equivalent, on a verbal level, to an act of cuckoldry (the improper, illicit joining of a wife with the "wrong" man). Some of Chaucer's fabliau "fathers" are very deliberately cuckolded by their wives and their wives' lovers linguistically, intellectually, as well as physically; they are encouraged to interpret the signs of their own humiliation in the "wrong" contexts. We experience pleasure in the subservient, "childish" characters' freewheeling, arbitrary interpretation of signs and their ability to make the "father" believe this interpretation, thereby putting themselves and their illicit intention on top. May, for example, doubly dupes January in the "Merchant's Tale," first by copulating with Damian in the tree, then by providing January with and convincing him to believe an outlandish context of interpretation that reverses the true meaning of the signs he has just witnessed, with the result that he consents, albeit unwittingly, to his own cuckolding. May convinces him that she was "struggling" with a man on a tree in order to restore her husband's eyesight according to an old remedy for blindness (E 2368–75). She authorizes her error by inventing an extraordinary proverbial recipe that, nevertheless, satisfies January.

There are also a number of French fabliaux in which the husband is fooled and dethroned in this way, by convincing him to accept a bizarre context of interpretation, thus misleading his intellect—hoodwinking him—and getting him to accept his replacement by another man. For example, in "Du Prestre ki abevete" ("The Priest Who Spies," MR, vol. 3, pp. 54–57), a priest makes a husband believe that the view through the hole in his door is false, because when the priest looks through it, he claims to see the husband and wife copulating, although they are really eating dinner. When the husband goes out to test the view through the hole, the priest seizes his opportunity, and the husband is none the wiser for having witnessed his own cuckolding. In "Du Vilain de Bailluel" ("The Rustic from Bailluel," MR, vol. 4, pp. 212–16), the husband is encouraged to believe that he is lying on his bed dead and thus can do nothing about the spectacle across the room of his wife making love with the priest.

In Chaucer's "Miller's Tale," the clerk Nicholas fools the old husband, who should know better (for God promised never again to destroy the world by water), into believing in and making ridiculous preparations for a second, this time flash, Flood—and all this after the husband has just prided himself at length on his ignorance and lack of curiosity:

> This carpenter to blessen hym bigan,
> And seyde, "Help us, Seinte Frydeswyde!
> A man woot litel what hym shal bityde.
> This man is falle, with his astromye,
> In some woodnesse or in som agonye.
> I thoghte ay wel how that it sholde be!
> Men sholde nat knowe of Goddes pryvetee.
> Ye, blessed be alwey a lewed man
> That noght but oonly his bileve kan!
> So ferde another clerk with astromye;
> He walked in the feeldes for to prye
> Upon the sterres, what ther sholde bifalle,
> Til he was in a marle-pit yfalle;
> He saugh nat that. But yet, by Seint Thomas,
> Me reweth soore of hende Nicholas.
> He shal be rated of his studiyng."
>
> (A 3448–63)

The jealous old husband's pride in his own stupidity heightens the comedy of his fall from the divine grace he believed was especially his—believed firmly enough to spend the night hanging in a trough in the rafters waiting for a second Flood, from which God would save him, like another Noah, with his wife (and his boarder, in lieu of sons). In Chaucer's "Summoner's Tale," on the other hand, it is the ill husband, Thomas, who misleads the "fatherly" friar's understanding by encouraging him to believe that the gift hidden in such a private place, which must be equally divided among the friars in the convent, must be very precious indeed. The friar should know better than to go feeling around Thomas's anus, but his own greed and Thomas's misleading suggestions encourage his total misinterpretation of the signs, which he understands in the context of a dying man's legacy—until Thomas rectifies this misinterpretation with a fart that proclaims, by providing its own unmistakably pungent context, what kind of "gift" Thomas intended.

In all the passages thus far discussed, the fabliau plot involves one or more "child" characters' mocking or dethronement, through their actions and words, of an authoritative, inhibiting "father," who may also be represented by one or more characters, but most commonly by a jealous old husband or a lascivious, middle-aged priest. There are, however, consolations to be had from fictive dethronements of a more abstract kind, in which the power or authority to be subverted and mocked is vested, not in a character, but in a prescribed code of language or conduct or in a literary genre or topos. The satisfactions to be had in breaking such rules will be the subject of the next chapter.

Chapter Five

Breaking Verbal Taboos

The Consolations of Fiction III

If, as is fairly generally accepted now, the fabliaux were not tavern fare, composed by the vulgar for the vulgar (certainly Chaucer's fabliaux were not), then it must be admitted that, just as the fabliaux's action of cuckoldry and physical aggression breaks the rules of polite peacetime behavior, so the raw vocabulary of many fabliaux infringes the rules of polite and courtly speech to which respectable bourgeois or courtly audiences would ordinarily conform. In the late medieval period, the rules of proper speech, which I call the "father" tongue, forbade the outright naming of sexual parts or open discussion of lower bodily functions such as sexual intercourse or excretion.[1] Furthermore, proper speech was supposed to be clear in a conventional way. It could be rich in ornamental, figurative expressions (rhetoric) and use euphemisms to avoid breaking the above-mentioned taboos, but proper speech could not be deliberately equivocal to the point of calling attention to itself as object, that is, to the point of materializing language.

On one level, the father tongue is conventional adult speech. In the Middle Ages, as today, children gradually had to give up what Freud has called the "pleasure in nonsense"—to which we might add the "pleasure in surplus sense," in richly equivocal evocations of meaning. I quote at length from Freud's description of the stages of giving up and covertly or rebelliously recovering the childish pleasures of using words idiosyncratically, of assimilating

74

language rather than accommodating oneself to conventional, adult linguistic codes:

During the period in which a child is learning how to handle the vocabulary of his mother-tongue, it gives him obvious pleasure to "experiment with it in play." . . . And he puts words together without regard to the condition that they should make sense, in order to obtain from them the pleasurable effect of rhythm or rhyme. Little by little he is forbidden this enjoyment, till all that remains [*sic*] permitted to him are significant combinations of words. But when he is older attempts still emerge at disregarding the restrictions that have been learnt on the use of words. Words are disfigured by particular little additions being made to them, their forms are altered by certain manipulations . . . , or a private language may even be constructed for use among playmates. . . .

Whatever the motive may have been which led the child to begin these games, I believe that in his later development he gives himself up to them with the consciousness that they are nonsensical, and that he finds enjoyment in the attraction of what is forbidden by reason. He now uses games in order to withdraw from the pressure of critical reason. But there is far more potency in the restrictions which must establish themselves in the course of a child's education in logical thinking and in distinguishing between what is true and false in reality; and for this reason the rebellion against the compulsion of logic and reality is deep-going and long-lasting. Even the phenomena of imaginative activity must be included in this [rebellious] category.[2]

Freud's observation about the restrictive effect of formal education is corroborated by some contemporary studies of children's use of language. These show that spontaneous metaphor decreases, and literalism increases, at school age, when children are under pressure to conform and follow rules. This verbal literalism, one study notes, "need not surprise us, as it has parallels in the domain of children's drawings, which become increasingly realistic (and decreasingly striking) after the preschool years."[3]

Private games of rebellion against reason such as Freud describes had public, ritual counterparts in the Middle Ages. The medieval game context of festive time, a bounded and regulated fiction that involved role-playing, could license the overt regression of the entire social body, adults as well as adolescents, and the temporary recovery of forbidden corporeal and linguistic pleasures.[4] Within the frame of festive time or outside it, the game contexts of certain medieval versified literary genres, such as, in French, the *fatras* or *fatrasie,* the *rêverie,* and the *sottie,* sanctioned the enjoyment of nonsense or surplus sense, the sheer sensual pleasure and the delight in mastery that comes from manipulating at will the matter of language to create patterns of sound, to evoke multiple senses in defiance of the censorious, rationalizing rules of correct grammar and clear expression.[5] Although I might quote a section from one of these French nonsense genres, translating it would be impossible in the conventional sense, for any translation would be idiosyncratic in the extreme. To an even greater extent than the facetious wordplay of some fabliaux, these nonsense genres rebel against the grammar of the father tongue. They may be full of bawdy-seeming combinations of syllables, but the target nonsense genres attack is the censoring *how to* of the father tongue, whereas a major intention of the fabliaux is to expose "Goddes pryvetee," that is, *what may not be said* in proper speech.

On another level, the father tongue was more than merely adult speech: it was the speech of those with power, and it was often, literally, a different language or dialect from the native or mother tongue. In the medieval Western Church, for example, in every land, the language of authority was Latin. For a long time after the Conquest, the father tongue in England was French, and those with ambition learned it, even if "after the scole of Stratford atte Bowe" (A 125). It was well into the fourteenth century in England before the father tongue became English again, with the teaching of English in schools and the elaboration of prescriptive, censoring codes such as Chaucer's fictional Knight had internalized:

> . . . of his port as meeke as is a mayde.
> He never yet no vileynye ne sayde
> In al his lyf unto no maner wight.
> He was a verray, parfit gentil knyght.
>
> (A 69–72)

If there are virtually no English fabliaux before Chaucer's time, this is in part because, until the mid-fourteenth century, there was no English father tongue for an English fabliau to dethrone with rebelliously, aggressively vulgar and equivocal, "childish" speech. The greater the pressure to conform to proper speech in the situations of everyday life, the greater the pleasure in the fictional subversion or flouting of the rules. This, one suspects, is the reason for the great popularity of fabliaux in French courts and polite society in the thirteenth and fourteenth centuries, at the height of the effort there to refine speech and manners, to adopt a courtly father tongue.[6]

Compared to many French fabliaux, Chaucer's are sparing in their use of vulgar, obscene expressions, and these are used less often to dethrone and mock an abstract father tongue or proper standard of speech than to mock and expose particular characters within the fictional structure of the *Canterbury Tales* (characters who may, however, represent other fictional characters or powerful social groups or individuals outside the fiction, in life). For example, Harry Bailly's response to the Pardoner's facetious invitation to worship his fake relics is an obscene and hostile joke that ineffectively masks with protestations of "just play" the Host's aggressive—indeed, castrating—and exposing intentions:

> "Lat be," quod he, "it shal nat be, so theech!
> Thou woldest make me kisse thyn olde breech,
> And swere it were a relyk of a seint,
> Though it were with thy fundement depeint!
> But, by the croys which that Seint Eleyne fond,
> I wolde I hadde thy coillons in myn hond
> In stide of relikes or of seintuarie.
> Lat kutte hem of, I wol thee helpe hem carie;
> They shul be shryned in an hogges toord!"
>
> (C 947–55)

The Pardoner, who is no fool, gets the point: with the obscene language of his joke, the Host tries to turn the Pardoner into a sexual object, to "expose" him in front of the other pilgrims, thus provoking laughter[7] and dethroning him, bringing the Pardoner down from his pulpit, putting an end to his power to fascinate the pilgrims and manipulate them with his words. The Host's joke is the verbal equivalent of the action of a fabliau such as "The Crucified Priest," in which the priest's castration takes place against a religious background—literally, as he is stretched out on the cross in a very unwilling *imitatio Christi*. In the Host's joking "castration" of the Pardoner, the vulgar, taboo terms he uses to expose his rival—"fundement," "coillons," "hogges toord"—have an explosive impact in the apparently sacred context created by the Pardoner's sermon, his invitation to worship the relics, and the Host's own naming of sacred objects of religious worship in the insult— "croys which that Seint Eleyne fond," "relikes," "seintuarie," "shryned."

The next time Harry Bailly uses the vulgar term "toord" to expose someone, it is Chaucer's pilgrim persona whom he "cuts off" in the act of telling the romance of "Sir Thopas":

> "By God," quod he, "for pleynly, at a word,
> Thy drasty rymyng is nat worth a toord!
> Thou doost noght elles but despendest tyme."
>   (B² 2119–21)

Chaucer's verse, Harry judges, is no better than excrement. The Host's verbal insult is the equivalent, in terms of fabliau action, of a fart in the face. Why, we might ask, does Chaucer do this to "himself"? I suspect that Chaucer can hardly have been oblivious to how people responded to his wonderful fluency with languages, his power over words and, through them, over other people. Harry Bailly reacted to the Pardoner's verbal manipulations with resentment that he expressed openly in a joke intended to enlist others on his side and make a scapegoat of his rival. Chaucer uses Harry, the master of *japes,* to express our resentments against himself; this is a very clever ploy, because, of course, it is entirely controlled by Chaucer, who is playing all the roles.

The man whom we call the father of English poetry defuses jealousy and resentment by playing the clownish, impotent father. With his first attempt at a tale, "Sir Thopas," he strings together all the authorizing marks and conventions of courtly romance in an extremely awkward way, in a tale with little content other than these conventions. By telling "Sir Thopas," Chaucer, in effect, puts on the over-large, old men's trousers of the clown, the baggy, empty-looking trousers that draw our derision. Chaucer's friends and rivals in life would probably have been most appreciative of the release he offers them, for they would have had occasion to resent Chaucer's superior power with words. Nevertheless, modern students, "subjected" to Chaucer by the regulations of English departments, and medieval scholars, who inevitably feel inferior to the great master, also seem to get considerable pleasure out of Harry's verbal fart in Chaucer's figurative face. There are, after all, only two ways we can go in the face of genius. We can protect ourselves, in our relative weakness, by submitting to and identifying with the genius, as English professors very often do in teaching, "becoming" the genius through imitation, role-playing. The other alternative is to rebel against and belittle the genius in order to valorize ourselves. Although this is not an option that can be practiced overtly in most English departments, it is very often practiced covertly in lectures and scholarly writing wherein we "deconstruct" Chaucer or—less challengingly rebellious—"reconstruct" him, that is, explicate Chaucer, remake him in our own images, try to make him say what we mean, implicitly putting ourselves on top. We do this, not exactly out of a Bloomian "anxiety of influence," but, rather, out of that rivalry for power that has been played out on the field of literature for centuries, even across centuries, between poet and interpreter (poet, critic, scholar), a rivalry, an insistence on making anew, that has helped to produce what Paul Zumthor dubbed the "mouvance" or "movement" of the medieval text,[8] a movement that continues even in our print culture.

To challenge an Ur-father and to put oneself on top through interpretation may be an even more satisfying experience than to play the game of interpretation with a contemporary genius. What are our motives for looking ever further back in the study of literature? I doubt that most Chaucerians' only pleasure in explicating Chaucer is a vicarious enjoyment of Chaucer's power with words that comes from hearing those very words of the father of English poetry in our own mouths, seeing them flow from our pens or flicker across our word-processor screens. Indeed, I suspect that most of us have an ambiguous relationship with Chaucer the father, that we derive some pleasure from and valorize ourselves in both ways: by "becoming" our idol and by deposing him, by accommodating ourselves to Chaucer's text and by assimilating it in our own peculiar ways, the two modes alternating in an endless dialectic. Although we criticize and dethrone Chaucer in less obvious ways than he dethrones himself through the Host, we can nevertheless appreciate and laugh to hear our forbidden, punitive, "deconstructive" desires openly expressed in Harry Bailly's "nat worth a toord!"

Another situation in which Chaucer uses taboo or extremely

vulgar diction to expose and mock someone occurs in the prologue to the "Summoner's Tale," where the Summoner takes revenge on the friar by portraying friars as diminutive insects swarm-
ing into and nesting in the devil's presumably filthy asshole, which
is to them like the honeycomb to bees:[9]

> "'Hold up thy tayl, thou Sathanas!' quod he;
> 'Shewe forth thyn ers, and lat the frere se
> Where is the nest of freres in this place!'
> And er that half a furlong wey of space,
> Right so as bees out swarmen from an hyve,
> Out of the develes ers ther gonne dryve
> Twenty thousand freres on a route,
> And thurghout helle swarmed al aboute,
> And comen agayn as faste as they may gon,
> And in his ers they crepten everychon."
> (D 1689–98)

Here is another verbal equivalent of—indeed, in this case an introduction to—the classic fabliau deflation of a fart in the face. After
the friar in the fiction gets his from Thomas (D 2151), the impact
of the insult is multiplied by repetition when the problem of
equally dividing the fart among all the friars is taken up as a facetious, burlesque version of the courtly *demande* or love problem to
be debated at dinner (D 2214–86). The perfect solution Jankyn
imagines puts the friar down once again, this time with his nose
directly under a farting churl in a burlesque of conventional imagery of the descent of the Holy Spirit on Christ's disciples at Pentecost. The allusions to sacred imagery create a background of propriety, introduce the tension of an incongruity that maximizes the
comic impact of the final fart in the face. Jankyn's (and the Summoner's) intentions are to mock the authority of the preaching
friar, to bring him down by letting him "begin the board," a very
unsavory one, for his "worthiness":

> "The noble usage of freres yet is this,
> The worthy men of hem shul first be served;
> And certeinly he hath it weel disserved.
> He hath to-day taught us so muche good
> With prechyng in the pulpit ther he stood,
> That I may vouche sauf, I sey for me,
> He hadde the firste smel of fartes thre;

And so wolde al his covent hardily,
He bereth hym so faire and hoolily."
(D 2278–86)

Chaucer also uses extremely vulgar diction in the narration of Alison's exposure of her "hole" (to expose and ridicule Absalom by tricking him into kissing her "naked ers") and Nicholas's similar exposure of his private parts and his thunderous fart (that backfired instead of completely squelching the "somdeel squaymous" Absalom). However, this obscene language is aimed more at the Knight and other "gentils," with their maidenly proper speech, than at the characters in the Miller's fabliau. Absalom does not bear the brunt of the low *diction* but, instead, of the low *action:* being forced into or inadvertently kissing ass ("ful savourly, er he were war of this" [A 3732–35]) was just as great a humiliation as receiving a fart in the face, both being classic fabliau deflations.[10]

Censored as it now stands after the provocative lines "And hadde a wyf that heeld for contenance / A shoppe, and swyved for hir sustenance" (A 4421–22), the "Cook's Tale" promises more bawdy language at the outset than any other tale. All in all, though, the language of Chaucer's fabliaux is hardly as lewd as his "General Prologue" apology (A 725–42) would lead us to expect, especially if we are aware of the depths to which contemporary French fabliau diction might descend. The sole satisfaction of many French fabliaux seems to be the breaking of verbal and behavioral taboos, and relatively more of these have to do with sex than with excretion. A fabliau such as the "Four Wishes from Saint Martin" ("Les .iiii. souhais Saint Martin," MR, vol. 5, pp. 201–10) fulfills libidinous desires in an outrageous way. Saint Martin gives a devoted peasant four wishes, and the peasant's wife persuades him to let her make the first wish, which she uses to fulfill her deepest desire. She asks Saint Martin to cover her husband all over with erect penises to satisfy her sexual appetite:

—Je demant," dist ele, "en non Dieu,
Que vous soiez chargiez de vis,
Ne vous remaingnent oeil ne vis,
Teste, ne braz, ne piez, ne coste
Où partout ne soit vit planté.
Si ne soient ne mol ne doille,
Ainz ait à chascun vit sa coille;

Toz dis soient li vit tendu,
Si samblerez vilain cornu."
(p. 204)

"I ask," she said, "in the name of God, / that you be loaded with pricks, / that there not remain on you an eye, face, / head, arm, leg, or side / without everywhere having pricks planted on them. / And that these not be soft and tender, / but that each prick have its own balls, / and that at all times the pricks be extended, / so that you will resemble a horned peasant."

As we might expect, the husband's nose is the first place the penises start popping out on his body, which is soon covered with them. The narrator describes this metamorphosis at length, using a litany of taboo *vits*. As revenge for his grotesque transformation, the husband wishes the equivalent on his wife, that she be covered with vaginas, the description of which involves another blatant exhibition or exposure of taboo words, this time involving wordplay on the syllable *con* (cunt) in words such as "connue," conventionally meaning "recognized" but, according to facetious etymology or word formation, meaning either "naked cunt" (*con nu*) or "provided with cunt" (by analogy with the formation of *cornu*):[11]

Adonc fu ele bien connue
Qu'ele ot .ii. cons en la veüe;
.Iiii. en ot ou front coste à coste,
Et con devant et con d'encoste;
Si ot con de mainte maniere
Et con devant et con derriere,
Con tort, con droit et con chenu,
Et con sanz poil et con velu,
Et con pucel, et con estrait,
Et con estroit, et con bien fait,
Et con petit, et con aorce,
Et con parfont et con seur boce,
Et con au chief, et con aus piez.
Adonques fu li vilains liez:
"Sire," dist ele, "qu'as tu fait?
Por qoi m'as doné tel souhait?
—Je te dirai," dist li bons hom:
"Je n'avoie preu en .i. con
Puis que tant vit me doniiez.

> Bele suer, ne vous esmaiez
> Que jamès ne vendroiz par rue
> Que vous ne soiez bien connue."
>
> (p. 206)

Then she was well known, / because she had two cunts in her regard / and she had four on her forehead, side by side, / and cunts in front and cunts on the sides, / and she had cunts of all sorts, / and cunts in front and cunts in back, / crooked cunts and straight cunts and white-haired cunts / and cunts without hair and furry cunts / and virgin cunts and long cunts / and narrow cunts and well-made cunts / and small cunts and cunts on the bias / and deep cunts and cunts on top of humps / and cunts at her head and cunts at her feet. / Then the rustic was delighted: / "Lord," she said, "what have you done? / Why have you visited such a wish on me?" / "I'll tell you," said the good man. / "I had no profit from one cunt / after you had given me so many pricks. / Sister, don't be dismayed, / for never will you come down the street / without being instantly recognized."

Such an outrageous fictional fulfillment of forbidden desires tends in this case to provoke at least partial censorship by its audience. On the one hand, such constant repetition of the taboo words *con* and *vit* emphasizes the word itself in its various combinations with surrounding syllables in each ensuing line. We are caught up in the wordplay, in *vit* and *con* as linguistic objects (signifieds rather than signifiers), and we nearly forget their reference to sex organs. Furthermore, the grotesque image of a man covered with penises or a woman covered with vaginas provokes laughter whose purpose is to assert control and protect us by declaring the grotesque incongruity nonthreatening, unreal. Our laughter says, "It couldn't happen to us." Just as the fabliau wife and husband are relieved to get back to a state of normality (one sex organ per person) after this excessive wish-fulfillment, we are somewhat relieved to find ways of partially censoring and controlling such outrageous fulfillment of erotic desires. The concluding metafictional moralization of the fabliau firmly reasserts paternal authority:

> Par cest fablel poez savoir
> Que cil ne fet mie savoir
> Qui mieus croit sa fame que lui:
> Sovent l'en vient honte et anui.
>
> (p. 207)

By this fabliau it may be learned / that the man hardly behaves wisely / who trusts his wife more than himself. / Often shame and trouble come of this.

Taboos against talking about excretion (and related behavioral taboos as well) are broken in the fabliau of "The Little Turd" ("De la crote," MR, vol. 3, pp. 46–48). A peasant husband finds amusement while scratching himself at his hearth by starting a guessing game with his wife in which the correct answer requires her to name his genitals. On the wager of some wine, she in turn proposes a problem for him: in three guesses he must discover the identity of a little piece of her dried excrement. Touch and sight do not get the husband any closer to the correct response, but, at the comic climax of his last guess, taste resolves the enigma:

> Et cil en sa bouche dedenz
> La met et masche entre ses denz
> Que paor a que il ne perde.
> "Par le cuer bieu", fet il, "c'est merde;
> Je m'en puis bien apercevoir."
>
> (p. 48)

And he puts it in his mouth / and chews it between his teeth, / for he is afraid he will lose. / "By Gog," he says, "it's shit. / I'm sure of it."

This guessing game played by peasants at the hearth is a deliberately crude parody of didactic medieval question-and-answer games, such as *demandes d'amour,* which were played in polite society. The fabliau of "The Little Turd" thus dethrones a more authoritative genre, which we might call a "generic father." So do other medieval literary burlesques as, for instance, the outrageously scatological imitation *chanson de geste* known as "Audigier."[12]

Gautier Le Leu's "Debate between the Cunt and the Asshole" (MR, vol. 2, pp. 133–36) manages to break all the father tongue's verbal taboos against discussing sex and excretion and at the same time to parody in a mocking vein a much-appreciated high literary genre, the debate overheard in a dream vision. All it takes to evoke the dream-vision genre at the outset is one conventional line: "L'autrier me vint en avision" ("the other day it came to me in a dream"). The tale (*conte*) of this fabliau is an accounting (*conte*) that begins with the asshole's demand of a rent for services rendered to the cunt (*con*). The protagonists' arguments for their own respective merits mix crude names, vulgar, "kitchen" euphemisms for sex, and more courtly euphemisms such as caroling and kneeling in supplication. Gautier ends this highly irregular debate in the conventional manner of dream visions:

> De m'aventure n'i a plus.
> Seignor, ceste desputison,
> Qu'avez oï du Cul au Con,
> Si m'avint l'autrier en sonjant
> A mie-nuit en mon dormant.
> Tout issi com je me dormoie
> Si me prist une si grant joie
> Qu'il me prist talent de rimer
> Por ceste aventure conter;
> Mès onques plus je n'en oï
> Fors ce que j'ai conté ici.
>
> (p. 136)

There's no more to my adventure. / Lords, this debate / that you have heard between the Asshole and the Cunt / came to me the other day in a dream / in the middle of the night in my sleep. / And as I was sleeping, / such a great joy took me / that I felt the urge to rhyme / in order to narrate this adventure. / But I never heard any more of it / than what I have recounted here.

Such a fabliau not merely breaks verbal and behavioral taboos, but it does so conspicuously by imitating the high generic context of a dream-vision debate. This combination of high and low is analogous to deliberately ineffective censorship. Calling to mind the rules of proper speech and manners in order to break them heightens the pleasure in disobedience. Even a hint of censorship, such as a courtly euphemism, will heighten a comic climax. The more powerful the repression or censorship, the greater the energy of desire that must be mobilized to lift it, the greater the comic climax when no/yes explodes into the open in laughter.

A number of fabliaux employ extended euphemism to comic effect in plots that involve the seduction of a very proper young woman: "The Young Lady Who Could Not Hear Tell of Fucking" ("De la damoisele qui ne pooit oïr parler de foutre," MR, vol. 3, pp. 81–85); "The Virgin Who Watered the Colt" ("De la pucelle

qui abevra le polain," MR, vol. 4, pp. 199–207); "The Virgin Who
Wanted to Fly" ("De la pucelle qui vouloit voler," MR, vol. 4,
pp. 208–16); "The Crane" ("De la grue," MR, vol. 5, pp. 151–
56). These stories all begin by setting up the standard of proper
language to be subverted; they describe the strict parental guard-
ing of the young lady's body and/or tongue or the girl's own extreme prudishness. For example, the fabliau "The Squirrel" ("De
l'escuiruel," MR, vol. 5, pp. 101–8) begins with a very rich lady's
lecture to her daughter on how to behave. She is not to talk too
much and, above all, never to mention that "thing that men carry
hanging down" ("Que ja ne nommez cele rien / Que cil homme
portent pendant," p. 102). The daughter takes this as a riddle and
proceeds to guess at the true name of the unmentionable "thing":

> "Mere," dist ele, "dites moi
> Comment il a à non e qoi.
> —Tais toi, fille, je ne l'os dire.
> —Est ce la rien, qui à mon sire
> Entre les jambes li pent, dame?
> —Tesiez, fille, ja nule fame,
> S'ele n'est se trop male teche,
> Ne doit nommer cele peesche
> Qui entre les jambes pendeille
> A ces hommes. —Et quel merveille
> Est ore de nommer peesche?
> Est ce ore ce dont l'en pesche?"
>
> (p. 102)

"Mother," she said, "tell me / what name it has and why." / "Be quiet,
daughter; I don't dare say it." / "Is it the thing that on milord / hangs
between his legs, milady?" / "Silence, daughter, no woman, / unless she
is of bad character, / ought to name this sin / that hangs down between
the legs / of these men." "But how extraordinary / to name it 'sin' [or,
punning, 'fishing']. / Is it with this that they sin [or, punning, 'fish']?"

To curtail her daughter's increasing curiosity and outlandish
guesses, which, to the mother (as to us), have vulgar, punning
undersenses, the lady finally gives in and names the *vit,* a word
with which the naive daughter is delighted, apparently associating
it with a word that sounds much the same, *vie* (life), but which, as
opposed to *vit,* is perfectly proper and used by everyone all the
time without restriction:

"Vit," dist ele, "Dieu merci, vit!
Vit dirai je, cui qu'il anuit,
Vit, chetive! vit dist mon pere,
Vit dist ma suer, vit dist mon frere,
Et vit dist nostre chamberiere,
Et vit avant et vit arriere
Nomme chascuns à son voloir.
Vous meïsme, mere, por voir,
Dites vit, et je toute lasse
Qu'ai forfet que vit ne nommaisse?
Vit me doinst Dieus que je n'i faille!"
(p. 103)

"Life," she said, "God be thanked, life! / Life I will say, whoever it annoys, / life, poor thing! Life says my father, / life says my sister, life says my brother, / and life says our chambermaid, / and life before and life after, / everyone names just as he wants. / Even you, mother, in truth, / say life, and I, all weary, / what have I forfeited by naming life? / God give me life so that I will not die!"

This passage is nearly impossible to translate, because the litany of *vit*s means one thing to the naive daughter and another to her mother, for whom *vit* is a dirty word, and both to us, who catch all the equivocations, especially in the last line, where the pun seems right, affirming at once sex and life, subverting the censorious morality of proper speech and manners that insists on making distinctions and on clarity and singularity of intention.[13]

The upshot of all this harping on verbal taboos is that the naive daughter makes an easy target for seduction by young Robin, who has overheard the entire exchange between mother and daughter and cleverly perceives that he has but to give sex organs and acts a more proper, euphemistic name to get past courteous language taboos and satisfy his physical desires. Thus he presents the daughter with his erect member and tells her that it is a squirrel. When she explores further and finds his testicles, he elaborates the euphemism: this squirrel lays eggs. From here he invents an "allegory" of sexual intercourse as the squirrel hunts and pierces through to the nuts the girl has eaten—in what may be a burlesque, literal and material enactment of allegorizing exegesis, which involves searching for the "grain" or the "nut" of the figured sense beneath the exterior shell of the literal sense.[14]

The euphemisms in this fabliau and the name of the clever young man, Robin, also evoke an idealized rustic—or pastoral—world. In other fabliaux of this nature, the euphemisms may evoke romance plots, as for instance in "The Young Lady Who Could Not Hear Tell of Fucking," in which a young cleric tricks a supercilious and prudish girl by using the exegetical techniques clerics were skilled in to allegorize the sex act, and she is perfectly willing to let his "colt" drink at her "fountain" in the "meadow" guarded by her "trumpeter" (MR, vol. 5, pp. 24–31). Indeed, these prissy young ladies actively take part in euphemistic naming and in elaborating the allegory of sexual intercourse. They have nothing against the act itself, even when illicit, but only against naming it frankly. For instance, when the cleric, David, responds to the girl's invitation to water his "colt," he says he fears her "trumpeter," and it is she who offers the solution: if the "trumpeter" threatens, have the "two marshals" beat him well (p. 31).

Such fabliaux of extended euphemism mock the superficiality and hypocrisy of courtly language codes and of the authoritarian fathers (the Church, noble society, parents, guardians) who believe they can control the desires of their "children," that is, of all subordinates, by censoring "low" words from their vocabulary. These fabliaux dethrone the father tongue of courteous speech by exposing the underside of courtly euphemism. The gambit is daringly provocative and rebellious and creates more tension than a matter-of-fact description of the sex act that does not explicitly challenge the powers of censorship. As I have already suggested with respect to Augustine's allegorization of a line from the Song of Songs and to modern scholarly moralizations of Chaucer's works, figurative interpretation—and this goes as well for euphemism and other ways of displacing meaning from one word or verbal structure to another of one's own creation—is a way of sublimating desire. It explicitly denies or forbids the desire too openly expressed in the "dangerous" text by relegating this text to the status of a subtext. However, at the same time, figurative interpretation secretly preserves the pleasure of this subtext by transferring its forbidden meaning to the new, more proper text of extended euphemism or allegory that figuratively represents the hidden subtext.

Courtly euphemism involves the same sort of interpretive process, the overt denial and covert affirmation of dangerous desires. It is this contradiction—this attempt to have it both ways, to appear proper but not to be so or to truly give up the dangerous desire—that fabliaux such as "The Young Lady Who Could Not Hear Tell of Fucking" play to the hilt, thereby unmasking courtly euphemism. Both texts (supra and sub) are made explicit, the vulgar text being voiced by the narrator of "The Young Lady," the proper text being voiced by the fabliau characters. These two linguistic registers, so far apart, nevertheless describe the same action, and we may jump abruptly from a high register to a low one and back again in a few lines, as at the climax of the fabliau:[15]

> Cele respont: "S'il en dit mal,
> Bien lo batent li mereschal!"
> Daviz respont: "Ce est bien dit!"
> Atant li met el con lo vit;
> Si fait son boen et son talant
> Si qu'ele nel tient pas à lant
> Que .iiii. fois la retorna,
> Et se li cornerres groça
> Si fu batuz de .ii. jumaus.
> A icest mot faut li fabliaus.
>
> (MR, vol. 5, p. 31)

She answered, "If he threatens, / let the marshals beat him well!" / David answered, "Well said!" / Immediately he put the prick in her cunt / and did her pleasure and his desire / so that she did not consider it boring / that he turned her over four times, / and if the trumpeter complained, / he was beaten by the two twins. / With this word the fabliau ends.

By bringing the subtext out of hiding, by openly restoring this forbidden meaning to the supratext of euphemism, these fabliaux expose the prurient intention behind the censorship that characterizes courtly linguistic codes. Jean de Meun does much the same thing in the scandalous ending of his *Roman de la rose,* where he depicts the female sex organs as a religious "relic" and thereby proves correct Reason's earlier argument that obscenity lies, not in the word itself, but in our own prurient understanding of it.[16]

None of Chaucer's fabliaux makes such extensive use of courteous euphemism as to turn the plot of the fabliau into an allegory of obscenity. However, Chaucer does write passages of slightly protracted euphemism, such as the wife's use of mercantile terms (debt, tally, pay, score) as metaphors for sexual intercourse at the end of the "Shipman's Tale" (B^2 1603–14). Fabliau wives, like poets, are accomplished at double-talk; they are extremely good at inventing figures and extended euphemisms (such as that of the "lady leech" or May's "struggle with a man upon a tree") in order to deceive their husbands about the true nature of their actions and desires. Even though Chaucer does not construct whole fabliau plots as extended euphemisms, he does, in conventional fabliau fashion, frequently engage in a comic unmasking of specific courteous euphemisms by using them in such crude contexts or to describe such rude actions that their obscene subtext sallies forth, exposing the flimsiness and impotence of the euphemism's censorship, subverting the father tongue. Such is Chaucer's punning use in the "Miller's" and "Shipman's" tales of "queynt" and "aqueyntaunce," wordplay for which he had ample precedent in thirteenth- and fourteenth-century French fabliaux.

The French adjective form *cointe* (English cognate, *queynt*) is used to describe both attractive young men and women in the fabliaux, and it usually connotes refinement of dress or behavior, that is, an attention to personal aesthetics, ornament, coquetry—a subtly equivocal attempt to turn oneself into an object of desire— that we might associate with gentility or aspirations in that direction. In "The Lady Who Asked for Oats for Morel" ("C'est de la dame qui aveine demandoit pour Morel," MR, vol. 1, pp. 318– 29), a fabliau of extended euphemism for copulation, the lady falls in love with and marries

> . . . un vallet fort et legier,
> Bel et gent, et mignot et cointe;
> Forment avoit chier son acointe.
>
> (p. 318)

. . . a young man strong and agile, / handsome and genteel and elegant and refined; / she held his acquaintance very dear.

This young husband demonstrates his refinement or *cointise* by inventing the euphemism of feeding oats to the horse, Morel, in order to enable his wife to ask inoffensively for sex. As we might expect in a fabliau plot, she wears her husband out with "feedings" until he decides he has had enough of this feeding euphemism and renders it unpalatable with an extremely vulgar, punning action. He literally defecates on his wife and explains that he has no more oats to offer, only "bran" (which means both "straw" and "shit").[17] So much for this young man's *cointise*.

In "Gombert and the Two Clerks" (MR, vol. 1, pp. 238–44), an analogue to the "Reeve's Tale," *cointe* describes women, the wife and daughter of the peasant Gombert. One of the clerks loves the wife, but he does not know how "to acquaint" (*acointier*) himself with her, because she is so pretty and refined in appearance: "Mès ne set coment s'i acointe, / Quar la dame est mingnote et cointe" (p. 238). The next line gives this rustic's wife the crystal-bright eyes—"Les iex ot vairs come cristal"—of the idealized lady of romance. A few lines later, the narrator intervenes:

> Quar sa fille est et cointe et bele,
> Et je di qu'amor de pucele,
> Quant fins cuers i est ententiex,
> Est sor toute autre rien gentiex.
> (p. 238)

Because his daughter is polished and beautiful, / and I say that the love of a virgin, / when a refined heart aspires to it, / is more genteel than anything else.

The narrator uses this courtly linguistic register to introduce a tale of cuckoldry in which the clerks themselves, whose love is anything but refined, use the lowest possible registers, blatantly vulgar terms followed by kitchen euphemisms, to describe their nocturnal sexual exploits:

> —Par le cul bieu, je vieng de foutre,
> Mès que ce fu la fille l'oste;
> Pris en ai devant et encoste;
> Aforé li ai son tonel,
> E se li ai donné l'anel
> De la paelete de fer."
> (p. 243)

"By the rear end of Gog, I come straight from fucking / the host's daughter. / I took her from the front and the side; / I pierced her keg for her / and I gave her for this the ring / from the iron skillet."

Both the action of this fabliau and the vulgar diction of its characters unmask the courtly euphemism of the narrator's *cointe*s and expose the erotic motive behind the clerk's desire for "acquaintance" with these "ladies."

As Larry Benson has explained, proper metaphoric or euphemistic substitutes for obscene words, when these are often employed, gradually lose their duplicity; that is, the euphemism loses the original field of meaning that served to mask the obscene one:

> Our most offensive words are those which in effect have no meaning other than the offensive one. That was apparently what happened to the verb *swyven;* the Anglo-Saxon verb *swifan* . . . had no sexual connotations at all; sometime before the beginning of the fourteenth century it began to be used—presumably originally as a euphemism—for the act of copulation. By Chaucer's time the older meanings of the verb had disappeared, and it had become one of the most offensive words in Middle English.[18]

This is apparently also what was happening to the verb *acointier* and its adjective form *acointement* in certain thirteenth- and fourteenth-century fabliau contexts. The courteous sense of the verb connotes a degree of mutual knowledge or intimacy similar to being on "familiar" (familylike) terms, a much less casual relationship than is suggested by the modern English word *acquaintance.* Like the French *acointier,* the Middle English term *aqueynted,* as used in the opening of the "Shipman's Tale," describes a very close, "familiar" relationship between the monk and the merchant, an intimacy based on the monk's claim of blood relation (everyone from the same village being in one way or another likely to be cousins):

> This yonge monk, that was so fair of face,
> Aqueynted was so with the goode man,
> Sith that hir firste knoweliche bigan,
> That in his hous as famulier was he
> As it is possible any freend to be.
>   And for as muchel as this goode man,
> And eek this monk of which that I began,
> Were bothe two yborn in o village,
> The monk hym claymeth as for cosynage,
> And he agayn, he seith nat ones nay,
> But was as glad therof as fowel of day,
> For to his herte it was a greet plesaunce.
> Thus been they knyt with eterne alliaunce,

And ech of hem gan oother for t'assure
Of bretherhede whil that hir lyf may dure.

(B² 1218–32)

Although the "proper" meaning of *acointier* or *aqueynte* is "to become familiar with," in fabliau contexts where *acointier* describes
a familiar relationship between a cleric or priest and a wife, an improper meaning is never far from the surface: "to have sexual intercourse," to "know" in the biblical sense. This is what the word
both covers and discovers in the monk's ingratiating overture to
the merchant's wife later in the "Shipman's Tale":

> "He is na moore cosyn unto me
> Than is this leef that hangeth on the tree!
> I clepe hym so, by Seint Denys of Fraunce,
> To have the moore cause of aqueyntaunce
> Of yow, which I have loved specially
> Aboven alle wommen, sikerly."
>
> (B² 1339–44)

When a French fabliau context features illegal or immoral copulation, the illicit connotation of *acointier* as "to have coitus" subverts the word's conventionally courteous denotation. For example, in "The Priest and Alison" ("Du prestre et d'Alison," MR,
vol. 2, pp. 8–23), a lascivious priest who covets a pretty young
bourgeoise is tricked by the mother into paying to go to bed in the
dark with the local prostitute, who plays the obedient virgin mar-
tyr to the priest's desire. When she is stretched out beneath and
joined with him, then he "gets to know" her:

> En sus de lui est traite et jointe,
> Et li Prestres vers lui s'acointe.
>   Une fois la fout, en mains d'eure
> Que l'en éust chanté une Eure.
>
> (p. 20)

Underneath him she is stretched out and joined, / and the priest gets familiar with her. / He fucked her once in less time / than it would have
taken to sing an Hour.

In such a context, with the frank word *foutre* in the following line
in a comparison of the speed with which the priest copulates to
that with which he sings his Hours, the euphemism of "s'acointe"
does not mask much.

The same is true in "The Priest Who Was Put in the Larder"
("Du prestre qui fu mis au lardier," MR, vol. 2, pp. 24–30), a
fabliau the narrator introduces by announcing that he will make us
"laugh about a cobbler without using any vulgar words":

> Mos sans vilonnie
> Vous veil recorder
> Afin qu'en s'en rie
> D'un franc Savetier.
>
> (p. 24)

The euphemisms the narrator uses a few lines later to describe the
cobbler's beautiful wife's relationship with the priest avoid vulgarity only in the technical sense by avoiding explicit naming of
the sex act: "she became familiar with a handsome priest" ("ele
s'acointa d'un Prestre joli") who, when her husband was away,
was quick to rush to her house to "polish her little ring" ("a la
Savetière fourbissoit l'anel"). The censorship of these euphemisms,
slight as it is, nevertheless raises the tension and adds to the plot's
suspense, just as does the whispered Latin prayer, "me delibera,"
of the priest hiding inside the larder that the husband sells for a fine
profit to another priest (because a Latin-speaking larder is such a
rare prize). The wily husband is willing to preserve—for a high
price—the proper veil of this final euphemism. Both we and he
know what lies under the lid of the Latin-speaking larder and what
the wife's "acqueyntaunce" with the priest so flimsily conceals.
Likewise, in the fabliau of "The Bourgeoise of Orléans" (MR,
vol. 1, pp. 117–25), the wife's appreciation of the "courtesy" and
the "company" of a young cleric arouses the husband's suspicions
and ours too:

> .I. en i ot de grant ponois,
> Qui moult hantoit chiés .i. borgois;
> S'el tenoit-on moult à cortois;
> N'ert plains d'orgueil ne de bufois,
> Et à la dame vraiement
> Plesoit moult son acointement;
> Et tant vint e tant i ala,
> Que li borgois se porpenssa.
>
> (pp. 117–18)

There was one of them of high status / who often frequented the house
of a bourgeois, / and he was considered to be very courteous. / He

wasn't proud or boastful, / and his company really / pleased the wife very much, / and he came and went so often / that the bourgeois got to thinking.

Whatever their use in more courtly contemporary genres, in the context of the opening lines of fourteenth-century French fabliaux, *cointe* or *acointier* and their derivative forms virtually announced cuckoldry or adultery to come. In addition to the examples previously discussed, the fabliau of "The Bishop Who Blessed the Cunt" ("De l'evesque qui beneï lo con," MR, vol. 3, pp. 178–85) features a bishop "who very eagerly got to know / married and unmarried ladies" ("Qui mout volantiers s'acointoit / De dames et de damoiseles," verses 2–3), and the fabliau of "The Fucker" ("Du Fotéor," MR, vol. 1, pp. 304–17) presents the "hero" considering "how he could manage / to get to know the lady" ("Comment il porroit esploitier / De soi à la dame acointier," p. 307). The purpose of euphemisms has always been duplicitous: to reveal what they apparently attempt to conceal. But by dint of too frequent or too blatant revelation in certain contexts, we tend to forget, as in the case of *cointe* and *acointier* in French fabliaux, that these words ever tried to conceal anything. Indeed, the spelling *acoitemant* (for *acointement*) in one version of the fabliau of "The Bourgeoise of Orléans"[19] suggests that at least one medieval reader understood *coît* (coitus) as the true root of *acointement,* just as we might, by means of a similar folk etymology, understand *cunt* as the true root of *queynte* or *aqueyntaunce* in some of Chaucer's fabliau contexts. Benson notes that the scribe of a Cambridge manuscript of the "Wife of Bath's Prologue" writes "the frank obscenity [*conte*] in place of *queynte.*"[20] Benson also suggests that this *conte* may possibly be "an error (omission of 'i') for *cointe,* which appears as a variant [French] spelling for *queynte.*" We might add that even in this case the omission may be deliberate and is, indeed, characteristic of playful, goliardic or jongleuresque interpretive deformation of words, which could produce either *conte* (cunt) or *coîte* (coitus) from *cointe* (refined).

As I have shown, it was fairly common in medieval French fabliaux to label the illicitly desired and desiring characters *cointe,* and this had become a sign of imminent cuckoldry. In translating *cointe* to the English context of his "Miller's Tale," Chaucer amplified and refurbished its censorious value as a euphemism, as a

proper cover for obscenity. Chaucer does not explicitly label
Nicholas *cointe,* but he describes at considerable length the hopeful
young clerk's *cointise,* his refinement and aspirations: Nicholas's
study is on the stars, an apparently high aim; his room and his person are "ful fetisly ydight"; he is twice called "sweete" clerk, and
his demeanor is "maidenly meek" (A 3202), rather like Chaucer's
Knight's. As Beryl Rowland has pointed out, with his nightly
song of "angelus ad virginem," Nicholas plays the role of the an-
gel Gabriel in the act of Annunciation to the Virgin.[21] Furthermore,
this "hende," genteel clerk knows the art of "deerne love," that is,
courteous love, love kept secret. From the opening description,
Nicholas seems to be the epitome of Oxford student refinement,
with some angelic overtones. On the other hand, what *cointise*
there is in the dress, toilette, and deportment of Alison-of-the-
polished-forehead is periodically undercut during the course of her
initial description by animal and erotic imagery, from the implicit
innuendo of her "likerous ye," possibly "nether" (cf. A 3852), to
the narrator's explicit comment:

> She was a prymerole, a piggesnye,
> For any lord to leggen in his bedde,
> Or yet for any good yeman to wedde.
>   (A 3268–70)

Having established Nicholas's refinement at length, even going
to the extent of an angelic allusion, Chaucer makes short work of
disillusioning us about the true nature of Nicholas's aspirations: not
high, but low, and right at hand. Nicholas's seduction of Alison
bears all the marks of crudity—to "rage and pleye" in a rambunc-
tiously rustic fashion; to call Alison by the base term "lemman"
(cf. "Manciple's Tale," H 220); to catch and hold her "harde by the
haunchebones" (A 3279). Words that we had earlier taken as signs
of Nicholas's refinement are now reframed by Nicholas's vulgar
gestures, which bring low connotations to the surface subversively
to unmask courteous euphemisms: "hende" now suggests "handy"
or "good with the hands"; "prively" now suggests where Nicholas grabbed Alison, in the private parts; "spille" and "dye" may
now suggest ejaculation; Alison's conventional cry of "out, har-
row, and allas" now suggests an attempt at forced entry (rather
like January's similar response to the sight of Damian's entry into

May, E 2366); and, of course, the second "queynt" (literally, Alison's "refinement") now suggests "cunt."

Although Chaucer has set up the interpretive situation so that we can hardly do otherwise, even if we fancy ourselves "gentils," it is we, and not the narrator, who break the taboo and mockingly expose the father tongue of courteous euphemism when we openly express our illicit understanding of "queynte" here or of the monk's use of "aqueyntaunce" with reference to the wife in the "Shipman's Tale." Some of the more courteously, equivocally admiring portraits of the "General Prologue" place us in similar interpretive situations. As Jill Mann pointed out with respect to the "General Prologue" portraits, Chaucer puts the responsibility for judgment on us.[22] It is we who think the vulgar thoughts and do the critical exposure, if we are so inclined. Chaucer's "naive pilgrim" is the persona of a man who is an accomplished politician and diplomat, a man who leaves to us both the pleasure and the responsibility or blame for dethroning authority, wherever it is vested: in "fatherly" characters, in courtly codes of speech or gesture, in high literary genres, authoritative—especially biblical—texts, or proverbial expressions. But Chaucer gives us the same excuse for our aggressions that he gives himself: they are "not serious" because this is "just play," and no one is his real self in play.

Chapter Six

"Straw for Youre Gentillesse"

Symbolic Rebellion in the
Canterbury Tales

The social context in which a medieval comic tale was performed might provide an implicit standard of propriety or gentility against which a jongleur could detonate the low language and manners of his narrative. This implicit standard might, however, be very low in certain performance contexts, and it would vary considerably from performance to performance as the jongleur moved about and settings, audiences, and occasions changed. Thus many fabliaux, in one way or another, set up their own standards of propriety to subvert, their own rules to break. They build the "father" into the text in order to dethrone him, chiefly, as we have seen, by burlesquing the plot, the linguistic register (especially the euphemisms), or other easily recognized conventions of the authoritative, "serious" genres of romance, epic, courtly love lyric, or dream vision debate. Even if performed in a tavern or on a popular festive occasion in a permissive context that allowed the freest sort of speech and behavior, such fabliaux could still quite effectively use low, taboo language or action to dethrone and mock the inhibiting authority conjured up by their parody of high genres, biblical episodes, and courtly euphemisms.

This puts in a slightly different light Per Nykrog's thesis that the medieval fabliaux are the antithesis, the mocking parody, of courtly romance.[1] Indeed, they are that, but the target the fabliaux truly

aim to bring down—if only temporarily and playfully, in fiction—
is not a genre, but repressive authority in general. We do, of
course, find this repressive authority epitomized in courtly codes
of behavior and speech, which are inscribed in the literature of
courtly romance, as well as in other sorts of exemplary, "pathetic"
fictions that, as I have shown, involve the trials of a hero or heroine and his or her and (through identification) our eventual accommodation to authority. The rebellion against repressive authority,
the vicarious satisfaction of erotic and aggressive desires that relatively refined medieval audiences enjoyed in the imaginary world
of the fabliau and in nonsense forms such as the *fatras* or *fatrasie*
gave them pleasurable, temporary release from real-life repres-
sions. The antithesis of the fictive world of the fabliau or the lyric
fatras, the world they truly oppose, is, properly speaking, the real
world, and not the fictional world of an idealizing literary genre
such as courtly romance or love lyric.

This is especially clear for the extreme case of the *fatrasie,* the
best-known writer of which was Philippe de Beaumanoir, the
thirteenth-century compiler and author of the *Customs of Beau-
vaisis,* a professional "man of law" who filled a series of important
posts as seneschal and *bailli* for the French Crown.[2] For Philippe it
must have been a great pleasure, in leisure time, to defy the laws of
reason and convention in composing a grotesque *fatrasie,* a strophe
of eleven verses rhyming a a b a a b b a b a b, in which the major
condition is that words must be combined in incongruous ways so
as constantly to break the rules of proper usage. From the example
of Philippe, I see no reason to doubt that the Gautier Le Leu who
wrote some of the most obscene and sacrilegious surviving fabliaux was the "Waltier Li Leus, échevin de Valenciennes," who
signed his name to a cartulary in 1296. Charles Livingston goes to
considerable trouble, using other evidence, to date and place the
fabliaux in the same region of Valenciennes at exactly the same period, only to insist that "our jongleur and the Valencienne burgher
are two different people, because it is very hard to see any resem-
blance between the mentality of our author and that of the serious
magistrate of a large city."[3] There were, nevertheless, throughout
the course of the Middle Ages, many respectable ecclesiastical,
royal, or civic officials—men whose discourse normally supported

the law—who turned occasionally to the composition of blatantly "foolish" verses.

If Rabanus Maurus could versify the *Cena Cypriani;* if Alexander Neckam could write a series of goliardic poems in praise of wine; if that stern magistrate, Philippe de Beaumanoir, could write *fatrasies;* if Eustache Deschamps, royal *bailli* and self-appointed "old counselor," could compose facetious verses for a foolish *Ordre des Fumeux;* if fifteenth-century *rhétoriqueurs* and official historians for the house of Burgundy, such as Jean Molinet, could pun so licentiously in rhyme;[4] if that eminent Clerk of the King's Works, Geoffrey Chaucer, could write "The Miller's Tale," there is no reason why a city magistrate of Valenciennes might not write obscene fabliaux, leaving their performance to a jongleur whose foolish persona both masked and protected the author, much as Chaucer's "naive" pilgrim and Miller personae protected him. Indeed, there is a certain logic to these reversals of modern expectations, these irregularities on the part of respectable gentlemen. The logic lies in the therapeutic, cathartic uses of fiction, in fiction as play that allows the writer—and his audience—to satisfy in game the desires forbidden in adult life and especially in "gentil" society and in serious, responsible positions or professions. Such fictive flouting of authority was surely safer than the real flouting of fatherly authority of *raptus.*[5]

To a far greater extent than most writers of French fabliaux, Chaucer builds the authority to be dethroned into the text of his *Canterbury Tales.* He makes authoritative standards explicit by writing them into individual tales; by defining the tales' audience, their standards of speech and behavior and their devotional goal; and by posing, himself, as historian of the pilgrimage endeavor. We have already seen how Chaucer uses and even emphasizes courteous euphemisms before subverting them with vulgar actions and how he uses biblical allusions or parodies, such as, in the "Miller's Tale," references to the Flood, the Annunciation, the Holy Family, and the Song of Songs, in order to "raise" characters whom he is building up for a mocking fall. Thus John, the husband, is implicitly compared to Joseph and Noah before his cuckolding and fall; Nicholas is compared to Gabriel before accosting Alison so crudely; and Absalom is compared to Christ as mystic bridegroom before getting his unsavory kiss. To similar effect,

Chaucer uses classical, epic, and scriptural allusions, high style, and parody of scholastic debate to inflate characters and situations in preparation for comic deflations. Just when we had begun to believe we were in the castleyard, Chaucer reminds us that the characters we are empathizing with are chickens in the chickenyard "enclosed al aboute," not with fortifications and moat, but "with stikkes, and a drye dych withoute" ("Nun's Priest's Tale," B² 4037–38). Sometimes Chaucer builds up a repressive father figure through description before dethroning him, as at the beginning of the "Reeve's Tale" with the description of the miller as a walking armory, pugnacious, jealously possessive of his women, proud of his lineage. But Chaucer not only underlines and calls attention to repressive authority within the text of his tales; he also defines and intermittently calls our attention to the censorious authority that lies outside the tales in the "gentil" standards of a part of the audience of Canterbury pilgrims.

By framing the *Canterbury Tales* as he does, describing the reality, albeit fictive, in which the tales are told, Chaucer defines a rule of proper speech and behavior against which certain characters, such as the Miller and the Cook, and even the Host, rebel. Likewise, at the end of the "General Prologue" (A 725–46) and in his narratorial intervention prior to the "Miller's Tale" (A 3167–86), Chaucer fictionalizes his real audience (which includes us) by apologizing for his verbatim repetition of vulgar language, that is, his deliberate deviation from the censorious norm of our polite standard of speech. The "gentil" standards of his pilgrim audience Chaucer defines partly by means of the "General Prologue" portraits of individuals who are especially proper in their speech and manners, pilgrims such as the Knight, who had never spoken a vulgar word in his life to any man (A 70); the Prioress, with her fair and "fetys" French (A 126), a lady whose "gretteste ooth was but by Seinte Loy" (A 120); or the Clerk, whose speech was always "sownynge in moral vertu," "seyd in forme and reverence, / And short and quyk and ful of hy sentence" (A 305–7). Already in the "General Prologue" portraits, Chaucer is setting up the conflict between such prescriptive rules of courteous or gentle speech and the much freer speech of churlish characters: of the great-mouthed Miller, "a janglere and a goliardeys, / And that . . . moost of synne and harlotries" (A 561); the Friar, who deliberately deformed his English by a wanton lisping intended to seduce (A 264–65); or the Summoner, who mechanically, crazily parroted Latin legal phrases when he got drunk (A 636–46).

The methods Harry Bailly uses in his aggressively tendentious jokes, his *japes,* also tend to separate and set the gentles against the churls among the pilgrim audience. Just as Chaucer's admiring description of the pilgrims in the "General Prologue" is more subtly equivocal in the case of the more gentle pilgrims such as the Prioress, so Harry's *japes* are more subtly mocking in the case of gentles. The Host permits himself to deride the Miller outright by calling him a fool (A 3135) and to disparage the Cook's storytelling ability (and his honesty) with a joke comparing the Cook's stories (which will presumably be farcical fabliaux) with his fraudulent practices in making and selling meat pies and other stuffed (farsed) dishes:

> "Nowe telle on, Roger; looke that it be *good,*
> For many a pastee hastow laten blood,
> And many a Jakke of Dovere hastow soold
> That hath been twies hoot and twies coold.
> Of many a pilgrym hastow Cristes curs,
> For of thy percely yet they fare the wors,
> That they han eten with thy stubbel goos;
> For in thy shoppe is many a flye loos.
> Now telle on, gentil Roger by thy name."
>   (A 4345–53; my italics)

Considering the Host's characteristically derisive humor in asserting his authority to choose the next speaker, we may suppose that he is mocking the Cook here by calling him "gentle." Indeed, the Host's tendentious humor often turns on the issue of gentility. In this case, he is calling a churlish fellow "gentil," an ironic fiction that derides the churl; but he may also, somewhat less obviously, be deriding gentles by implying that Robert, the seller of warmed-over pies and dishes that look good but are not, is gentle in the sense that gentility involves just such a duplicitous use of signs.

Much of the Host's aggressive humor takes the form of "exposure" of individual pilgrims as he puts them on the spot by asking for their tales. His treatment of the Cook in the farcical interchange that precedes the "Manciple's Tale" is bullyingly blatant.

He accuses the sleepy Cook of being drunk, of having spent the night scratching at fleas, or of having spent it with a prostitute:

> "Awake, thou Cook," quod he, "God yeve thee sorwe!
> What eyleth thee to slepe by the morwe?
> Hastow had fleen al nyght, or artow dronke?
> Or hastow with som quene al nyght yswonke,
> So that thow mayst nat holden up thyn heed?"
>
> (H 15–19)

Before all the other pilgrims, Harry makes the Cook, who has fallen asleep on his horse, into a scapegoat, and he easily draws the Manciple into the game of baiting the Cook, until the latter falls off his horse in anger. At this point, the Host urges that the Manciple, if he does not want to bear the brunt of the Cook's "real-life" revenge of exposing his fraudulent accounts, make peace and reestablish the game context. This the Manciple promptly does by denying a seriously critical intention ("I seyde it in my bourde," H 81) and by giving the Cook a draught of his good wine, which sweetens the Cook's humor and turns "ernest into game" (H 100).

The Host's joking assaults on the Monk and the Nun's Priest take the form of embarrassing sexual exposures; he treats these men, who have willingly taken vows of chastity, as great studs. There is a world of difference between Chaucer's pilgrim persona's admiration of the Monk for his manliness and the Host's. Harry draws the Monk out of retirement, ordering him to "ryde forth," guessing at his name and his position, commenting on his skin and muscles and, finally, on his sexual potency:

> "I pray to God, yeve hym confusioun
> That first thee broghte unto religioun!
> Thou woldest han been a tredefowel aright.
> Haddestow as greet a leeve as thou hast myght
> To parfourne al thy lust in engendrure,
> Thou haddest bigeten ful many a creature.
> Allas, why werestow so wyd a cope?
> God yeve me sorwe, but, and I were a pope,
> Nat oonly thou, but every myghty man,
> Though he were shorn ful hye upon his pan,
> Sholde have a wyf; for al the world is lorn!
> Religioun hath take up al the corn
> Of tredyng, and we borel men been shrympes.

> Of fieble trees ther comen wrecched ympes.
> This maketh that oure heires been so sklendre
> And feble that they may nat wel engendre.
> This maketh that oure wyves wole assaye
> Religious folk, for ye mowe bettre paye
> Of Venus paiementz than mowe we;
> God woot, no lussheburghes payen ye!"
>   (B² 3133–52)

The sexual payment from religious men's purses (scrota) is no false coin (indeed, no coin at all). Harry's tendentious joke is a fiction that involves role-playing. Harry pretends to be a feeble pro-creator and to admire the monk's and all religious men's superior capacity in this line. That he is playing is obvious, and he insists on the protection of game, of fiction and laughter that proclaim "this is not serious," to embarrass the monk, who "took al in pacience." The Monk's response is, not to get even by telling a fabliau, which is what Harry hopes to provoke him to, but to stand on his dignity by telling a series of short tragedies about historical people, from Adam to contemporary rulers, with an implicit lesson (man's powerlessness to control his life on earth) that is antipathetic to the Host and to an atmosphere of festive rebellion.

After the Host, with a bold and rudely familiar manner, invites the Nun's Priest to tell a tale and mocks his "foul and lene" horse (B² 4005), the Nun's Priest tells a beast fable that turns ludicrously around the issue of whether a cock can control its own destiny:

> Wheither that Goddes worthy forwityng
> Streyneth me nedely for to doon a thyng—
> "Nedely" clepe I symple necessitee—
> Or elles, if free choys be graunted me
> To do that same thyng, or do it noght,
> Though God forwoot it er that I was wroght;
> Or if his wityng streyneth never a deel
> But by necessitee condicioneel.
> I wol nat han to do of swich mateere;
> My tale is of a cok, as ye may heere,
> That tok his conseil of his wyf, with sorwe.
>   (B² 4433–43)

The "Nun's Priest's Tale" is in some respects a burlesque of the Monk's tragedies of the falls of illustrious men. Even though the

Nun's Priest's heroic cock has a certain amount of trouble controlling its desires (B^2 4350–61), Chauntecleer triumphs in the end
over fate, foxes, and females. The "Nun's Priest's Tale" celebrates
the victory of Chauntecleer the cock, "Venus' man," the victory
of *eros* and enterprise. This mock-heroic beast fable is a comic
riposte to the pessimism of the Monk's tragedies of painful accommodation to destiny. It is fitting that Chaucer's only clear reference
to the Peasants' Revolt (B^2 3394–96) should occur at the comic climax of this implicitly rebellious, life-affirming tale.

In praising this "murie tale," in an epilogue that Chaucer seems
to have written and later cancelled, the Host once again tries to put
himself on top, this time by exposing and embarrassing the celi-
bate Nun's Priest:

> "Sire Nonnes Preest," oure Hooste seide anoon,
> "I-blessed be thy breche, and every stoon!
> This was a murie tale of Chauntecleer.
> But by my trouthe, if thou were seculer,
> Thou woldest ben a trede-foul aright.
> For if thou have corage as thou hast myght,
> Thee were nede of hennes, as I wene,
> Ya, moo than seven tymes seventene.
> See, whiche braunes hath this gentil preest,
> So gret a nekke, and swich a large breest!
> He loketh as a sperhauk with his yen;
> Him nedeth nat his colour for to dyen
> With brasile ne with greyn of Portyngale."
>
> (B^2 4637–49)

The Host deliberately, facetiously paints the Nun's Priest, whose
lifestyle should encourage pallor and minimal muscle development, with the colors and the physique of a fine breeding (and
fighting?) cock. To describe the brown, brawny, fierce Shipman in
these terms would not be particularly funny, but the incongruity
between the Nun's Priest's probable appearance and the Host's flat-
tery of his fine, cocklike physique is humorous, and we laugh at
the Nun's Priest's expense. By giving him fictive feathers (describing him as a fine cock), the Host effectively plucks the Nun's
Priest, exposing him for his lack of virility.

The Host's mocking exposure of Chaucer the pilgrim also involves embarrassing references to his body and his love life—spe-

cifically to his great girth (his belly), which, rather than his status, gives him the right to a spacious place, but also makes it difficult for any small woman to embrace him. Harry comically "enlarges" Chaucer the pilgrim at the same time as he "reduces" him—to a "popet" (puppet or doll). Chaucer's pilgrim persona, like all the other gentles, is reticent and tries to avoid Harry Bailly's selective eye for as long as possible. As is the case in most games, no one wants to be "it," but the general reluctance is reinforced in this game because no one wants to brave the mocking exposure of the Host's *japes:*

> . . . oure Hooste japen tho bigan,
> And thanne at erst he looked upon me,
> And seyde thus: "What man artow?" quod he;
> "Thou lookest as thou woldest fynde an hare,
> For evere upon the ground I se thee stare.
>
> "Approche neer, and looke up murily.
> Now war yow, sires, and lat this man have place!
> He in the waast is shape as wel as I;
> This were a popet in an arm t'enbrace
> For any womman, smal and fair of face.
> He semeth elvyssh by his contenaunce,
> For unto no wight dooth he daliaunce.
>
> "Sey now somwhat, syn oother folk han sayd;
> Telle us a tale of myrthe, and that anon."
> "Hooste," quod I, "ne beth nat yvele apayd,
> For oother tale certes kan I noon,
> But of a rym I lerned longe agoon."
> "Ye, that is good," quod he, "now shul we heere
> Som deyntee thyng, me thynketh by his cheere."
>   (B² 1883–96)

As we shall see, "deyntee" is the word the Franklin uses to compliment the Squire ("of thy speche I have greet deyntee," F 681), a compliment that brings the Host's ridicule down on the Franklin's head. Now the Host uses the same word, which connotes pleasure in refinement, facetiously to compliment Chaucer the pilgrim in advance on his tale. Chaucer the pilgrim's response to being made the butt of the Host's jokes about his body, his reticence, and his genteel refinement is, much like the Franklin's and other gentle pilgrims', to profess unworthiness. As opposed to the others, Chaucer the pilgrim then proceeds to prove that his protest is no mere modesty topos. He claims to know only one old rhyme, which turns out to be the ridiculously inept romance of Sir Thopas. After this lame performance, the Host no longer bothers with subtle mockery but berates Chaucer the pilgrim roundly in a tirade that I have earlier compared to a verbal fart in the face: "Thy drasty rymyng is nat worth a toord!"

The Host deliberately minces words, jests equivocally, in putting the Franklin on the spot and back in his place: "Straw for your gentillesse!" (F 695). On the one hand, with a facetiously obsequious epithet ("youre gentillesse"),[6] the Host either literally or figuratively hands the Franklin a straw, which means it is his turn to tell the next story, that his "cut" is up, now determined by the Host instead of by chance. But with the same phrase that builds the Franklin up, the Host puts him down through a derogatory second sense: "[I don't give a] straw for your gentility." As in the case of Chaucer's "queynte" pun in the "Miller's Tale," which Benson pointed out,[7] modern readers have generally gone straight to the point, to the punning subtext, missing the facetiously courteous sense of the Host's intervention, which might be accomplished in performance with an exaggerated bow. Both senses, polite and impolite, are supported by the larger context of the interchange that follows between the Host and the Franklin:

> "Straw for youre gentillesse!" quod oure Hoost.
> "What, Frankeleyn! Pardee, sire, wel thou woost
> That ech of yow moot tellen atte leste
> A tale or two, or breken his biheste."
>   "That knowe I wel, sire," quod the Frankeleyn.
> "I prey yow, haveth me nat in desdeyn,
> Though to this man I speke a word or two."
> "Telle on thy tale withouten wordes mo."
>
> (F 695–702)

The Host mockingly pretends to obsequiously solicit the next tale from the Franklin, but the reaction that provoked the Host's "What, Frankeleyn!" and the Franklin's reference to the Host's disdain both suggest that the Franklin realizes immediately what is going on: the Host is making him the butt of a joke for his presumption in complimenting the Squire's genteel eloquence, his emotional elocution:

"In feith, Squier, thow hast thee wel yquit
And gentilly. I preise wel thy wit,"
Quod the Frankeleyn, "considerynge thy yowthe,
So feelyngly thou spekest, sire, I allow the!
As to my doom, ther is noon that is heere
Of eloquence that shal be thy peere,
If that thou lyve; God yeve thee good chaunce,
And in vertu sende thee continuaunce,
For of thy speche I have greet deyntee."
                                        (F 673–81)

The Franklin is moved by pathos in delivery (and pathetic fictions
of accommodation) as a gentleman ought to be according to the
Squire's proverb (which is a version of his father the Knight's):
"pitee renneth soone in gentil herte, / Feelynge his similitude in
peynes smerte" (F 479–80). The Franklin's compliment to the
Squire is thus meant not only to halt the Squire's tale courteously
but also to be a demonstration of the Franklin's own gentility.

Following the Host's *jape,* the Franklin backs down in the prologue to his own tale and pictures himself as considerably less of a
connoisseur of eloquence:

But, sires, by cause I am a burel man,
At my bigynnyng first I yow biseche,
Have me excused of my rude speche.
I lerned nevere rethorik, certeyn;
Thyng that I speke, it moot be bare and pleyn.
I sleep nevere on the Mount of Pernaso,
Ne lerned Marcus Tullius Scithero.
Colours me knowe I none, withouten drede,
But swiche colours as growen in the mede,
Or elles swiche as men dye or peynte.
Colours of rethoryk been to me queynte.
                                        (F 716–26)

By playing the rube with this long modesty topos and deferring to
the Host's superior judgment, the Franklin may be trying to turn
the tables on the Host and to make him the butt of his own joke
about presumption:

"I wol yow nat contrarien in no wyse
As fer as that my wittes wol suffyse.

I prey to God that it may plesen yow;
Thanne woot I wel that it is good ynow."
(F 705–8)

As the Franklin demeans himself in order to set the Host up even further than the Host has presumed to do, the Franklin's tongue must be in his cheek, for an innkeeper's aesthetic judgment is hardly above reproach. What is good enough for Harry is decidedly not good enough for the gentles among the pilgrim audience, even though they have agreed, in a sort of burlesque of royal acclamation demanded by Harry ("Hoold up youre hondes, withouten moore speche," A 783) to be subject to and abide by the judgment of the beefy Southwark innkeeper, whose profession is to provide the most physical kinds of *solas* (food, drink, sleep) and who is something of a Lord of Misrule. (In the medieval French comic plays of the *Jeu de la feuillée* and the *Jeu Saint Nicolas,* tavern-keepers are also chosen as arbiters, the ruler of the tavern, of the "lower" world, replacing the legitimate political ruler temporarily in play.)

As Alan Gaylord has pointed out from the "General Prologue" description of the Host,[8] the terms by which this "myrie man" introduces the storytelling game are overwhelmingly weighted against *sentence* and toward "myrthe" and merriment (A 756, 759, 764, 766, 767, 778, 782, 802) and other analogous words such as "play" (758, 772), "confort" (773, 776), "ese" (768), and "disport" (775). Harry's proposal for fun, quickly assented to by all the pilgrims, who do not think it worthwhile to consider the pros and cons at length ("Us thoughte it was noght worth to make it wys," A 785), involves an inversion of the usual social order, a leveling of all ranks of society (Knights, Prioresses, Men of Law included) under the absolute, but temporary, rule of a bold Southwark innkeeper, their "governour, / . . . juge and reportour" (A 813–14). Harry exercises his power in comic ways, exposing and embarrassing his temporary "subjects" with his *japes* and encouraging among the pilgrims an aggressive competition that involves cudgeling one's rival with words and putting oneself on top implicitly, in fiction, in "just play."

The only person over whom Harry is incapable of exercising power, so he tells the other pilgrims in the interludes between tales, is his own wife "Goodelief," whose name may suggest both "beloved" and "willful" (in the sense that she does what she pleases, takes her own "good leave"). In a comic inversion of the proper order of things, Harry's wife is decidedly "on top." Above the jesting Lord of Misrule, there is a Lady of Misrule. Harry's wife is, he tells us, a "labbyng shrewe" about whom he dares not complain in much detail for fear that it will get back to her (E 2429–40). He would give one barrel of ale if she could hear the Clerk's exemplum of Griselda's obedience (E 1212^{a-g}) and another if she could hear Chaucer's story of Melibee's peacemaking wife Prudence. Harry depicts himself in the wake of "Melibee" as a long-suffering husband whose holy terror of a wife wears the pants in the family and is, if not a husband-beater, not far from it, for she is "byg in armes" (that is, bigger than Harry), constantly subjects him to a stream of demeaning, feminizing verbal abuse, and urges him to acts of physical violence against those who cross her:

> "By Goddes bones, whan I bete my knaves,
> She bryngeth me forth the grete clobbed staves,
> And crieth, 'Slee the dogges everichoon,
> And brek hem, bothe bak and every boon!'
>   "And if that any neighebor of myne
> Wol nat in chirche to my wyf enclyne,
> Or be so hardy to hire to trespace,
> Whan she comth hoom she rampeth in my face,
> And crieth, 'False coward, wrek thy wyf!
> By corpus bones, I wol have thy knyf,
> And thou shalt have my distaf and go spynne!'
> Fro day to nyght right thus she wol bigynne.
> 'Allas,' she seith, 'that evere I was shape
> To wedden a milksop, or a coward ape,
> That wol been overlad with every wight!
> Thou darst nat stonden by thy wyves right!'
>   "This is my lif, but if that I wol fighte;
> And out at dore anon I moot me dighte,
> Or elles I am but lost, but if that I
> Be lik a wilde leoun, fool-hardy.
> I woot wel she wol do me slee som day
> Som neighebor, and thanne go my way;
> For I am perilous with knyf in honde,
> Al be it that I dar nat hire withstonde,
> For she is byg in armes, by my feith:

That shal he fynde that hire mysdooth or seith—
But lat us passe awey fro this mateere."
(B² 3087–113)

Harry's description of his home life reminds us of the playful, reversed world of medieval marginal grotesques, where women often have the upper hand; the victorious wives of fabliaux; the seasonal festivities of ritual status inversion in which wives vanquish husbands and men disguise themselves and play the roles of women; literary inscriptions of such ritual inversions, Hugue d'Oisy's burlesque *Tournament of Ladies* (*Tournois des dames*), the numerous *Female Gospels* (*Evangiles aux femmes* [or of *Quenouilles*]), and, nearer to hand, the reversed world of "woman on top" of the "female gospels" of the "Wife of Bath's Prologue."[9]

As master of the revels and cowed husband, Harry Bailly is a Lord of Misrule; his order is a rejuvenating antithesis, a playful reversal of conventional social orders. In a mirthful springtime revival, he rebels against the restrictions of pious, introspective, penitential pilgrimage, of pilgrimage as religious service, an ordeal of self-denial and accommodation to higher authority: "to ride by the weye doumb as a stoon" (A 774). Harry also overturns the hierarchy of proper medieval processional order, both religious and secular. On the occasion of a royal entry, a civic riding, or an ecclesiastical celebration, each group had its assigned place in the procession that symbolized the rightly ordered social body. Stations or halts in the orderly progress of the official procession were well planned in advance and devoted to the kind of seriously imitative pageantry that explicitly reinforced the power of rulers and the status quo. Participants usually did not get out of line, out of order, during these stations.

Harry Bailly's pilgrimage order subverts conventional processional orders in several ways. The lowly Miller leads off to the tune of his bagpipes, while the Summoner sets a mood of foolish revelry by wearing a leafy garland on his head "As greet as it were for an ale-stake"[10] and by making a buckler of a cake (A 666–67) in a burlesque of knighthood. Furthermore, the stations of this pilgrimage, their duration and place, are determined in an impromptu fashion by Nature and human nature—by Harry's judgment of the angle of the sun, by his and the Pardoner's need to wet their whistles at the nearby alehouse, by other pilgrims' desires for immediate fictive revenge for fictive insults. The forward progress of the Canterbury pilgrimage is arbitrarily halted by game as Harry chooses someone to be "it" and urges him to "ride forth," to come up front and face his audience, which presumably circles around to hear, thus turning the linear procession temporarily into the anti-processional form of a theater. Even the sequence of fictions told at each station or rest stop tends to subvert authority, rather than to support it, when fabliaux and beast fables unmask and deconstruct the sublimations of more courteous, high-cultural genres such as romances and secular and religious saints' lives. As temporary Lord of Misrule, Harry himself debases "gentillesse," deliberately breaks the rules and decorum of polite, pious society. On the one hand, he swears outrageously and uses taboo words such as "toord" and "coillons"; on the other hand, he facetiously mimes *politesse* to comic effect.

In his invitation to the Prioress to tell a tale, the Host explicitly defers to her will four times and phrases his own will in a hypothetical way:

> . . . and with that word he sayde,
> As curteisly as it had been a mayde,
> "My lady Prioresse, by youre leve,
> So that I wiste I sholde yow nat greve,
> I wolde demen that ye tellen sholde
> A tale next, if so were that ye wolde.
> Now wol ye vouche sauf, my lady deere?"
> (B² 1635–41)

When the character described by Chaucer's pilgrim persona as "boold of his speech" (A 755), the master of the comic insult, puts on such a display of courtesy, we may detect an edge of ridicule of gentility or of the manners of the gentle pilgrim Harry mimics in such an exaggerated fashion.

The Host's preachy excursus on lost time, descending from a Senecan proverb to one on Malkyn's maidenhead (B¹ 16–32), is similarly incongruous; with such a sermon the Host probably means to twit the Man of Law about the delaying tactics of his profession. Harry mimes a judge to hold the Man of Law to his promise, forcing him to do his duty, and thus—so the Host implies—keeping him honest for a change:

> "Sire Man of Lawe," quod he, "so have ye blis,
> Telle us a tale anon, as forward is.
> Ye been submytted, thurgh youre free assent,
> To stonden in this cas at my juggement.
> Acquiteth yow now of youre biheeste;
> Thanne have ye do youre devoir atte leeste."
>
> (B¹ 33–38)

Harry's preaching is facetious impersonation, for he is against sermons. He advises the Clerk, for example, not to preach

> ". . . as freres doon in Lente,
> To make us for oure olde synnes wepe,
> Ne that thy tale make us nat to slepe."
>
> (E 12–14)

It is especially from the ecclesiastical characters—the Clerk, the Pardoner, the Monk, the Nun's Priest—that Harry, reversing the usual order of things, demands a merry tale. Even from the solemn Parson he requests a fiction, a "fable." Furthermore, he mocks learned pilgrims for their gentle behavior and language. He makes a *jape* about the Clerk for remaining as silent and reticent as a new bride and for privately musing on sophisms rather than participating in the general amusement:

> "Sire Clerk of Oxenford," oure Hooste sayde,
> "Ye ryde as coy and stille as dooth a mayde
> Were newe spoused, sittynge at the bord;
> This day ne herde I of youre tonge a word.
> I trowe ye studie aboute som sophyme;
> But Salomon seith 'every thyng hath tyme.'
> "For Goddes sake, as beth of bettre cheere!"
>
> (E 1–7)

The Host will have a "murie thyng of aventures" from the Clerk, without any "quaint" language, none of "youre termes, youre colours, and youre figures, / Keepe hem in stoor" (E 16–17). Likewise, in his mock-pious response to the "Physician's Tale," the Host makes fun of the professional paraphernalia, the badges of authority, of the Physician:

> "I pray to God so save thy gentil cors,
> And eek thyne urynals and thy jurdones,
> Thyn ypocras, and eek thy galiones,

> And every boyste ful of thy letuarie;
> God blesse hem, and oure lady Seinte Marie!"
>   (C 304–8)

The Host's imitation of gentle speech and intentions also has a
tendentious, mocking purpose when he addresses the Pardoner as
"beel amy" (C 318) in order to request a tale that is churlish: "Telle
us som myrthe or japes right anon" (C 319). This request immediately draws a protest from those gentle pilgrims who want to
distinguish themselves from the Pardoner and to censor any *japes*
or immorality he might tell:

> But right anon thise gentils gonne to crye,
> "Nay, lat hym telle us of no ribaudye!
> Telle us som moral thyng, that we may leere
> Som wit, and thanne wol we gladly heere."
>   (C 323–26)

Although both epithets for the Pardoner, Chaucer's pilgrim persona's "gentle Pardoner" (A 669) and the Host's "beel amy,"
equivocate, they do so on different tones to *explicitly* different purposes. Chaucer's pilgrim persona bends over backward to be lik-
able and to treat everyone as he would like to be treated, or even
better. Thus he calls the Pardoner "gentle" because he sings a love
duet and because of his hairdo, and he calls the Summoner "gentle
harlot" (A 647) because the Summoner knows two or three Latin
phrases. The Host, on the other hand, *mimes* various pilgrims'
speech and manners in addressing them in order to mock their
pretensions or folly, to reveal the fraud of their professions, to expose them and make them the butt of his jokes. Chaucer's pilgrim
persona is a Placebo ("And I seyde his opinion was good," A 183);
the Host is his opposite, a master of the comic degradation, an aggressive joker.

   In the interludes between tales, Chaucer's Host is continually
heating up the conflict between gentles and churls, either by
ridiculing the speech and behavior of the gentles in various ways or
by facetiously calling churls gentles. For example, following the
"Man of Law's Tale," in an interlude that appears in many manuscripts, although not in Hengwrt or Ellesmere, the Parson attempts to censor the Host's blasphemous oaths, and the Host responds by ridiculing the Parson's ascetic earnestness and lack of

humor, calling him a Lollard and announcing a sermon with a defiant oath for emphasis:

> "Now! goode men," quod oure Hoste, "herkeneth me;
> Abydeth, for Goddes digne passioun,
> For we schal han a predicacioun;
> This Lollere heer wil prechen us somwhat."
>
> $(B^1\ 1174-77)$

This time it is a churl's turn to put a stop to the moralizing of a gentle. A pilgrim who prides himself on not knowing any "quaint" Latin terms of philosophy or medicine or law breaks in:

> "Nay, by my fader soule, that schal he nat!"
> Seyde the Shipman, "Heer schal he nat preche;
> He schal no gospel glosen here ne teche.
> We leven alle in the grete God," quod he;
> "He wolde sowen som difficulte,
> Or springen cokkel in our clene corn.
> And therfore, Hoost, I warne thee biforn,
> My joly body schal a tale telle,
> And I schal clynken you so mery a belle,
> That I schal waken al this compaignie.
> But it schal not ben of philosophie,
> Ne phislyas, ne termes queinte of lawe.
> Ther is but litel Latyn in my mawe!"
>
> $(B^1\ 1178-90)$

Just as the drunken Miller interposed to cut off the Monk and "quite" with his own churlish tale the Knight's tale, much appreciated by the "gentils everichon," so this churlish pilgrim (Shipman? Summoner? Squire?)[11] cuts in to cut off a sermon and to "quite" the Man of Law's pathetic romance with his own rousing tale, which promises to be a fabliau. With the Host urging the two sides on, there is a contest between gentles and churls, opponents distinguished, not solely by their actual social status, as Lindahl has argued,[12] but by their ambitions and their willingness and capacity to sublimate erotic and aggressive desires.

Gentles and churls tell very different kinds of tales. The gentles, such as the Knight, the Prioress, the Second Nun, the Monk, the Clerk, or the Man of Law, tell serious, "pathetic" fictions that emphasize accommodation to exterior reality/morality at the expense of overt satisfaction of individual desires. The consolation or *solas* of such fictions is an alleviation of anxiety through the controlled, imaginative repetition of painful situations of powerlessness, but also, more important, a covert illusion of power that comes from the imaginative playing of the powerful roles as well as the weak ones, that is, from identification with the same power or authority that thwarts the fulfillment of the hero's desires. In pathetic fictions, the young hero or "child" figure (sometimes a wife) secretly triumphs by internalizing the will of the "father," thereby implicitly becoming and replacing him. Our pleasure comes from identifying with the implicit interloper.

The consolation or *solas* of the churls' fabliaux and fables involves a more obvious kind of wish fulfillment or fictive accomplishment of forbidden desires. The fabliau hero, like Nicholas in the "Miller's Tale," grabs straightforwardly for the object of his desire and sates himself with it. The heroes of the Miller's, Reeve's, Merchant's, and Shipman's tales are also "child" figures, young clerks or squires or monks or wives sheltered under the "fatherly" roof; however, their triumph over the father figure is completely open. In order to satisfy their own desires against the "father's" will, they mock and dethrone him both physically and intellectually. If there are gods or supreme powers in a fabliau, they are not frightening, thwarting paternal figures such as Saturn in the "Knight's Tale," but, rather, child figures themselves, *enfants terribles* such as the shrewish wife Proserpina in the "Merchant's Tale," who regularly reverses the patriarchal order of things in her own marriage to old Pluto, bringing spring with each of her rebellions against his constraint. Proserpina gives May and all earthly women the ability to *do what they want and get away with it,* to satisfy their illicit desires and put themselves "on top" (E 2266–75). The Merchant's fabliau inverts the paternalistic hierarchy of both earth and heaven. The fictions of the churls are as rebellious as the fictions of the gentles are obedient.

Even though the *Canterbury Tales* are unfinished, and although the sequence of the tales differs somewhat among the surviving manuscript collections, Chaucer's intention seems to have been to organize the tales so that there is repeated subversion of gentle tales by churlish ones, of seriously accommodating fictions by comically rebellious ones. The "Miller's Tale" "matches" the Knight's by deconstructing its illusions, such as chivalry and refined love, through burlesque imitation. Although somewhat less neatly, the "Merchant's Tale" subverts the "Clerk's Tale," and the "Nun's Priest's Tale" mockingly parodies the Monk's tragedies (and perhaps also Chaucer's conciliatory, accommodating "Melibee").

Some tales deconstruct themselves. The "Franklin's Tale," for instance, proceeds to make earnest out of game in "gentle" fashion by taking seriously the jest "in play" of Dorigen's promise to Aurelius (F 988–98). The Franklin gets as much pathos out of this jesting promise as possible—and competes with the Squire in speaking "feelingly" and eloquently—by giving Dorigan a long complaint filled with classical examples of powerless women who chose to die rather than lose their honor (F 1342–1456). After this complaint, however, the story takes another turn. According to his "General Prologue" portrait, the Franklin is a man who competes at being accommodating ("Seint Julian he was in his contree," A 340), as long as this does not involve any renunciation of his own pleasures ("For he was Epicurus owene sone," A 336). His egocentric satisfaction of the desires of the flesh puts the Franklin on the side of the churls rather than on that of the gentles. Harry Bailly recognizes a fellow churl with his "Straw for youre gentillesse." Although the Franklin's closing question imitates the *demande* or question for courteous debate (F 1621–22), it nevertheless turns a pathetic romance of accommodation centered on the predicament of a powerless heroine into a game of deciding which of three men gave up the most, who was most generous or accommodating in a more vulgar, materialistic sense of the word. Chaucer's Clerk also turns earnest into game at the end of his tale, but he goes even further; he burlesques his own tale of a patient, obedient wife with a martial closing "song" rallying wives to marital battle:

> And lat us stynte of ernestful matere.
> Herkneth my song that seith in this manere:
> . . . .
>   Ye archewyves, stondeth at defense,
> Syn ye be strong as is a greet camaille;
> Ne suffreth nat that men yow doon offense.
> And sklendre wyves, fieble as in bataille,
> Beth egre as is a tygre yond in Ynde;
> Ay clappeth as a mille, I yow consaille.
>   (E 1175–1200)

If the so-called fragments or linked tales in the surviving manuscripts of the *Canterbury Tales* represent the stations of the pilgrimage, that is, storytelling sittings (rather like those of Boccaccio's *Decameron*), Chaucer's general intention seems to have been to create dialogical, contestatory relationships between the tales and links within each sitting. What this means in terms of most fragments is that they begin with "gentle," pathetic fictions, which are subsequently subverted or reversed in some way: by their own endings, by "churlish" interruptions and disputes, by the fictive "quitting" of comically rebellious fabliaux or beast fables. In this light, "quitting" takes on another meaning, that of leaving and bringing to an end. We know that in antiquity, comical farces and mime plays were often used to bring the performance of tragedies to an end. The logic of such a play structure is a logic of balancing the emotions in order to stabilize them.

The most effective way to contest and match a noble tale such as the Knight's was to deconstruct its illusions through burlesque imitation, which is what the Miller does in his fabliau (and to some extent also the Merchant, with his homespun version of the gods in which wives are on top [Proserpina cows old Pluto with a tongue-lashing] and divine intervention into human affairs amounts to giving women the ability to do it themselves, to talk themselves out of any scrape). The relationship between the "Knight's Tale" and the "Miller's Tale" is like that between an idealizing vignette at the top of an illuminated manuscript page and the grotesque drawings at the bottom of the same page, both of which may be visual interpretations, albeit in deliberately opposite registers, of the same inscribed text.

The "Knight's Tale" is a serious fiction of the pathetic variety that depicts the accommodation of the "child" figures to the will of the "father(s)." At the outset, the narrator establishes the benevolently rigorous paternal authority of Theseus, king of Athens. Theseus curtails and represses outrageous, unlawful, erotic and aggressive desires: first, he conquers the Amazons and turns their queen, Ypolita, into his obedient wife; then, waving the banners that recollect his earlier conquest of the Minotaur (that grotesque offspring of illicit female desire), Theseus conquers the "bad father," the Theban tyrant Creon. In this battle, two young Theban princes, Palamon and Arcite, half-dead, are discovered by pillagers, handed over to Theseus, and imprisoned by him for life. These two heroes, confined to their prison tower, are powerless, conflicted child figures par excellence. They are subject not only to fate and Theseus but also to their own emotions and desires—to love and hate. When they see Emelye walking in the garden below their prison, both of them fall in love with her instantly and completely, and "sibling" rivalry begins for the right to possess the female love object, which is unattainable not only because Theseus has imprisoned the two young men, but also because Emelye "belongs" to Theseus, her sister's husband, who has the paternal authority—and the right of the conqueror—to dispose of her person.

Instead of openly expressing their resentment at Theseus for preventing the fulfillment of their desires, the two young men turn their anger against each other, expressing it, even so, in relatively genteel, sublimated forms such as verbal dispute and, later, in formalized, secret battle to the death for the love object. The young heroes lament their inability to control their fate in Boethian monologues, but they do not defy Theseus to the extent of abducting or trying to seduce Emelye or even telling her how they feel. On the contrary, when Theseus releases Arcite from prison at the request of a mutual friend, but exiles him on pain of death, Arcite redoubles his obedience and servitude to paternal authority. He returns in disguise to spend long years in the humble role of servant in Theseus's household, in physical proximity to Emelye, but without ever revealing his desire to her. When Theseus discovers the two princes fighting alone in the forest one May morning, Palamon voluntarily confesses their disobedience (his own for breaking out of prison and Arcite's for coming back in disguise) and asks Theseus for the death penalty they both deserve:

> This Palamon answerde hastily
> And seyde, "Sire, what nedeth wordes mo?
> We have the deeth disserved bothe two.
> Two woful wrecches been we, two caytyves,
> That been encombred of oure owene lyves;
> And as thou art a rightful lord and juge,
> Ne yif us neither mercy ne refuge,
> But sle me first, for seinte charitee!
> But sle my felawe eek as wel as me;

> Or sle hym first, for though thow knowest it lite,
> This is thy mortal foo, this is Arcite,
>
> . . . .
>
> I make pleynly my confessioun
> That I am thilke woful Palamoun
> That hath thy prisoun broken wikkedly.
> I am thy mortal foo, and it am I
> That loveth so hooté Emelye the brighte
> That I wol dye present in hir sighte.
> Wherfore I axe deeth and my juwise;
> But sle my felawe in the same wise,
> For bothe han we deserved to be slayn."
>   (A 1714–41)

When the ladies succeed in allaying Theseus's anger, he takes pity on the youths, and they both obediently accept the conditions Theseus lays down for winning Emelye in a public battle after a delay of one year. Theseus channels and sublimates individual desire—abstracts and symbolizes it almost beyond recognition—into the pageantry of a theatrical contest in a specially constructed arena between two teams of a hundred men each, with everyone playing the game by the rules that Theseus lays down. Right before the contest, he announces a series of prohibitions aimed at preventing any killing. The protagonists are not to use certain kinds of deadly weapons or engage in certain kinds of dangerous battle actions, and the winner will be the one who forces his opponent to the stake.

Both Palamon and Arcite and their teams, headed by the kings of Thrace and India, play by Theseus's rules, and the outcome of the contest is determined by the gods. Neither of the heroes wins what he wants directly by his own physical efforts, or even by those of his team; instead, he wins because his prayer has found favor with a god. Arcite wins the battle, as he had requested of Mars, but Palamon eventually gets Emelye, as he had requested of Venus. After Arcite wins the battle, the gods dispose of him in order to grant Palamon's prayer. Arcite falls off his rearing horse and dies of internal injuries. As Arcite's body is reduced to ashes on a grand funeral pyre in another sublimating public pageant, the narrator forcefully reminds us that he is in control of this pathetic story; in a long series of negations, he lists what he will *not* tell us about the funeral celebrations.

The "Knight's Tale" ends with an authoritative sermon by Theseus on the subjection of every living thing to the will of the "father"—that is, to the First Mover, the progenitor, the creator. Theseus concludes that it does no good to complain or rebel against the will of the father. It is best to believe in, to identify with, his wisdom, to believe that everything is for the best, to accept whatever restrictions authority imposes—even death—in short, to make a virtue of necessity, to give up foolish individual desires and accommodate "reality" (the will of the father):

> "Thanne is it wysdom, as it thynketh me,
> To maken vertu of necessitee,
> And take it weel that we may nat eschue,
> And namely that to us alle is due.
> And whoso gruccheth ought, he dooth folye,
> And rebel is to hym that al may gye."
>
> (A 3041–46)

On this note, Theseus decides to marry Emelye to Palamon, and the couple are perfectly obedient to his will. Having learned their lesson, they live happily ever after without any "jalousie," strife, or complaint of any sort.

Reeling drunkenly, refusing to doff his hood, cursing in a loud, overbearing voice—with such unruly behavior the Miller, that "unaccommodated" man, rebelliously insists on telling his fabliau, which challenges the repressive authority of the "Knight's Tale" and of the gentles who find *solas* in such a noble tale. In the "Miller's Tale," the sibling-rival figures, Nicholas and Absalom, approach their common love object, the carpenter's wife Alison, with considerable impunity, especially the "handy" Nicholas. Even the foppish Absalom does not hesitate to serenade Alison while her husband is sleeping at her side:

> The moone, whan it was nyght, ful brighte shoon,
> And Absolon his gyterne hath ytake;
> For paramours he thoghte for to wake.
> And forth he gooth, jolif and amorous,
> Til he cam to the carpenteres hous
> A litel after cokkes hadde ycrowe,
> And dressed hym up by a shot-wyndowe
> That was upon the carpenteris wal.
> He syngeth in his voys gentil and smal,
> "Now, deere lady, if thy wille be,

I praye yow that ye wole rewe on me,"
Ful wel acordaunt to his gyternynge.
This carpenter awook, and herde him synge,
And spak unto his wyf, and seyde anon,
"What! Alison! Herestow nat Absolon,
That chaunteth thus under oure boures wal?"
And she answerde hir housbonde therwithal,
"Yis, God woot, John, I heere it every deel."
                                              (A 3352–69)

Absalom is more indirect than Nicholas in his attempts to win
Alison; yet Absalom's indirection—serenades, go-betweens, promises of love service, gifts of food, monetary bribes, and even master-
ful playacting (A 3371–84)—does not stem from fear of reprisals
from the jealous husband, but, rather, from his desire (entirely inappropriate in this case) to imitate the "courteous" or "gentle"
lover.

Whereas age triumphs over youth in the romance of the
"Knight's Tale," the Miller reverses the equation in his fabliau,
wherein the child characters (including the desirous Alison) easily
escape the "father's" control to satisfy their own erotic desires
(with each other) and their aggressive, punitive ones as well. They
mock and ridicule the wisdom of the "father," make him into a
fool in the public view, subvert his authority. It is the rebellious
child figures who set in motion the comic mechanism of the tale's
ending, and not the gods. Arcite may be unhorsed and killed by a
fury sent up from hell by Pluto at the command of Saturn, father
of the gods, but Nicholas *himself* produces the "thonder-dent" of a
fart that blinds Absalom and provokes his counterblow with the
red-hot coulter, which burns and unseats Nicholas from the shot-
window with cries of "water," which, in turn, causes the carpenter (who was perhaps first awakened by Nicholas's flatulent
"thonder-dent") to cut the rope that precipitates his own fall. The
chain of cause and effect is inexorable, but youth, not age or di-
vinity, is the First Mover; youth acts to set the chain reaction of
fabliau events in motion, which climaxes, inevitably, in the embarrassing exposure of the "father's" impotence.

In the combative dialogue between gentles and churls of the
Canterbury Tales, it takes three short fabliaux—the Miller's, the
Reeve's, and the Cook's fragment—to "quite" the repressive grav-

ity of the lengthy "Knight's Tale." But even within the larger debates of the current groupings of tales, there are local debates. For
example, given his "General Prologue" description, we would not
expect the Reeve to tell a fabliau, for he is no child eager to expose
the father's impotence; instead, as a type of the miser, we associate
the Reeve with inhibiting, jealous, irascible paternal authority. Indeed, to get back at the Miller for exposing his "impotence," the
Reeve initially launches into a confessional sermon on the vices of
old age, which would put the Reeve and the "spirit" back on top
over the Miller and the flesh by proving the Reeve's witty self capable of criticizing and mocking his physically decrepit, fleshly
self and all old men:

> "We olde men, I drede, so fare we:
> Til we be roten, kan we nat be rype;
> We hoppen alwey whil that the world wol pype.
> For in oure wyl ther stiketh evere a nayl,
> To have an hoor heed and a grene tayl,
> As hath a leek; for thogh oure myght be goon,
> Oure wyl desireth folie evere in oon.
> For whan we may nat doon, than wol we speke;
> Yet in oure asshen olde is fyr yreke."
>
> (A 3874–82)

The effect of this sermon, after the release of tension in laughter at
the comic climax of the "Miller's Tale," is to raise tension again by
recollecting piety, propriety, and authority. As the Reeve begins to
sound more and more like Pope Innocent III "on the wretched
engendering of mankind," the Host pulls his imaginary pulpit
abruptly out from under him:

> He seide, "What amounteth al this wit?
> What shul we speke alday of hooly writ?
> The devel made a reve for to preche."
>
> (A 3901–3)

The Reeve thus has no alternative but to "shove force off with
force" and get even with the Miller by means of a fabliau riposte
that begins by building up the tension again with a description of
repressive fatherly authority in the pugnacious, jealous, vain miller (*cum* Miller), who will be cuckolded and even beaten by his
own wife in the end.

Because the motivation for creating—as well as reading or re-playing—fictions is so often the need to gain a sense of control in the conflictual situations of everyday life by imaginatively playing *all* the roles, the theme of much fiction has always been *mastery*. This theme is made explicit in fictions of contest or war and is generally left more implicit in fictions of love. In Chaucer's *Canterbury Tales,* as I have been demonstrating, the theme of mastery lies very near the surface of all the tales. The pathetic fictions of his gentle pilgrims focus on self-mastery (repression, sublimation, ennoblement of character) through identification with the master(s), thereby psychologically becoming and replacing them and maintaining the status quo. The comic fictions of his churlish pilgrims focus on a rebellious but temporary mastery and dethronement of the repressive father or authority figure by the child figure and a wish-fulfilling overt satisfaction, often to the point of gluttony, of erotic and aggressive desires. Moreover, Chaucer makes the theme of mastery explicit within the symbolic context of marriage, not only in the Wife of Bath's prologue and tale but also, as scholars have long recognized, in other tales, such as the Clerk's, Merchant's, and Franklin's, which explicitly discuss the politics of power in marriage and present variations on possible balances of power between husbands and wives.

Fabliau rebellions against repressive paternal authority produce temporary inversions of the social order with child figures, including wives and nubile daughters, momentarily on top. However, the "Wife of Bath's Tale" represents a more dangerous kind of inversion of the paternal hierarchy, not just a temporary rebellion. Feminine authority, that is, a female version of censorious, preachy gentility, permanently replaces paternal authority in her fiction. The Wife tells a serious, pathetic—indeed, an explicitly gentle—romance featuring the trials of a hero (like the Clerk's and Man of Law's tales), but her hero is masculine, not feminine. The self-mastery her young knight (and former rapist) learns—through a year of searching for the answer to the question posed by the queen, on the gage of his life, "What thyng is it that wommen moost desiren?"—is to put himself completely in the hands of women and to identify with the power and authority of his old wife to such an extent that he is able, Griselda-like, to concede:

"My lady and my love, and wyf so deere,
I put me in youre wise governance;
Cheseth youreself which may be moost plesance
And moost honour to yow and me also.
I do no fors the wheither of the two,
For as yow liketh, it suffiseth me."
"Thanne have I gete of yow maistrie," quod she,
"Syn I may chese and governe as me lest?"
"Ye, certes, wyf," quod he, "I holde it best."
(D 1230–38)

Once her young husband concedes that his only desire is to do as she wishes, the old wife, like a benevolent monarch, does what is best for both of them so that they may live happily ever after in youth, beauty, and perfect harmony—in other words, in perfect stability.

By changing the sex of fatherly authority, the Wife of Bath reverses the usual order of things in the pathetic fiction of her gentle romance; in this way, she puts herself and all women on top in a more seriously subversive way than she might have done with the momentary comic reversal of a fabliau fiction such as the "Shipman's Tale." This alteration of the conventional pattern of a fiction of status elevation is prepared for by the autobiography of the Wife's prologue, in which she flaunts her five marriages to ever younger men (which would make her a prime target, at least on the Continent, for the derision of a charivari or cacophonous ritual imitation, in controlling play, of the disharmony of a marital union between age and youth, experience and inexperience, sterility and fertility).[13] Through her fictions, the Wife of Bath puts herself gloriously on top for a while. In the "female gospels" of her "Prologue," she contests with female *experience* the wisdom of the "fathers" (especially St. Paul's) and repressive patriarchal *authority* in general. The trial of accommodation of the hero of her romance, and ours to the extent that we identify with him, involves identification with the will of a woman. The young knight's quest is a precarious one, threatening at every moment to turn into comedy because of the possibly equivocal meaning of the question—"What *thyng* is it that wommen moost desiren?"—especially in light of the Wife of Bath's prologual proclamation of her strong "Venerien feelynge" (D 609–26). Nevertheless, the authority of romance conventions forces us to repress this subversively facetious interpretation. The Wife both tempts and masters us, making us identify with repressive *female* authority, which knows what is best for us. Even so, the Wife of Bath's and woman's ascendancy is temporary after all; it occurs in the unreal play time and space of the Wife's stories, for which she is duly reprimanded by the next speaker, the Friar, who does not admire the presumption she has shown in preaching and abrogating authority to herself:

> "Dame," quod he, "God yeve yow right good lyf!
> Ye han heer touched, also moot I thee,
> In scole-matere greet difficultee.
> Ye han seyd muche thyng right wel, I seye;
> But, dame, heere as we ryde by the weye,
> Us nedeth nat to speken but of game,
> And lete auctoritees, on Goddes name,
> To prechyng and to scoles of clergye."
>
> (D 1270–77)

The dialogical structure of the *Canterbury Tales* involves a contest between gentles and churls engaged on the playing ground of fiction, with the churls' fabliaux and beast fables repeatedly overturning with blatantly infantile desire the repressive authority embodied in the gentles' fictions, and with the gentles ever reasserting the powers of censorship and sublimation through their romances, saints' lives, tragic exempla, and sermons. I believe that Chaucer constructed this playful debate between reason and desire with a therapeutic, equilibrating intention. The major problems faced by Chaucer and his contemporaries were political, social, and economic instabilities, and these must have seemed particularly acute to courtiers and royal servants. Economic depression, intermittent warfare with France, schism in the Church, the Peasants' Revolt and other signs of unrest in the lower classes, as well as power struggles within the ruling classes, had an unsettling impact on Chaucer's personal life, as Donald Howard has suggested:

the years during which Chaucer planned and began *The Canterbury Tales* were likely the somberest of his life. His job was unsteady: he left the Customs during this period, probably in a political shake-up, moved from London, was Justice of the Peace in Kent (1385–1389) and a member of the Parliament (1386), and was sent on a mission abroad. Gloucester's party was gaining control over the young king, so that the king's appointees must have been in a parlous circumstance. John of Gaunt, whose influence he could count on, was chiefly out of the country, waging wars in Scotland (1386) and Castile (1386–88). During these years Chaucer fell into debt, and, at about this time, his wife died.[14]

Instability is one of the major thematic preoccupations of the verse of Chaucer's friend, John Gower, and Chaucer, too, treated the problem openly in lyrics such as "Lak of Stedfastnesse," addressed to Richard II:

> O prince, desyre to be honourable,
> Cherish thy folk and hate extorcioun.
> Suffre nothing that may be reprevable
> To thyn estat don in thy regioun.
> Shew forth thy swerd of castigacioun,
> Dred God, do law, love trouthe and worthinesse,
> And wed thy folk agein to stedfastnesse.
>
> (Benson, p. 654)

Men could not learn self-mastery by identifying with a master who (because he was himself young and foolish) did not exercise authority, did not brandish the paternal sword to censure and correct individuals who tried to aggrandize themselves and satisfy their own aggressive desires.

As opposed to Gower or to Eustache Deschamps, the latter in his self-appointed poetic role as "old counselor" to the young Charles VI of France,[15] Chaucer, whether temperamentally unsuited to the role or out of a sense of its futility, did not pursue this hortatory, fatherly method of stabilizing society by trying to make the king into a better exemplar of paternal authority. Instead, following a more primitive logic and a long festive tradition, Chaucer offered in the *Canterbury Tales* a means of restoring social stability, at least for a while, through the symbolic play of his fictions.

When society is sick and in need of renewal, primitive consciousness often seeks a solution in regression, *reculer pour mieux sauter*. This may be a logic of the body based on the observed relationship of cause and effect in certain bodily movements or gestures, such as drawing the arm back in order to throw an object forward. Medieval life seems to have been organized dialogically, as Bakhtin has pointed out, around a similar principle. The pater-

nal, rational order of everyday life was regularly broken and subverted by the alternate order of festive disorder, which involved a
kind of sanctioned regression en masse. Within the safe bounds of
festive time, adults playfully reverted to infancy, and, in the guise
of youths, women, or fools, gleefully rebelled against the "will of
the father" to satiate flagrantly, on many levels, aggressive and
erotic desires that would in ordinary times have to be repressed.
During such festivities, people played the rebellion of youth
against age and in so doing expressed and temporarily purged
themselves of their frustrations with authority.

If such festive behavior reaffirmed the oneness of the social
body, as Bakhtin has argued, it was not the oneness of the individual with something bigger than himself in the sense of the sublime (as in *sublimation*), that is, the total accommodation of the individual to the extent of losing his selfhood in society. On the contrary, rebellious medieval festivity encouraged the assimilation of
society to the individual self; this involved a regressive, infantile,
physical sense of oneness of the individual with the social "body"
analogous to (indeed, probably originating in) the infant's inability
to distinguish the mother's body from his own and his consequent
belief that "every-body" is "himself."

Such periodic medieval festive play produced the illusion of renewing society (through youth's dethronement and replacement of
age), and it also stabilized the regular social order by satisfying, if
only temporarily and in game, powerful individual desires for self-
assertion that had to be curtailed by the authorities in ordinary life
for the common good. Chaucer, like Boccaccio before him, had a
problem to solve with his heterogeneous collection of stories that
included so many fabliaux. Chaucer's problem was the instability
of late-fourteenth-century English society. His solution was the
play of the *Canterbury Tales,* in which a group of pilgrims, repre-
sentative of major classes and estates of contemporary society, led
by a Lord of Misrule, engage in a festive, springtime game of
storytelling, a game that temporarily, intermittently subverts the
piety of pilgrimage and the hierarchy of real life and enables many
of the churls to express their aggression and frustrated rivalry
against gentles or against other churls, harmlessly, through the
minifictions of tendentious jokes and through the more elaborate
fictions of their comic tales, which dethrone the father and satisfy
illicit desires.

To the extent that we, Chaucer's audiences, identify with these characters and read our own frustrated desires in theirs, we too may be purged and sated by such festive rebellion, and we may presume that Chaucer himself found some of the same consolations through the repetitive reversals of the dialogical structure of his play. That Chaucer's ultimate aim was, nevertheless, to promote social stability is suggested by the lengthy and highly serious religious treatise that anchors all his preceding fictions. The "Parson's Tale" is not really a tale, for the Parson refuses to play Harry's game and tell a fiction, a fable. Instead, he buckles up Harry's proverbial bag of fictions and, with the definitive closure of his sermon, Chaucer's Parson reestablishes proper order and authority.

Chapter Seven

De*author*izing the Text

Setting Up the Game of
the *Canterbury Tales*

In an article entitled "Le Carnaval de Bâle ou l'histoire inversée," Peter Weidkuhn presents a photograph of the Paris street riots of May 1968 in which a group of young men in white masks smeared with red hang a policeman in effigy and carry the "corpse" of a comrade (which consists of an almost comically empty pair of jeans with shoes sticking out of the legs). Are these young men using the symbolic language of festive rebellion, outside festive time, with a seriously revolutionary intent? Or are they, in this May rebellion, using the masks and the puppets, the fictive lynching of a policeman instead of a real lynching, to signal that their contestation of power is temporary and not intended to be seriously destabilizing? Peter Weidkuhn, an ethnographer, concludes the latter: "they are playing at revolution. . . . the structuralist accommodates himself to that which grieves the historian."[1] In order to contest authority, to deauthorize sacred texts or symbols of power with some degree of impunity, one must put on a mask to signal that the threat is not real after all. This mask serves to deauthorize the text of aggressive actions or words by pointing out the pretense involved, by framing them off from the real world as a fiction. All of us do this on one level or another.[2]

For example, I find it next to impossible to elaborate on the sacrilegious innuendos Chaucer evokes concerning "Goddes pryvetee" in the "Miller's Tale" when sitting on my desk three feet away from a naive and corruptible undergraduate class that really wants to take me for a "gret auctorite." It is less difficult to say the same things from the distance of a podium in the vaguely carnivalesque context of a convention, in the role of "woman on top" (or *Mère Folle*) before an audience of knowing fellow scholars.[3] In writing—and especially in doubly disembodied writing on a word-processor screen—it is easier to express such sacrilegious interpretations, because writing involves the even greater distance of absence as well as the assumption of fictive personae: my I's (which include the personae of the medieval interpreter and Chaucer the author and even the Wife of Bath and other pilgrims whose roles I play), as well as my imagined audience, are fictions; I am not really speaking to you. At the same time, whenever I emerge from the game world of writing, I realize that in spite of—indeed, liberated by—the denying devices of critical-scholarly writing, I am telling the truth, that there is, as Harry Bailly puts it, "truth in game." I am saying things that do reveal the "real" me and also, I am relatively sure, something about real medieval interpreters and about Chaucer; furthermore, I know that what I write will appear in authoritative, permanent print, that real audiences will read it, and that I am not able to control their interpretations.

Although he was composing in a manuscript culture, which made controlling his audience's interpretations even more difficult, Chaucer surely must have had many of the same problems in profaning the sacred that I have in explicating his profanation (thereby making it, in effect, my own). Although not a university professor, Chaucer was part of the Establishment; his word was supposed to support that Establishment, the English monarchy and its governmental bureaucracy. As I have just tried to do with mine, Chaucer deauthorized his own texts—and thereby protected himself from reprisals (of conscience or higher authorities)—by blatantly assuming fictive personae and also by pointing out in the end, in his "Retraction," that he is different from his personae. But as with any game, the player is constantly aware of the pretense, of the illusion (otherwise the game would turn into a delusion). Games enable such doubling, such fictive liberation from the constraints of everyday life; they are equi-vocal, equi-gestural. The player knows that he is himself, although temporarily pretending to be another, to exist in another world. I know that the voice of the *Canterbury Tales* as I reenact and replay the tales in this book is really my voice, although I may pretend it is Chaucer's. And Chaucer knew that the voice of the *Canterbury Tales* was really his own, although he might pretend temporarily that it was the voice of his pilgrim persona or that of other pilgrims, also his personae, for he was playing all the roles.

Nevertheless, in order to play any game, we must give its fictions at least partial credence, and this is also true for the spectator (viewer or reader) as player. The soccer fan who knows perfectly well that he is just watching the tiny screen of his television set participates in the contest in his imagination. In order to play the game of the *Canterbury Tales,* we must acquiesce in its pretenses (although never entirely), because this permits us to identify with the various characters and their conflicts and to experience the consolations of Chaucer's various fictions. These he has carefully arranged within each station or sitting of the *Canterbury Tales* into a contest between gentle and churlish tellers whose stories form a repetitive pattern of inversions, first encouraging gentle or accommodating behavior, then encouraging churlish or egotistical (assimilating) behavior. The gentle, pathetic tales of trial and submission, as we have seen, encourage identification with authority and the covert illusion of becoming and replacing the father, of a permanent status elevation for the neophyte. These gentle tales are interrupted or "quitted" and symbolically, ritually reversed by churlish, comic tales of rebellion against authority involving the "father's" temporary dethronement and desecration. In this same way a child plays to console itself in its conflict with parental authority. The game the child invents to alleviate anxiety and to gain control is often a dialectical series of plays involving accommodation and assimilation; the child will alternately play the roles (or masking figures thereof) of the parent punishing the child and of the child punishing the parent.[4] Chaucer's *Canterbury Tales* are an extremely sophisticated, highly sublimated and disguised version of the child's consolatory dialectic of playlets involving repeated role-reversals.

Chaucer has set up the game of the *Canterbury Tales* in order to give himself and his audience the most varied and satisfying experiences of identification while constantly reminding us that we are "just playing." This prolonged equivocation, this divided state of consciousness as we live in two or more worlds or contexts at once, seems to free us partially from the restrictions of reality, to enrich our experience. In this chapter I would like to lay bare some of the techniques Chaucer uses in the "General Prologue" to set up his interpretive game, to place us at the crossroads of intentions (or associations). This needs doing because the history of interpretation of the *Canterbury Tales* shows that we have tended to overlook some of the signs that announce play while overprivileging others that announce history. We have also, it seems, taken some of Chaucer's signs to mean just their opposite. This is not surprising, considering the complexity of Chaucer's play and also the anachronistic context that a twentieth-century reader inevitably brings to Chaucer's text.

Virtually all readers of the *Canterbury Tales* acquiesce, at least intermittently, in the "realism" of its fictions, giving them credence as if they were real. And so we should—but not entirely. As I have just explained, this willing suspension of disbelief is necessary to play any game. No scholar takes the *Canterbury Tales* as a true historical account of Chaucer's travels to Canterbury with just the set of companions under just the circumstances he describes, but we do consider the journey and the contest *possible* (some of us even calculate the itinerary), and virtually all of us find ourselves, at one time or another, as I was doing in the preceding chapter, discussing the pilgrims' motivations and personalities as if they were real people. In short, we tend to read through Chaucer's words as if they were transparent, taking them for serious representation of the words and actions of Canterbury pilgrims.

Modern scholars have attributed the realistic effect of the *Canterbury Tales* to the dramatic frame of the "General Prologue" and the links between the tales wherein Chaucer introduces the pilgrim characters and depicts them interacting with one another before each delivers the dramatic monologue of his tale. Most modern audiences tend to think of dramatization as a technique for bringing a text to life, making it seem more real. When we go to see a play, we generally do not want to be made aware of the illusion; we want to believe that the player *is* the character he plays; in other words, we want to be deluded. G. L. Kittredge's famous analysis of the *Canterbury Tales* as "roadside drama" reflects this relatively

modern assumption that the purpose of dramatization is always serious imitation of reality, "realism." In his analysis Kittredge
moves rapidly from "personae" to "persons":

The Canterbury Pilgrimage is . . . a Human Comedy, and the Knight
and the Miller and the Pardoner and the Wife of Bath and the rest are the
dramatic personae. The Prologue itself is not merely a prologue: it is the
first act, which sets the personages in motion. Thereafter, they move by
virtue of their inherent vitality, not as tale-telling puppets, but as men
and women. From this point of view, which surely accords with Chaucer's intention, the Pilgrims do not exist for the sake of the stories, but
vice versa. Structurally regarded, the stories are merely long speeches, expressing, directly or indirectly, the characters of the several persons.[5]

Kittredge has it reversed. The "General Prologue's" formal resemblances to an historical account encourage us to read its language
as if it were transparent and to believe that the pilgrim characters
are real people. On the other hand, the "General Prologue's" formal resemblances to medieval dramatic prologues and imperson-
ated literature encourage us to focus on the game of interpretation
and on the opacity of language—on the equivocal richness of possible significations of Chaucer's double- or multi-voiced texts,
spoken by Chaucer/his "short-witted" pilgrim persona/other pilgrim personae/characters in "their" tales.[6]

The "General Prologue" to the *Canterbury Tales* gives contradictory directions for understanding what follows. Chaucer deliberately depicts the narrator of the *Tales* as a kind of Janus figure
frowning gravely in one direction, smiling impishly in the other;
he places himself, and consequently us, at the crossroads of intentions, between history and play, earnest and game. His opening
account of the who, when, where, and why, his claim to be an
eyewitness (*auctor*) and participant in the action, his profession of
truthful intentions and apology for his deficiencies as a writer, all
seem to signal that the *Canterbury Tales* is history. These are the
authenticating conventions of historical writing, and especially of
Chaucer's religious and secular historical models, the Gospels
(Christ's life reported by disciples who participated in the events)
and the Troy story (as told by the eyewitness Dares and translated
and retold by Benoît de Sainte-Maure and Guido delle Colonne).[7]
If we take the "General Prologue" as the introduction to an his-

torical account, then we must not expect any verbal play, trusting that Chaucer is sincerely trying to make the word resemble the deed. We must read the spring topos opening, for example, as a florid rhetorical delineation, in the manner of Guido's description of the Greeks setting sail for Troy,[8] of the people, place, and period of the historical narrative (and not read for the pleasure of the poetic language, for erotic innuendo and equivocal meanings of pilgrimage).

And yet Chaucer's prologual voice, for all his imitation of authoritative historical models, is not quite that of an historian. It was not a convention of medieval historical narrative for the writer to claim to be repeating other men's words nearly verbatim, as Chaucer does in his long apology for his plainspokenness near the end of the "General Prologue":

> But first I pray yow, of youre curteisye,
> That ye n'arette it nat my vileynye,
> Thogh that I pleynly speke in this mateere,
> To telle yow hir wordes and hir cheere,
> Ne thogh I speke hir wordes proprely.
> For this ye knowen al so wel as I:
> Whoso shal telle a tale after a man,
> He moot reherce as ny as evere he kan
> Everich a word, if it be in his charge,
> Al speke he never so rudeliche and large,
> Or ellis he moot telle his tale untrewe,
> Or feyne thyng, or fynde wordes newe.
> He may nat spare, althogh he were his brother;
> He moot as wel seye o word as another.
> Crist spak hymself ful brode in hooly writ,
> And wel ye woot no vileynye is it.
> Eek Plato seith, whoso kan hym rede,
> The wordes moote be cosyn to the dede.
> Also I prey yow to foryeve it me,
> Al have I nat set folk in hir degree
> Heere in this tale, as that they sholde stonde.
> My wit is short, ye may wel understonde.
>
> (A 725–46)

This apology may seem to modern readers to guarantee the historical accuracy of the narrative. However, in the Middle Ages such faithful imitation—or mime—was the task, not of the composer, but of the *performer* of the text, that is, the jongleur who performed it orally or the scribe who performed it in writing (or, to a lesser extent, its translator). In preface to his French translation of Boethius's *Consolation,* Jean de Meun apologizes to those who criticize that he has not translated "word for word" by explaining that he is fulfilling King Philip IV's command to translate the *sentence* (or meaning) plainly, without following too closely (to the point of obscurity) the Latin wordings.[9]

The historian's more sententious task was to teach by selecting significant episodes for the purpose of revealing and preserving historical or moral truths. In the prologue to his "Melibee," Chaucer adopts an attitude toward language that is more typical of the medieval historian: what matters is the *sentence,* not the words per se. The example Chaucer uses to illustrate this is the Gospels, which use different words to say the same thing about Christ's Passion:

> ". . . ye woot that every Evaungelist
> That telleth us the peyne of Jhesu Crist
> Ne seith nat alle thyng as his felawe dooth;
> But nathelees hir sentence is al sooth,
> And alle acorden as in hire sentence,
> Al be ther in hir tellyng difference.
> For somme of hem seyn moore, and somme seyn lesse,
> Whan they his pitous passioun expresse—
> I meene of Mark, Mathew, Luc, and John—
> But doutelees hir sentence is al oon.
> Therfore, lordynges alle, I yow biseche,
> If that yow thynke I varie as in my speche,
> As thus, though that I telle somwhat moore
> Of proverbes than ye han herd bifoore
> Comprehended in this litel tretys heere,
> To enforce with th'effect of my mateere;
> And though I nat the same wordes seye
> As ye han herd, yet to yow alle I preye
> Blameth me nat; for, as in my sentence,
> Shul ye nowher fynden difference
> Fro the sentence of this tretys lyte
> After the which this murye tale I write."
>
> (B[2] 2133–54)

Like Benoît de Sainte-Maure, who promises a vernacular translation of the sense of the Latin text of the Troy story, while reserving the right to add some "bon dit" (proverbs or exempla) if any occur to him,[10] Chaucer in his preface to "Melibee" promises the same *sentence* in his English rendition of the story, but with additional proverbs pointing it. Exact replication or repetition of language was not the medieval historian's goal, because his audience was supposed to be interested in content; they were supposed to read through his words to a truth about or applicable to life.

For the late medieval historian, keeping good notes, analyzing them to extract the lessons of history, and conveying these lessons in a clear, distinguished style were the way to achieve authenticity and authority[11]—not performing prodigious feats of memory such as Chaucer seems to imply he is performing in repeating nearly verbatim all of the spoken tales of the Canterbury pilgrims.[12] For example, Chaucer's contemporary, the historian Jean Froissart, did not depend for many hours on his memory of events he had witnessed or of information he had gleaned from eyewitnesses. Froissart claims that whenever he had the chance he wrote down key facts in the form of a *mémoire* or notes:

With the words that Sir Espaing de Lyon told me I was completely delighted . . . and I retained them all very well, and as soon as we had entered a hostel along the road that we were travelling together, I wrote them down, either in the evening or in the morning, in order to have a better remembrance in the future, for there is no more accurate keeper than writing.[13]

These notes he later worked into the more exemplary, embellished, and rhetorical form of his prose *Chronicles*. Benoît de Sainte-Maure, likewise, assures us that Dares took notes, and Benoît authenticates his own "translation" by emphasizing in his preface how long Dares' eyewitness account had been lying in *writing* in a book cabinet until Sallust's learned nephew found and translated the Greek into the Latin history that he, Benoît, found in a "hardly worn" manuscript and translated, in turn, into French.[14] Chaucer, on the other hand, prefaces his book by suggesting that he is relying chiefly on his memory of other men's spoken words.

It was the jongleur, not the historian, who told his tale "un-

trewe" if he invented new words for those he had been commissioned to perform. The jongleur who performed a literary text
was not responsible for the vulgarity or innuendo of its language.
The irresponsibility of the mere performer is what Jean de Meun's
foolish Lover claims in a passage that Chaucer was probably
imitating:

> "Si m'a mes mestres deffendu,
> car je l'ai mout bien entendu,
> que ja mot n'isse de ma boiche
> qui de ribaudie s'aproiche.
> Mes des que je n'en sui fesierres,
> j'en puis bien estre recitierres;
> si nomeré le mot tout outre." [15]

"Indeed, my master [the God of Love] has forbidden— / because I understood him very well— / that any word leave my mouth / approaching
ribaldry. / But as long as I am not the maker [composer], / I can very well
be the reciter; / thus I will name the word out loud."

John Fleming finds the Lover's argument absurd: "The prohibition
against uttering dirty words applies only to new words—that is, I
presume, to words that one makes up oneself. As long as you are
not the maker (*fesierres*) of a dirty word, but only its reporter, you
have committed no sin against Cupid." [16] The word *fesierres* in this
passage probably refers instead to the act of poetic composition (to
the poet as maker), [17] hence to poetic composition involving vulgar
syllables or words, rather than to the invention of neologisms,
new dirty words. Nevertheless, Fleming is right that the situation
is an absurd one. It is precisely this denial of responsibility for
meaning on the part of a naively foolish performing persona, who
is just "rehearsing," that sets up the interpretive game of many a
medieval love lyric by giving the text two separate voices or contexts, thereby licensing equivocation. [18]

Another sign of game that undercuts the historical pretensions
of the "General Prologue" is Chaucer's rhyming of his "history,"
for late-fourteenth-century serious historical writing was usually
couched in prose. In early medieval lay society, as in other oral cultures, rhyme and alliteration were methods of locking words together more memorably, and they were regularly used to preserve
the memory of secular historical events. As the written word became more commonplace and authoritative, rhyme was increas-

ingly identified with game. Leonine verse and rich end rhymes, which constantly equivocated and foregrounded the aural, sensual matter of language, were censured by conservative churchmen who associated them with frivolity, with goliards and jongleurs and their comically subversive intentions.[19] Given his rhymed literary output before writing the *Canterbury Tales,* Chaucer must have been famous for the facility with which he rhymed. Indeed, jongleurlike, he mocks himself as a rhymester twice in the *Canterbury Tales,* not only through the alter ego of Harry Bailly after the fiasco of "Sir Thopas," but also through the persona of the Man of Law, who disparages Chaucer's rhyming ability but praises him for being prolific and for his circumspection in avoiding "wikked" tales (ones that Gower told in his *Confessio Amantis*):

> "I kan right now no thrifty tale seyn
> That Chaucer, thogh he kan but lewedly
> On metres and on rymyng craftily,
> Hath seyd hem in swich Englissh as he kan
> Of olde tyme, as knoweth many a man;
> And if he have noght seyd hem, leve brother,
> In o book, he hath seyd hem in another.
> For he hath toold of loveris up and doun
> Mo than Ovide made of mencioun
> In his Episteles, that been ful olde.
> What sholde I tellen hem, syn they been tolde?
> . . . .
> "But certeinly no word ne writeth he
> Of thilke wikke ensample of Canacee,
> That loved hir owene brother synfully—
> Of swiche cursed stories I sey fy!—
> . . . .
> "But of my tale how shal I doon this day?
> Me were looth be likned, doutelees,
> To Muses that men clepe Pierides—
> *Methamorphosios* woot what I mene;
> But nathelees, I recche noght a bene
> Though I come after hym with hawebake.
> I speke in prose, and lat him rymes make."
> (B[1] 46–96)

In spite of this elaborate apology for a prose tale, the "Man of Law's Tale" appears in the manuscripts in rhymed stanzas. Are we to believe that Chaucer had intended to revise the prologue to this tale? I think not.

No pilgrim, with the exception of Chaucer the pilgrim, announces that he will tell a rhymed tale, although several pilgrims' prologues imply or specify that their tales will be in the plain speech of prose. The Parson clearly rejects both alliterative verse ("geeste") and rhymed verse, and, like the Man of Law, promises a tale in prose—as does Chaucer the pilgrim in his second attempt at a pleasing tale. The Host's general attitude toward rhyme seems to be that it is a waste of time and needlessly complicates comprehension of the story; he tells the Clerk to cut the colors (a rhetorical term that could refer to sound patterns and rhyme), the figures, and other quaint terms, and to speak plainly (which the Clerk agrees to do):

> "Telle us som murie thyng of aventures.
> Youre termes, youre colours, and youre figures,
> Keepe him in stoor til so be that ye endite
> Heigh style, as whan that men to kynges write.
> Speketh so pleyn at this tyme, we yow preye,
> That we may understonde what ye seye."
>
> (E 15–20)

On the other hand, we might well imagine that the Clerk's short, closing battle "song" (E 1174, 1176) for contemporary wives was delivered in rhyme, albeit alliterative meter would have been more appropriate to its bellicose sentiments. Although the Franklin compliments the Squire's eloquence and emotional delivery, he makes no mention of rhyme, and in the introduction to his own tale his shift from the term "lay" to "tale" may be significant (F 709–28). The Franklin disclaims all knowledge of "colors" and muses and promises a bare and plain tale couched in rude speech, although drawn from his memory of an old Breton lay that was originally both rhymed and sung or chanted. The Monk also mentions the original form of the hundred tragedies he keeps in his cell, some in hexameters, some in other meters and in prose, but his apology for not remembering the proper order of the tragedies suggests that he will not be able to remember their form either and that he will paraphrase them in prose (B^2 3161–80). From the Prioress's use of the word "song" (B^2 1677) to describe her story, we might think that she told her tale in rhyme, but religious songs (or *laudes*) were not generally rhymed, and the Prioress is probably using the word "song" to signal her devotional, laudatory intent in telling a miracle of the Virgin. In short, I find no convincing evidence that Chaucer ever meant us to believe—or to suspend disbelief of the possibility—that most of the Canterbury pilgrims told their stories on the spot in verse.

In his "General Prologue" apology, Chaucer allows himself some leeway in his attempt at repetition of the other pilgrims' words, however vulgar:

> Whoso shal telle a tale after a man,
> He moot reherce *as ny as evere he kan*
> Everich a word, if it be in his charge,
> Al speke he never so rudeliche and large.
> (A 731–34; my italics)

This leeway we have generally supposed to be a reference to defects of memory, but it might also refer to the difficulties and the inevitable distortions involved in versifying and rhyming other men's texts. Chaucer's position as rhymer of other men's tales is similar to that of the turn-of-the-fourteenth-century jongleur (or Valenciennes burgher) who wrote under the name of Gautier Le Leu. In the opening of one of his bawdy fabliaux (which involves kissing a *cul* in the night, trying to feed its "mouth," and mistaking farts for bad breath), Gautier explains the story's provenance:

> Saciés de fit que Li Goulius
> Le raconta en tamains lius
> A Saint Amant et a Marcienes.
> Uns bacelers de Valencienes,
> Qui avoit esté ens el leu,
> Le raconta Gautier Le Leu
> Et il mist le fablel en rime.
> Dix en a fait, ves ci l'onsime.[20]

Be it known for a fact that the Glutton / told it in many places / at St. Amand and Marchiennes. / A young gentleman from Valenciennes / who had been there at the time / told it to Gautier Le Leu, / and he set the fable to rhyme. / He has composed ten; here is the eleventh.

Gautier Le Leu deauthorizes his bawdy tale by refusing to accept responsibility for its content or language; he claims to be merely repeating and rhyming the matter of other men's words, that is, the words of the Valenciennes gentleman reporting those of "Li Goulius."

Although we know that Chaucer was not really repeating and rhyming the words of other Canterbury pilgrims, as he claims to be doing, he *was,* in the tales proper, repeating and rhyming the matter of other men's words, that is, of earlier versions of these stories. There is a certain amount of truth in his historicizing game. Furthermore, the writing process Chaucer describes in the *Canterbury Tales* is not so very different from that he describes in his dream visions and his "history" of Troilus: in every case he claims that the verbal matter is given (in a dream, in an earlier book, in oral stories) and states or implies that he is merely its reporter or English translator and its *rhymer.* Chaucer's "General Prologue" apology presents him embarking on the writing of a rhymed history of a pilgrimage game. That he rhymes the "Man of Law's Tale" (after the Man of Law, anxious about Chaucer's "influence," promises prose) playfully points out that Chaucer the prolific rhymer comes after, as well as before, the Man of Law, improving upon the Man of Law's prose "hawebake."

Unlike the jongleur/performer, the medieval historian was entirely responsible for the words and style in which he chose to convey his story. Furthermore, the medieval historian would be sure to set people in their proper social positions throughout his narrative. He might ignore people's exact words, but not their social rank, for a major purpose of medieval historical narrative was to legitimize rank. Moreover, in order to authorize their accounts, most medieval historians pointed out their own merits in one way or another. Benoît de Sainte-Maure, for example, begins his prologue to the *Roman de Troie* with a *sentence* from Solomon stating that men should not hide their understanding but show it to the world to win honor, which is why, Benoît says, he has decided to work on the translation of the *Roman.*[21] Medieval historical writers might capture the audience's goodwill by apologizing for their general deficiencies as writers and calling upon their readers to correct any inadvertent errors, but they did not stretch the humility topos into self-mockery, as Chaucer does at the end of his "General Prologue" apology when he calls himself short-witted. Medieval historians might emphasize their impartiality, but Chaucer the pilgrim's amiable and unquestioning, Placebo-like acceptance of widely varying values and behaviors overshoots the historian's impartiality and might be interpreted as an excessive desire to please, a foolish abdication of judgment. The Trojan historian Dares, so Benoît and Guido assure us, tried not to lean toward one side or the other in recording the events of the Trojan war; to this end, Dares made a great effort during periods of truce to get to know the key leaders on both sides in order to portray them accurately in a preface to his narrative of events, beginning with the Greeks' choice of a leader and their setting sail.[22] In his self-appointed role as historian of the Canterbury pilgrimage, Chaucer the pilgrim also makes an effort to get to know the chief participants—"And shortly, whan the sonne was to reste, / So hadde I spoken with hem everichon / That I was of hir felaweshipe anon" (A 30–32)—and he sets down their descriptions in preface to his narrative of the journey and contest. Chaucer, however, presents himself as a burlesque version of Dares: Chaucer the pilgrim-historian tries so hard to be unbiased and comprehensive that he substitutes jongleuresque mime for history and comes off as foolishly lacking in discrimination.

Such self-mockery was the province of the jongleur or player, who used it to create a foolish persona that masked and de*au*thorized the aggression of his derisive jokes and stories. In his thirteenth-century *Livres dou trésor,* Brunetto Latini described the jongleur as "one who laughs and jokes and mocks himself, his wife and children, and everyone else."[23] By pointing to his own "short wit," Chaucer creates an irresponsible persona who will rehearse a series of stories as nearly verbatim as memory and the rigors of rhyming them will allow, writing/speaking them all through different masks, like a jongleur with a large repertoire. His narrative persona combines the historian with the player, for, as no medieval historian would do, he equivocates by interposing unreliable personae between himself and his audience. Thus he licenses his own wordplay and our game of interpreting his words. Such role-playing partially circumvents the restrictions of conventionally serious (cognitive, referential) linguistic usage; the role-playing speaker deauthorizes the text by declaring, in effect, "*I* am not speaking," and this frees both the speaker/writer and his audience to play with language.

That it is Chaucer the writer-rhymer of the tales playing all the roles becomes especially apparent in cases where a pilgrim claims to be "writing" his tale, as the Second Nun does in the apology of her prologue ("Yet preye I yow that reden that I write," G 78), or in the many other cases of what Donald Howard has called "unimpersonated artistry," when we think we hear Chaucer's authorial voice instead of a fictive pilgrim's.[24] These instances remind us that Chaucer is merely impersonating the pilgrims, that they do not really exist, that his history is a game of writing: he is doing the writing and pretending to be they. Some of these apparent slips may well be deliberately equivocating (in an almost Brechtian sense); by means of them Chaucer makes his masks obvious and forces us to think of the same words in at least two contexts at once, thereby enriching our interpretive experience, which tends to become impoverished as we gradually give in—even more readily if our experience of the fiction comes from reading letters on a page—to the delusion that we are interpreting history.

The major high-medieval generic distinction, which signaled either history or play, was whether or not deauthorizing, fictive personae were interposed between author and audience, either by the author in the way he conceived and composed the text, or by performers transforming it. The spoken word or the gesture did not carry authority unless the speaker witnessed to its authenticity by speaking it in his real historical identity. The same is true today. Serious historians never hide behind masks (or at least not behind deliberately obvious masks). When medieval speakers or writers assumed fictive personae, especially comic or errant ones such as, to name but a few, Golias or the foolish lover or passionate female festive disguises, they both disclaimed responsibility for the meaning of their words and gestures and signaled rebellious intentions. Chaucer's Nun's Priest reminds his audience, in order to smooth any ruffled feathers, "Thise been the cokkes wordes, and nat myne" (B² 4455). The irresponsible—in this case brute, animal—persona interposed between author and audience enabled all sorts of subversive play, indeed, licensed the interpreter to participate in subversion of the "authorities" as well.

Chaucer begins his "General Prologue" apology in an historicizing vein—"Now have I toold you soothly, in a clause, / Th'estaat, th'array, the nombre, and eek the cause / Why that assembled was this compaignye" (A 715–17)—but he ends the apology playfully and equivocally. Authoritative history is dethroned by game. After drawing a highly legitimizing analogy between his own plain speech and Christ's, and thus between the written text of the *Canterbury Tales* and the Scriptures (A 739), Chaucer cites a classical authority to substantiate his "rehearsal" of vulgar language: "Eek Plato seith, whoso kan hym rede, / The wordes moote be cosyn to the dede" (A 741–42). We expect this *sentence* to convey some immutable truth, but it turns on us. What does it mean that words should be "cousins" to deeds? Although "cousin" could perhaps not yet pun on the verb *cozen,* still it might suggest a duplicitous, self-serving relationship.[25] Cousinage was ambivalent, involving distance as well as proximity, especially in medieval families that recognized very distant cousins. Words that are cousins (or co-signs) to deeds may not be very closely related to the deeds or represent them very accurately. This ambiguity about what the *sentence* means subverts its authoritative formulation, turning it into something of a riddle, a game of interpretation. But even more may be going on here. This maxim, which Chaucer quotes in an apparent attempt to authorize his repetition of other people's vulgar words, had already been used and deauthorized through erotic innuendo (understanding *chose* ["thing"] as a euphemism for the genitals and sexual intercourse) in Jean de Meun's famous defense against those who accused him of using bawdy or foolish language.[26] For interpreters who are aware of Jean's playful subversion of the authority of this *sentence,* which Jean attributes to Sallust, not to Plato, Chaucer's choice of authorities is equivocal.

Chaucer uses the same *sentence* on the proper relationship between words and deeds again later in the *Canterbury Tales,* voicing it this time through the persona of the Manciple (H 210) in a local context that explicitly treats the subject of sexual duplicity and linguistic euphemism and in a tale where, as Donald Howard has written, "the ideal of an accord between word and action is destroyed by the crow's harsh experience with telling the truth."[27] Chaucer often plays facetiously with sententious statements in this way, deauthorizing them by repeating them in new, inappropriate contexts. For example, the Knight's "pitee renneth soone in gentil herte," which describes Duke Theseus's temperance of his anger (A 1761), is played in a much lower register by the Merchant, who uses the *sentence* to describe the "gentle" May's rapid decision to "take pity on" her husband's serving man—and take him for her lover. In this vulgar context, after May has just read and disposed of Damian's love letter in the privy and submitted to a second bout of her husband's unappetizing lovemaking, the Merchant's proverb, "Lo, pitee renneth soone in gentil herte!" (E 1986) is a ludicrously ill-fitting, gaping linguistic cover-up for a fabliau wife's decision to satisfy her sexual appetite in adultery.

Just as it is possible to authorize one's own text by intercalating a supporting *sentence* from an authority or a piece of proverbial wisdom, so it is also possible to deauthorize a proverb or *sentence* by using it in a context that conduces to "mispointing," that is, to distorting or misinterpreting its conventional or earlier meaning. The technique of turning *sentence* into *solas* by means of comic impersonation—voicing the maxim through an incongruous persona or in an incongruous situation—seems to go back at least as far as the Roman empire. The mime Publilius Syrus is reported to have brought down the house with well-known epigrams offered, one guesses, in the most ridiculously apt yet inept situations.[28] This is the basic technique of comic parody or burlesque, which deauthorizes and debases a sacred text (understood in the broadest sense) by crudely replaying it or prominent parts of it in a partially similar but nevertheless profoundly "wrong" context—such as, in Chaucer's Miller's and Merchant's tales, Nicholas's playing of Gabriel's song of Annunciation to Mary, or the division of Thomas's fart after the manner of the Descent of the Holy Spirit.

To encourage us to play with his words, and to absolve himself from responsibility for their meaning, Chaucer, in his "General Prologue," interposes between himself and us a short-witted, self-mocking, jongleuresque persona appropriate for the voicing of a comic or satirical text, a persona who reminds us, "This is game," and licenses the discovery of subversive subtexts in at least some of the pilgrims' portraits. At the same time as he points out the illusion, it is Chaucer's genius to be able to delude us, to make us disbelieve and believe at the same time, to make us oscillate between attitudes of game and earnest, to return us constantly to that crossroads of intentions that is the point of richest interpretive experience. Although we know Chaucer's jongleuresque pilgrim-persona is an irresponsible narrator, we still tend to read his descriptions of the pilgrims, at least part of the time, as objective descriptions of real people, and we even tend to interpret Chaucer the pilgrim's amiability as an uncalculating naiveté that makes his descriptions more objective, because he seems incapable of distorting "reality." Knowing that he is unreliable, we nevertheless want to and do at times give Chaucer the pilgrim-historian credence; we debate the behavior and psychology of the pilgrims, as depicted in their "General Prologue" portraits, in a search for meaningful *sentence* that focuses especially on the moral issue of whether certain pilgrims were behaving "as they should."

I will conclude this chapter with a brief discussion of these contradictory interpretive postures in modern readings, including my own, of the portrait of the Prioress in the "General Prologue." The *realist* identifies with the characters, privileging the signified over the signifier, whereas the *ironist* maintains a deconstructive distance from characters and objects represented and focuses instead on the verbal matter of the text, privileging signifier over signified; the realist accommodates, whereas the ironist assimilates; the realist takes a serious attitude, the ironist a playful one. Florence Ridley has summarized past scholarly arguments over the character of the Prioress:

G. G. Coulton thinks a Prioress's wimple should not be fluted; Sister Madeleva, that a "pinched" wimple was simply part of the Benedictine dress, its wearing a matter not of vanity but of duty and tradition. Kemp Malone thinks the cloak too elegant, an indication of worldliness as is the garb of the Monk and the Friar. Sister Madeleva defends the elegance of the cloak on the grounds that it is an indication of a commendable desire for cleanliness and of the typical nun's typical regard for her holy garment. . . . And so it goes; critical opinion as to whether the Prioress's behavior is appropriate for a nun seems hopelessly divided, with almost as much said for it as against it.[29]

Whether these scholars find the Prioress moral or immoral, their debate on her behavior proceeds from the realist's assumption that the words of the "General Prologue" portrait represent a person (and not a persona), a character whom we try to understand and judge according to our notions of human psychology and moral ideas such as the proper conduct of a prioress. Indeed, to the extent that Chaucer leads us to believe that he is serious about writing the history of a storytelling game that happened during a pilgrimage, he encourages us to take this realistic approach. From this point of view, whether or not we think she behaves as a prioress ought, Chaucer's fastidious Prioress is definitely one of the gentles on the pilgrimage who does the most to set standards of courteous speech and behavior—those imperfectly censoring sublimations of desire—against which churls such as the Miller rebel. However, to the extent that Chaucer mocks himself and assumes the jongleuresque persona of a short-witted rhymer who wants to be the historian of the journey, a *naif* who valiantly, but inappropriately, tries to be unbiased and withhold judgment, merely echoing other men's words ("And I seyde his opinion was good" [A 183]), he encourages us to take the language of the portraits in game, to hunt for equivocal meanings in the body of the text—the body of the Prioress—in an inter- and intra-textual game world. From this ironic perspective, the Prioress is not a person, but a playground, a *locus amoenus* for interpretive play—like a good many of the more facetious troubadours' "ladies."

Jill Mann has explored in detail the equivocal language of Chaucer's "General Prologue" portraits, although she does not discuss the traditional satirical techniques of foolish impersonation that license such play; and Terry Jones has done a thorough job of representing the ironist pole of interpretation on the Knight's portrait; indeed, Jones begins his facetious interpretation by saying, "I could never quite see the Knight as a real person."[30] A host of other scholars too numerous for separate mention here have pointed out equivocal words or passages in individual portraits, including the Prioress's. Interpreters *in malo* have found that the language of the Prioress's portrait abounds in covert erotic innuendos suggested by literary allusions, symbols, and puns: for example, the language describing the Prioress's table manners recollects the Old Bawd's advice, in the *Romance of the Rose,* to young women who want to make themselves attractive to men; the coral of the Prioress's beads may turn her rosary into a love amulet;[31] the motto of their pendant brooch, *Amor vincit omnia,* may refer to spiritual or physical love. This wood has been hunted so often that there would seem to be little game left in it. Nevertheless, we might cast our nets a little wider in trying to flush out the innuendos of the name Eglantine, which has been called that of a romance heroine.

Medieval names are likely places to look for hidden meanings; the serious exegetes were the first to do so, and facetious interpreters were always prepared to find game in a name. Thus the French translator of the goliardic Latin *Pamphilus* play warned (and cued) his audience in his prologue: "Brother, many names are equivocal" ("Frère, maint nom sont équivoque").[32] The code names or *senhals* for the troubadours' lady-loves were often suggestive—Pretty Rider, Sweet Pleasure, and the like. Not only did medieval interpreters find names hidden in texts, but texts hidden in names. Eglantine is the Old French name for the wild briar- or dog-rose, a prickly bush that flowers in May or June, the sort of bush beside which shepherdesses of *pastourelles* sit (if not under hawthorns, pine trees [with needles], or olive trees [known for their white flowers and black thorns]).[33] Readers of the *Romance of the Rose* need not be reminded that the "flower among thorns" has a symbolic sexual import involving the lure of the unattainable or difficult to approach. The word *eglantine,* especially in conjunction with the phrase "simple and coy" (which is often applied to the shepherdesses of *pastourelles*),[34] suggests the sexual quest and love-making outdoors—especially with a peasant girl (a "wild rose"). These erotic connotations of the word *eglantine* may account for its use as the name of a young woman in a late-twelfth- or early-thirteenth-century Old French narrative poem, two different versions of which Chaucer could have known.

The longer version of "Bele Aiglentine" survives only in the *Roman de la rose ou de Guillaume de Dole,* where a young knight performs the lyric to entertain his fellow knights during pre-tournament celebrations.[35] The poetic fiction features feats of masculine prowess, the fulfillment of many a young knight's fantasies.[36] Count Henry makes love with the beautiful Eglantine, impregnates her, and, after her mother suggests *raptus* (as a solution to the predicament of the pregnancy and the difference in their ranks, for Eglantine is of royal lineage), Henry summons a knightly band and gleefully carries his prize off to his own territory to be his wife. Eglantine is love's victim, a willing one.

The other Eglantine lyric, a short motet, also seems to contain sexual innuendos and may have inspired the longer, much more

explicit, and cruder version.[37] Both lyrics open with bedroom
scenes in which Eglantine has a love problem. In the longer version, the suspicious mother discovers the pregnancy and forces a
resolution, whereas in the motet a solitary Eglantine complains in
the conventional language of the distraught lover:

> En une chambre cointe et grant,
>   Se sist bele Eglentine
> Deseur .i. lit riche et plesant
>   Et enclos de cortine;
>   En sospirant
>   Va regretant
>   Ce qu'aime d'amor fine;
>   Puis va disant:
>   "Dieus! por qu'aim tant
>   Celui qui tant
>   Va demorant,
> Quant set que j'ai dolor si grant
>   Que nuit ne jor ne fine?
>   Or n'i sai medecine,
>   Se plus atent."

In a chamber, elegant and large, / sits the beautiful Eglantine, / upon a
bed, luxurious and pleasing, / and enclosed with curtains. / Sighing, /
she laments / that she loves with a refined love. / Then she exclaims, /
"God! Why do I love so much / the one who / delays so long, / when he
knows that I have such suffering / that it never ceases night or day? /
And now I know no cure for it / if he waits any longer."

If this lyric was not composed in burlesque imitation of lyrics
about refined love, its syntax nevertheless makes it an easy target
for burlesque mispointing. Late medieval poetic word order can be
extremely convoluted for the sake of rhyme. The possible innuendo about the nature of Eglantine's love "ailment" (a pregnancy
growing ever more obvious?) may be set up by pausing before the
adjectival phrases in the first and third lines. Is it the bedchamber
that is "elegant and large," or is it—like Chaucer's pilgrim name-
sake, who "was nat undergrowe"—Eglantine herself? Is it the bed
that is "luxurious and pleasing," or is it Eglantine? The meaning of
such a lyric depends entirely on how the interpreter punctuates
and inflects it with his voice. Furthermore, a feminine voice might
point the *chanson de toile* in a pathetic direction, while the mas-

culine voice of a foolish jongleuresque persona (or that of the young knight in the *Roman de la rose ou de Guillaume de Dole*) might point and amplify it in the "wrong" direction, toward burlesque. I suspect that Chaucer knew this example of playfully motivated *mouvance*.

As we focus on the baser associations of the name Eglantine in the Prioress's portrait, Chaucer's repetitious "ful" becomes pregnant with meaning. Common as the Middle English adverb *ful* (meaning "very") may be, Chaucer's use of it eleven times in the course of the fifty-four lines of the Prioress's portrait may be deliberate. Her demeanor is "ful symple and coy," "ful semely" and "ful plesaunt"; the sounds she produces are "ful semely" and "ful faire"; her dress is "ful semyly" and "ful fetys"; her mouth is "ful smal." No other pilgrim's portrait echoes with the word *ful* in this way. Although Chaucer uses the word three times in the short space of three lines (A 589–91) to describe, ironically, the "sclendre" Reeve, the count for the Wife of Bath's portrait, for example, is a mere two uses in thirty-one lines. The effect of such juggling repetition of a word in slightly different contexts is to draw attention to it and to its possible connotations. The *Middle English Dictionary* gives no listing of *ful* meaning "pregnant" or "voluptuous" in the fourteenth century.[38] However, Chaucer uses *ful* to describe a horn of mead and a "jubbe" of wine in the "Knight's Tale" (A 2279) and the "Shipman's Tale" (B 1261). As long as *ful* could be used in this concrete, materialistic way to describe the state of repletion of a vessel, the figurative connotations of "full" or "pregnant" might emerge from a context such as the Prioress's portrait, which abounds in covert suggestions of female sexuality. In such a context, mispointed by a short-witted, jongleuresque narrator, fleeting connotations may subvert or dethrone more orthodox denotations.

Outrageous as this interpretation of the subtext of the Prioress's portrait may seem, in festive, ritualistic inversions of the conventional order of things, medieval goliards and jongleurs practiced just this kind of profanation of the sacred (as well as facetious sanctification of the profane). Furthermore, praise of a lady had become a traditional locus of medieval interpretive play. As early as the twelfth century, the troubadours were interpreting lyrics and inventing ones that could be interpreted in at least two ways, *in bono* and *in malo,* with respect to "good" love and "bad" love. On festive occasions of ritualized status inversion, even the conventional phrases and epithets of Mariolatry might be temporarily turned upside down by understanding them in a rude and materialistic way. Goliards played with the possible fleshly connotations of *plena* (as in Gabriel's phrase of annunciation, "Ave Maria, gratia plena") in the same way we might play with those of *ful* in Chaucer's explicitly laudatory portrait of the Prioress, and in much the same way that spectators of the fourteenth-century play *The Miracle of the Pregnant Prioress* might savor erotic puns and innuendos and the burlesque "Virgin birth" at the play's ending.[39] It must be admitted, however, that not all of the "General Prologue" portraits lend themselves easily to this kind of playful interpretation that focuses closely on the language of the portrait rather than on the distant "person" the words supposedly represent. Chaucer alternates portraits such as the Prioress's with others, such as the Parson's, that do not seem equivocal but, rather, remind us of the historical claims of the pilgrim-narrator and encourage us to ignore the medium of language and to identify with the person described. By means of such alternations, which occur also within individual portraits, Chaucer returns us again and again to the crossroads of intentions, where history and game seem to meet.

The *Canterbury Tales* as Stabilized and Stabilizing Structure

In trying to arrange the corpus of a medieval poet's works into chronological order when there is no reliable external evidence for dating, as is so often the case, modern scholars tend to work on psychological assumptions: we assume that young writers will be rebellious, mature ones more circumspect, old ones pious and sententious. Thus we arrange any bawdy fictions in a writer's youthful period or student days, accounting for them as wild oats or student rags; this cordons them off and enables us to arrange the more serious (pathetic, tragic, accommodating) fictions where we feel they are most appropriate, that is, later in the poet's career. This is, for example, how Gaston Raynaud tries to take care of all of Eustache Deschamps's facetious verse, even though some occasional pieces are dated by the poet himself as late as 1385 and 1400, when Deschamps was in his late thirties and early fifties and held responsible official positions. Raynaud generalizes:

From 1366 president of the Society of the Quarrelsome under the name of John Quarrel, he took in turn, in his burlesque occasional poems, the titles of Emperor of the Quarrelsome (1370) and Sovereign of the Tipplers (1372). It is the most joyful period in the life of the poet, that of his amorous and often bawdy or more-than-bawdy lyrics when, young and active, free of all bonds, not yet knowing any of the worries about money and health that haunted him throughout much of his life, he enjoyed an optimism that did not last long.[1]

Speaking through the persona of old Oswald the Reeve, Chaucer gives the lie to this logic—if we believe him—in the "Reeve's Prologue":

> "We olde men, I drede, so fare we:
> Til we be roten, kan we nat be rype;
> We hoppen alwey whil that the world wol pype.
> For in oure wyl ther stiketh evere a nayl,
> To have an hoor heed and a grene tayl,
> As hath a leek; for thogh oure myght be goon,
> Oure wyl desireth folie evere in oon.
> For whan we may nat doon, than wol we speke."
>
> (A 3874–81)

Older men represent in words the follies they would do if they still could.

A rough chronology of Chaucer's own writings seems to support Oswald's view rather than that of more conservative idealists, medieval and modern, the Philippe de Navarres and Matthew Arnolds of the world, who believe that adult men holding respectable, official positions should not indulge in rebellious fictions.[2] Chaucer's poetic career, as we know it, appears to head in just the opposite direction. Chaucer begins by translating, adapting, and writing consolatory fictions of the almost exclusively pathetic, accommodating sort (*Boece [The Consolation of Philosophy], Anelida and Arcite, The Book of the Duchess . . .*). He ends by cutting these pathetic fictions with comedy: the comedy of Pandarus the go-between playing the courtly lover in an incongruously low register, in effect, burlesquing Troilus; the comedy of the *Canterbury Tales* in which the churls with their vulgar fabliaux and tendentious *japes* rebel against the restrictions of gentility, authority, and hierarchy. In its general outline, Chaucer's career as a poet begins with tragedy and ends with comedy. He signals this direction himself in the "envoy" to posterity of his *Troilus:*

> Go, litel bok, go, litel myn tragedye,
> Ther God thi makere yet, er that he dye,
> So sende myght to make in som comedye![3]
>
> (5.1786–88)

Yet even in Chaucer's "tragedy" of *Troilus,* laughter plays an important part. The tragic action of Troilus's accommodation to the authority of the "other" (a fiction of status elevation) begins with, is periodically cut by, and ends with laughter. We see Troilus first as a carefree young bachelor, egotistically laughing and making tendentious jokes at the expense of his lovestricken comrades (1.190–203). Next comes the pathos of Troilus's painful and gradual accommodation to the rules of society—of courtly love, of war, of proper conduct, of the common good (all symbolized by the authority of the God of Love, because love is what makes possible the psychological transference and accommodation to the will of the "other," the "father"). However, this pathos is intermittently punctured by Pandarus's distancing *japes* and burlesques of the courtly lover and by comic scenes in which Troilus submits to Pandarus, which is an accommodation in the "wrong" direction—not in the direction of the authoritarian "father" but in that of the solicitous and provocative "mother" (for Pandarus's role of go-between or bawd is more conventionally in medieval comedies, such as *Pamphilus,* a female role). After closing the story of Troilus's sufferings for love, Chaucer adds a sort of dialogical epilogue to the fifth book that restores Troilus's ability to laugh *post mortem* (5.1821). This disembodied, cosmic laughter denies the world and signals Troilus's final mastery over it, his imperviousness to any pains the world—the "other"—might inflict. Troilus's laughter from the distancing perspective of the heavens further diminishes the world, which appears below him as a "litel spot of erthe":

> And in hymself he lough right at the wo
> Of hem that wepten for his deth so faste,
> And dampned al oure werk that foloweth so
> The blynde lust, the which that may nat laste,
> And sholden al oure herte on heven caste.
>
> (5.1821–25)

Too much submission and sublimation or diversion of egotistical desires—to the point of Troilus's exemplary and anonymous death fighting for father and city—had to be balanced by a rebellion, and so Chaucer makes Troilus's spirit laugh. But what this disembodied laughter enables—in us "lovers" who identify with Troilus—is further "service," and on a higher level of symbolization or sublimation, service now to the heavenly Father:

> O yonge, fresshe folkes, he or she,
> In which that love up groweth with youre age,
> Repeyreth hom fro worldly vanyte,
> And of youre herte up casteth the visage
> To thilke God that after his ymage
> Yow made, and thynketh al nys but a faire,
> This world that passeth soone as floures faire.
>
> (5.1835–41)

Troilus's last laugh and the burlesque inversions performed or perpetrated by the comically pragmatic Pandarus only temporarily interrupt our identification with the suffering hero in Chaucer's longest fiction of accommodation and status elevation. The greatest consolation of *Troilus and Criseyde* comes, not from the momentary rebellions of laughter, but from Troilus's "elevation," the progressive ennoblement of his character through loving and his final heavenly resting place (and our own, to the extent that we identify with the hero). The pious, devotional ending of the *Canterbury Tales,* the ballast of the didactically religious "Parson's Tale," also demonstrates the ultimately accommodating intention behind Chaucer's cycle of fictions, although the proportion of accommodating and rebellious fictions in the *Canterbury Tales* as they now stand, incomplete, seems more equally balanced than in *Troilus,* and even, in the middle, weighted toward comic rebellion. Whereas the central action of *Troilus* involves the hero's painful accommodation to "authority," the great middle section of the *Canterbury Tales* is filled with fabliau rebellions against and subversions of authority and with the spiel of "experience" opposed to authority, with the Wife of Bath "on top."

The logic—the medieval mentality—behind the structure of Chaucer's *Canterbury Tales* is a Carnivalesque one: the best way to stabilize a structure at dangerous points of necessary transition or change is to exteriorize tension at these points by destabilizing the structure symbolically in controlled and controlling play. There were always those who condemned such apparently rebellious fictions, wherever they appeared: in playful status inversion at the New Year or other times of transition or seasonal change; in literary versions of festive inversion (which were often partial transcriptions of actual social rituals, or simulacra for these); in the ludic, grotesque or burlesque marginal drawings surrounding blocks of the serious or sacred text on the pages of medieval manuscripts; at the pressure points, structural transitions, and interstices of medieval religious buildings. St. Bernard's questions in his famous letter to the Abbot of St. Thierry sometime after 1120 are rhetorical questions, not real ones: "in the cloister, under the eyes of the Brethren who read there, what profit is there in those ridiculous monsters, in that marvellous and deformed comeliness, that comely deformity? To what purpose are those unclean apes, those fierce lions, those monstrous centaurs, those half-men?"[4] Bernard probably knew perfectly well what purpose such monsters on column capitals were intended to serve—not to warn people against sin and evil, but to stabilize the structure of the cloister itself (as building and as symbol of the monastic body).

By putting the "bottom" symbolically "on top," by inverting the order of things, externalizing tension in playful contests contained within a limited field (such as the circular or rectangular world of the column capital), medieval builders and "makers" intended to relax temporarily the tension of subordination (the column's subordination to its load, the monks' rigid discipline) at pressure points or points of structural transition. One thinks not only of the grotesque carvings of capitals on religious buildings, but also of leafy-headed masks at the places where the ribs of vaulted roofs join the ribs of the walls, of grotesque or monstrous caryatids, of the burlesque carvings under the seats of misericords supporting the weight of the buttocks of men (another variation of "bottom on top"). Points of transition on the exteriors of religious constructions were also subject to this ludic treatment, this externalization of tension in the forms of gargoyles and other "drôleries" (such as the lewdly exhibitionistic jongleur reliefs atop Modena cathedral) that deliberately display the "beast" or the bestial in man, which the discipline of Christian religious life ordinarily subordinates and represses.[5] Indeed, rather than understanding such images as animals behaving like people, as we have habitually done, we should take them for people behaving like animals. In allegorizing exegesis, we normally read figures "up," but in these instances of rebellious play, we should read the figures "down." Carved on a capital or a misericord or depicted in the margin of a manuscript, a fox preaching from a pulpit, for example, is an image of man as fox, of a foxy man and not of a manly fox.

These symbolic reversals at the transition points of artistic and

architectural structures—we might call them all texts—stabilize
the created structures not only by a kind of catharsis or exterior-
ization of dangerously destabilizing internal forces, as I have been
suggesting, but, through the mimesis of a reversal, they also encourage a renewal of the forces necessary to maintain the structure.
This seems to be the meaning of carvings on capitals of humans
copulating or of exhibitionistic, priapic or whorish caryatids.[6]
These images and others such as ostentatiously public defecation
and farting, which Gaignebet collects under the sacrilegious titles
of "anal offering" and "the soul fart," display deliberately regressive, fabliau-like behavior.[7] The logic here seems to be one of
reculer pour mieux sauter, of the refreshing, reanimating power of
regression, of breaking the rules—as long as the rebellion is carefully circumscribed in play—and its renewing energies are made to
bear up the building, or, in the case of gargoyles as drainspouts, to
divert excesses. This is the logic of Carnival.

The same mentality accounts for the organization of many a
medieval verbal edifice. Manuscript collections made up largely of
seriously accommodating longer genres such as saints' lives, romances, epics, and histories also tend to include shorter, comically
rebellious pieces such as fabliaux, exhibitionistically erotic love
lyrics, drinking songs, nonsense poems, and the like. These have
the effect of temporarily reversing order with a burst, narrowly
circumscribed by its very brevity, of deliberate insubordination
and regression. The literary edifice of Chaucer's *Canterbury Tales*
works like this. The first tale, the Knight's, is about accommodation to authority, explicitly in its Boethian speeches, but also in its
plot and even in its style. The "Knight's Tale" is relatively long
and trying for its audience, requiring an extended submission to
its disciplined structure, which Charles Muscatine has described as
its "symmetry of scene, action, and character grouping, the slow
pace of the narrative, the large proportion of static description, the
predominantly rhetorical kind of discourse"[8]—in short, to its conventionally authoritative and authoritarian style. In the design of
the *Canterbury Tales,* we might compare to weight-bearing pillars
Chaucer's long, pathetic fictions: the "Knight's Tale," the even
more symmetrically organized and subordinated "Clerk's Tale,"
the seemingly interminable "Man of Law's Tale" of the trials of
Constance . . .

Such fictions of accommodation test our patience and endurance, but not intolerably, because they are usually followed by rebellious, deliberately insubordinate fabliaux whose plots peak rapidly in the comic climax of a figurative dethronement of the "father."[9] It requires no great discipline on the part of the audience to appreciate these tales. Like a subversive pun or a witty joke, the fabliaux, as Howard Bloch has remarked, seem to us "gratuitous," as if they came "from nowhere."[10] Chaucer relieves the strain on his audience of being submissive throughout his long fictions of accommodation—and the metaphoric strain of weighty *sentence* on the pillar-fictions of his literary edifice—by means of the brief, rebellious interludes of his fabliaux, which serve much the same purpose as the grotesquely carved capitals or caryatids of medieval religious buildings: to externalize tension and renew forces by drawing on energies that can be directed to supporting the structure, thus maintaining and stabilizing it.

Not only do we experience a vicarious sense of power in seeing the child figure dethrone the father figure of the fabliau, but we also renew our sense of power over language, our power to signify, as we enjoy the fabliau's subversion of the father tongue of proper adult speech. The fabliaux—and even more so the rebellious lyric forms of goliardic and jongleuresque verse—take liberties with language and deliberately break the rules that limit signification. Let me take as an example a near-pun that I have played with in this book: *vie/vit* ("life"/"penis"). To identify the two words or to take one for the other is "wrong" because, as we have all been taught, these are two different words, the first feminine, the second masculine, not to be confused because they are pronounced with different ending sounds, as represented by their different spellings. Furthermore, to mention the vulgar *vit* at all is not "proper," which makes it especially outrageous to take *vie* for *vit*. These are the rules of the father tongue of correct speech, the language of authority that limits how sounds and spellings and words and all the other components of language may signify. But the father tongue is in many respects only a second language to us, even if we are talking about a single language of which we are native speakers. All of us as infants or little children, each in his own idiosyncratic ways, learn our native language by associating the meanings of similar-sounding words. Words such as *vie* and *vit*, whose predominant initial consonant and vowel sounds are the same, along with innumerable other near-puns, puns, and words that sound only slightly similar, are associated in the catalogues of our unconscious memories, along with their meanings, the "incorrect" early associations as well as the later "corrections."

Medieval goliardic and jongleuresque play—and much poetry in every age—licenses temporary linguistic regression that overturns the restrictive rules, the censorship, of the father tongue of correct speech by bringing out into the open again and speaking verbal associations that later schooling has taught us are wrong. We call these associations folk etymologies when they have a fairly wide currency, or free association when they are idiosyncratic; medieval people would probably have thought of them as "wild" or "natural" or "free" meanings. The rebellion of such facetious interpretation dethrones correct associations with incorrect ones. And the error becomes exhibitionistic when a vulgar and incorrect sense, such as *vit,* dethrones and replaces a proper sense, such as *vie.* Such temporary linguistic insubordination not only purges by externalizing the tension of repressing these wrong associations, but also, and more important, allows us to return to the father tongue refreshed and feeling more powerful in our ability and in our language's ability to signify richly, a capacity that is limited and diminished by the rules of correct, clear adult speech but is renewed in poetry, especially through the disorderly syntax and punningly rich rhyme of much medieval poetry.

We cannot blame the artisans, the students, and the little people exclusively for the ritual inversions the ascetics deplored but did not succeed in stopping. There were many mature and responsible medieval men in complicity, and even in the forefront, inventing rebellious fictions for enactment on festive occasions by the truly or the symbolically young. The author of the clever Latin play of *Babio* was more likely to be a middle-aged schoolmaster than a budding young Latin scholar. The fourteenth-century French kings all kept court fools, and the young Charles VI even dressed up as a savage. Eustache Deschamps, a royal officer responsible for keeping order, occasionally headed a facetious Order of the Quarrelsome; the lawyer Philippe de Beaumanoir wrote nonsense verse; Geoffrey Chaucer, the customs officer and keeper of accurate fiscal accounts for the king, spent his leisure time fabricating the "false accounts" of his fictions, his *contes* of Canterbury, so many of which were bawdy fabliaux.

Such irresponsible behavior in the "margins" of festive or free time must have been consolatory on a personal level, must have enabled Chaucer to go on serving. Chaucer's power over his fictional worlds was surely greater than his real power as a member of the royal household (or government), where he ranked higher than some, but lower than many others, in a hierarchy that required much subservience, much accommodation to the will of others. We will probably never know much about the intimate personal referents of Chaucer's fictions, that is, precisely how his fictions related to his personal life and helped him to rectify in play troubling imbalances of power. In any case, Chaucer's concerns, like his friend Gower's and like Deschamps's, reached beyond himself to fourteenth-century society, which seemed to be growing old as the end of the century approached, and to totter under the weight of war and of increasingly threatening imbalances of power between classes (which provoked peasants' revolts in both England and France) and between court factions (maneuvering in the absence of a strong king, for both Richard II and Charles VI were young).

In these unstable times, Chaucer wrote the *Canterbury Tales* to renew the productive forces of English society and at the same time, through controlling play, to stabilize the late-fourteenth-century social order. His opening description of the setting of his fiction, nature in the full swing of a springtime revival, with sap rising, breezes blowing, birds singing, suggests the revivifying part of his intention. However, his fictive pilgrimage is not only a rite of status reversal or "errance" but also a rite of passage, of status elevation through religious devotion and accommodation. The ending of the "Parson's Tale" amply testifies to this. Again and again, in variation upon variation, earnest is subverted by game in contests that exteriorize and exorcize social tensions: between gentles and churls and their respective kinds of fictions, between competitors in everyday life, between individuals who did not hit it off, in this egalitarian ritual *communitas* of pilgrims,[11] who nevertheless represent the ordinary hierarchy of the English social body, the order that Chaucer is trying to stabilize by destabilizing it in play. He built his literary structure to last; its strength and stability reside, not in its wholeness in the sense of the *finition* of the "perfect object," for it is not finished, but, rather, in the impression of completion—the satisfaction—evoked by Chaucer's dialogical alternation of *sentence* and *solas,* fictions of accommodation with fictions of rebellion, literary versions of rites of status elevation with rites of status reversal. The *Canterbury Tales* is a complete "play" because it is completely consoling.

Appendix

The *Troilus* Frontispiece and the Dramatic Presentation of Chaucer's Verse

The famous early-fifteenth-century frontispiece of the Cambridge Corpus Christi *Troilus* manuscript has long been the object of scholarly admiration and speculation.[1] (See Fig. 22.) It was once believed to represent Chaucer himself reading *Troilus* before Richard II's court, and efforts were made to identify members of the depicted audience.[2] The figure dressed in gold standing directly beneath the pulpit, for instance, was interpreted as Richard II. In short, we have tried to read the *Troilus* frontispiece as "history." More recently, scholars have stressed the idealizing aspects of the frontispiece and considered its relationship to other prefacing illuminations in late medieval manuscripts. According to James McGregor, Chaucer is being depicted as a sort of ideal secular counselor of princes as he *lectures* Richard, in radical reversal of the usual deferential dedicatory image of the kneeling poet presenting his work to his patron.[3] Such a reversal of positions of authority would be extremely daring—indeed, I think, too daring—even though "corrected" to some extent by an image of the prince on the ramp of the mountain above the poet's head. Derek Pearsall and Elizabeth Salter have argued that the figures do not represent individual historical persons; rather, the *Troilus* illuminator is merely using the iconographical conventions of preaching scenes in late medieval Continental manuscripts.[4] In Salter's judgment, "this is decisively signalled by the lack of text in front of the speaker, and by his familiar hand-gestures as he looks down from his portable, draped 'pulpit.'"[5]

In several fourteenth-century manuscripts of Guillaume de Deguileville's *Pèlerinage de vie humaine,* the first page is headed with a vignette that depicts the author standing in a raised pulpit addressing an audience.[6] The listeners closest to the pulpit are seated; standing behind them, the rest of the audience extends to the right, apparently beyond the frame, which cuts through figures for a slice-of-life effect. Some of the listeners engage in conversation with one another, eye a pretty lady, rest their heads on their hands in a gesture of boredom, or fall asleep. Such vignettes represent the conditions of medieval literary appreciation, but their mise-en-scène is also carefully designed to present the text of the *Pèlerinage* to its real audience, which is not the one pictured, but the reader who holds in his hands this book prefaced with an image of its performance. The absence of any book in the hands of the speaker in the pulpit of the vignette is probably deliberate; the reader has the book in his own hands. The illuminators of the vignettes of the *Pèlerinage* cleverly altered the traditional iconography of the medieval presentation scene, wherein a kneeling author offers the material object of his book to a standing or seated patron. This preaching presentation of some *Pèlerinage* manuscripts presents the text to the individual reader, who is supposed to imagine himself as part of the fictive audience, to imagine the text as it might be orally performed, and not to approach it solely as a valuable artifact or object of study. The illuminator of the *Troilus* manuscript adapts this new Continental presentation iconography, omitting the book in the speaker's hands, in order to present the manuscript of *Troilus* to the reader, who looks into the frame from behind the courtly figures seated in the foreground of the pictured audience. But what ought the reader to see—and what audience does he join? My answers to these questions are that I see a considerably idealized dramatic performance, after the medieval fashion, of *Troilus and Criseyde,* and I feel as though I had joined the audience of "lovers" of a medieval *puy.*

Skilled illuminators of deluxe manuscripts such as the Corpus Christi *Troilus* did not borrow iconographical conventions unthinkingly. They adapted the conventions to the particular context of the manuscript they were illustrating—in this case a five-part tragedy, as Chaucer himself labeled his work. To my eye, major differences present themselves between the composition of the preaching vignettes prefacing the *Pèlerinage* and the composition of the *Troilus* frontispiece. In the former, seated listeners are closest to the speaker in the pulpit, while other spectators stand behind the seated ones so as not to block the view. In the *Troilus* frontispiece, the space immediately in front of and below the speaker's pulpit is occupied by two finely dressed *standing* figures (one in cloth of gold and the other in blue) facing each other a small distance apart. According to the perspective of this image, seated spectators are drawn up in a semicircle around the pulpit and the two standing figures. Behind the seated viewers, on the far side of the semicircle, some figures stand. In effect, the *Troilus* illuminator has represented the semicircular arrangement of spectators in a medieval theater around a central pulpit.

In a passage from his *Troy Book,* Lydgate's convoluted syntax somewhat obscures his medievalizing conception of the classical theater as a semicircle with a raised pulpit in the middle:

> In the theatre ther was a smal auter
> Amyddes set, that was half circuler,
> Whiche in-to the Est of custom was directe;
> Up-on the whiche a pulpet was erecte,
> And ther-in stod an aw[n]cien poete.[7]

It is probably the theater, not the altar, that is half-circular. Lydgate does not mention an actual theater building here; indeed, the medieval understanding seems to have been that the spectators themselves, in their semicircular arrangement around the performer(s), could form the theater. John of Garland in his *Aequivoca* defined "theatrum" in the conventional etymologizing way, from *theorare,* "to see," hence "a spectacle or a place in which men, standing or seated, may see and hear well the gestures and words of singers or speakers or players."[8] In classical usage, as applied to drama, the word *pulpitus* meant "stage" or "platform," but early Christian interpreters such as Isidore understood the word, in terms more familiar to them from religious usage, as a place to read from, a "pulpit" or a "chair" or a small, houselike structure. The mid-twelfth-century etymological dictionary of a monk of Gloucester, the *Panormia* of Claudianus Osbern, glosses "pulpitum" with "analogium, lectrum vel legitorium"—places to read from.[9] In the Middle Ages, both religious sermons and more entertaining vernacular literature might be spoken from a pulpit, with or without accompanying mime by actors in the space immediately below (the orchestra, in classical terms). Secular dramatic practice seems to have resembled religious preaching practice, as G. R. Owst long ago claimed.[10] Thus the resemblances in the iconography of the manuscripts may be due not so much to the borrowing of visual icons but to attempts to represent actually similar techniques for oral performance of religious and secular texts.

In my judgment, the finely dressed figures standing beneath the pulpit in the *Troilus* frontispiece are engaged in miming the roles of Troilus and Criseyde, while the speaker in the pulpit above performs the text vocally. (See Fig. 23.) On the right, the blond-haired figure in blue may be playing the role of Criseyde, while the man in gold opposite her probably plays Troilus. Trojan princes, after all, might be supposed to dress splendidly, and Criseyde's "sonnysshe heeris" receive special attention in Chaucer's text (4.736, 816). The width of Criseyde's shoulders is not surprising if we are to imagine her role being played by a man; nor is the difference between her dress and that of female spectators necessarily significant if her costume is supposed to represent medieval notions of a noble Trojan lady's attire. Furthermore, the lack of definition of Troilus's facial features, which can hardly be an oversight in such a carefully detailed illumination, suggests that we are to imagine an actor wearing a mask, not a historical person, but a *persona*. Although Criseyde's head is turned away from us, I think I see the edge of the actor's mask in profile.

It is of course possible, but not fundamentally damaging to my argument, that I have misidentified the two characters involved. For example, the broad-shouldered blond in blue that I have identified as Criseyde might be Pandarus; nevertheless, it seems more likely that a frontispiece would feature the two characters after whom Chaucer's play is named. The *Troilus* frontispiece represents an idealized, fictive dramatization of the tragedy of *Troilus and Criseyde* before a medieval audience in much the fashion that Lydgate described in his anachronistically medieval account, in his *Troy Book,* of classical tragedy:

Al this was tolde and rad of the poete.
And whil that he in the pulpit stood,
With dedly face al devoide of blood,
Singinge his dites, with muses al to-rent,
Amydde the theatre schrowdid in a tent,
Ther cam out men gastful of her cheris,
Disfigurid her facis with viseris,
Pleying by signes in the peples sight,
That the poete songon hath on hight;
So that ther was no maner discordaunce
Atwen his dites and her contenaunce:
For lik as he aloft[e] dide expresse
Wordes of Ioye or of hevynes,
Meving & cher, bynethe of hem pleying,
From point to point was alwey answering—
Now trist, now glad, now hevy, & [now] light,
And face chaunged with a sodeyn sight,
So craftily thei koude hem transfigure,
Conformyng hem to the chaunt[e]plure,
Now to synge & sodeinly to wepe,
So wel thei koude her observaunces kepe;
And this was doon in April & in May,
When blosmys new, bothe on busche & hay,
And flouris fresche gynne for to springe;
And the briddis in the wode synge
With lust supprised of the somer sonne,
Whan the[se] pleies in Troye wer begonne,
And in theatre halowed and y-holde.
                         (pp. 170–71, verses 896–923)

According to Lydgate, then, the poet in the pulpit recited, while the actors directly below, with their faces disfigured by masks, represented his words by their gestures in a kind of pageant display. Whereas the person with text and baton in Jean Fouquet's well-known fifteenth-century illumination of the play of the *Martyrdom of St. Apollonia* (Condé Museum, Chantilly) is positioned, not in a pulpit, but on the ground among players whom he points to with a sort of baton that might perhaps be called a stylus, Lydgate would have his authorial persona read from a stationary pulpit raised above the playing area, sometimes with "stile enclyned," an

ambiguous phrase that I take to mean either "in a downcast manner or style" (suitable to tragic subject matter) or else "with stylus
pointed downward" (probably at the players beneath who were
"from point to point . . . alwey answering" his words with their
actions).

A similar performance method is depicted in two famous early-
fifteenth-century illuminations in manuscripts of the plays of
Terence.[11] (See Fig. 24.) These illuminations represent the text's
presentation twice. In the lower register, a seated Terence hands
over the bound book of his manuscript; in the upper register, his
play is performed in a circular theater before "populus romanus."
A figure labeled "calliopius" reads the play from a book as he sits
in a curtained pulpit labeled "scena," while masked men labeled
"joculatores" energetically mime directly in front of the pulpit. In
his commentaries on Seneca's tragedies, Nicolas Trivet also described such divisions of labor in dramatic performance: the poet
might recite to the accompaniment of mime, or the poet might introduce actors who both mimed and spoke their roles.[12] Medieval
people, like us, tried to understand past dramatic practices in terms
of their own. Chaucer, Dante, and other medieval writers used the
generic terms *comedy* and *tragedy* to describe works that we do not
consider dramatic, because they mix narrative with dialogue: the
Divine Comedy, the "tragedy" of *Troilus,* the "comedy" of the
Canterbury Tales (foreshadowed at the end of *Troilus,* 5.1788).
Nevertheless, by combining recitation with pantomime and dividing performance between a speaker and mimes, such works
could be dramatically performed according to medieval notions of
drama—and those notions are what matter, not our own stricter
idea of "true" drama.

When we look into the frame of the *Troilus* frontispiece, we
join the fictive audience of a dramatic performance of *Troilus and
Criseyde.* But who is this courtly-looking audience? Chaucer specifically addresses "loveres" in the opening stanzas of *Troilus* (1.22–
56). Closest to us and furthest from the pulpit, in the lower right
foreground, are a pair of lovers who profit from the gathering
(and the riveting of others' attention on the speaker) to sit and gaze
into each other's eyes. Medieval representations of audiences often
include lovers, usually at the back or on the fringes of the crowd.[13]

Figures 22–24

22. *Troilus* frontispiece, early fifteenth century. Cambridge, Corpus Christi College ms. 61 frontis. (photo courtesy of Parker Library, Corpus Christi College, Cambridge).

23. Dramatic performance of *Troilus*, detail of Cambridge Corpus Christi College ms. 61 frontis. (photo courtesy of Parker Library, Corpus Christi College, Cambridge).

24. Dramatic performance, *Terence des Ducs* manuscript, early fifteenth century. Paris, Bibliothèque de l'Arsenal ms. 664, fol. 1v, detail (photo by Bibliothèque Nationale, Paris).

We join them there. But this is not the only way the illuminator encourages readers to assume the imaginary role of "lovers."

Emblematically, the *Troilus* frontispiece represents a *puy* as the audience for Chaucer's play. The London *puy*, like most late medieval Northern French and Flemish ones, was a mutual aid society with explicitly amicable as well as devotional purposes. The *puy* was set up, under the patronage of Christ and the Virgin, to "aider, conforter, e conseiller lun et lautre en foi, et en loiaute, pais, amour et concorde, come frere en Dieu et en bon amour" ("to help, comfort, and counsel one another in good faith, loyalty, peace, love, and concord, as brothers in God and in charity").[14] In the thirteenth century, the London *puy* gave an annual feast that featured poetry competitions at composing *chansons royales* honoring the Virgin. Secular love lyrics were often adapted to this end. The stated purpose of the yearly celebration was to "nourish" and "enhance" among participants "friendship, delightful entertainment, and courteous pleasure, joy and tenderness" and, at the same time, to "discourage discord, annihilate vice, and make members forget their troubles." The regulations of some Continental *puys* also stated as their goal the promotion of (vernacular) letters. We know that fourteenth- and fifteenth-century medieval French *puys,* as at Arras and Amiens, sponsored more complex dramatic presentations, as well as lyric contests.[15]

The vernacular (French and Provençal) term *puy* (or *pui*) comes from the Latin *podium,* which meant "elevation" or "height." Regulations for some *puys* treat the decoration of the podium or pulpit from which verses will be read or sung.[16] The *puy* is both the association of men who gather around the podium or *puy* on festive occasions and the elevation from which the poet speaks. The word *puy* could also mean a conical hill or mountain or, more broadly, a steep incline or ramp, or even a support. Figuratively, the vernacular verb-form *puyer* (or *puier,* "to climb") suggests striving for betterment, elevation to a more honored position. All of these meanings seem to come into play in literary societies known as *puys,* which involved mutual support, self-betterment through letters and refinement of aspirations, and dramatic entertainments (lyrics, too, being a form of dramatic play) delivered from a podium or elevation of some kind.

The first use I know of *puy* as a literary society occurs in the mid-twelfth century in Peire d'Alvernhe's famous Provençal lyric burlesquing his fellow troubadours, "Cantarai d'aqestz trobadors." In the envoy he names the place where he has composed the verses: "Lo vers fo faitz als enflabotz / a Puoich vert, tot iogan rizen" ("The verses were made to the tune of the [bag]pipes, / at Puivert [or the green *puy*], in a spirit of play and laughter").[17] Nowadays Puivert is a place in Aude, a long way south of Auvergne. Place-names in medieval verse were often used for their symbolic value; "green" suggested youth and folly, while *puy* suggested the striving of the literary contest. In effect, Peire's burlesque, which treats a different troubadour in each strophe, creates a "green puy" (a foolish literary society) out of his fellows, who may or may not have come together at an actual place called Puivert (in Aude) for a contest. Literary *puys* seem to have begun in Southern France, with the "Puy Notre-Dame" of the town of Le Puy, situated on its volcanic cone, as the archetypal example. Englishmen who had experience with the literary societies of Aquitaine may have been responsible for founding the London *puy* in the thirteenth century. *Puys* seem to have been most prevalent in the late-fourteenth and fifteenth centuries in Northern France and Flanders. Although we have no records of the London *puy* at this period, it seems unlikely that it would have died out when such societies were flourishing across the Channel.[18] What does seem likely is that the London members' vernacular literary efforts would have expanded to include English and, as on the Continent, *jeu de mystère* and other dramatic forms.

Allegorical images and rebuses were the delight of some *puys*. Members played in a riddling, equivocating way with visual and aural signs and the relationship between these. According to surviving fifteenth-century regulations, lyrics praising the Virgin for the contest of the *puy* of Amiens had to be constructed around an allegorical refrain invented by the year's elected master, a refrain that usually played upon the master's name or his profession.[19] The Virgin's allegorical attributes thus depended on the identity of that year's master. For example, the magistrate Pierre Villain alluded to his own judicial office with the refrain, "Cour souveraine administrant justice" ("Sovereign court administering justice"), and the historian Adrien de Lamorlière hid his last name in the refrain, "Vierge qui vint *la Mort lier* au monde." Every year at Christmas,

the new master hung a picture in the cathedral in which the allegory of the refrain was represented in images (emblems explicitly
celebrating the Virgin, implicitly the master); in the lower register
of the painting there usually appeared an image of the master holding a banderole on which was inscribed the "inspiring" refrain for
that year's poetry competition. In 1517, in the hope of pleasing a
ruler and alleviating their taxes, the members of the *puy* of Amiens
had these allegorical pictures and the winning *chansons royales*
copied into a lavish manuscript (Paris, B.N. fr. 145) for Louise of
Savoy, Duchess of Angoulême, who had expressed curiosity about
the allegorical pictures mounted on the columns of the Amiens
cathedral.[20] Although conical mountains are visible in the background of some of these pictures, the favorite symbolic representation of the *puy* of Amiens (a city situated in a relatively flat landscape) was the *puits* or "well." The image of the Virgin holding the
Christ Child and standing beside or on a well appears in several
pictures, and, worked in silver, the well was the device that the
members of the *puy* carried in festive processions.[21]

Just as Picard, Northern French, and Flemish literary societies
played with rebuses and allegorical images based on equivocal
words, so does the illuminator of the *Troilus* frontispiece, although rather more straightforwardly. He uses the steep diagonal
ramp of a mountain in the upper register of the frontispiece to represent by means of a concrete mountain or *puy*—with courtly figures climbing it, and others coming down to give them a loving
welcome—the abstract notion of the *puy* as literary society involving friendship, striving, and aspiration (sublimation). The illuminator uses this symbolic device to designate a literary *puy* as the
audience for the dramatic presentation of Chaucer's *Troilus and
Criseyde,* which takes place in the lower register, spoken from a
pulpit-podium (which may also be termed a *puy*). There are thus
at least three different kinds of *puys* in the picture, all related: the
podium, the mountainous ramp, and the society. The courtly figures who gather around the speaker and actors of *Troilus,* as well
as those on the ramp of the mountain, represent in a symbolic,
idealizing fashion the literary *puy,* its aspirations and occupations.

I have found no very convincing iconographical precedents for
the diagonal ramp of the *Troilus* frontispiece. Those that Elizabeth
Salter has suggested from the "Itinerary" miniatures of the Lim-

bourg brothers are rather different in composition.[22] In the fourteenth and fifteenth centuries, cone-shaped peaks appear in exotic
landscapes in manuscripts of travel narratives illuminated by the
Boucicaut master and others. Such peaks may suggest ascesis
when pictured behind saints and martyrs in late medieval landscapes.[23] More significantly, with respect to the *Troilus* frontispiece, mountains regularly appear, from the tenth century on, in
images of the Nativity, where they represent Mary and the way to
paradise.

   In an excursus on the Nativity, Gertrud Schiller explains tenth-
century Byzantine pictorial symbolism:

The center of the mystery of salvation as here represented is the Mother
of God and next to her on the raised "manger altar" the Child wrapped in
swaddling bands. A high mountain rises behind the Mother of God, in a
cave of which she is shown lying on a large *kline*. Another tradition
shows her seated at the entrance to the cave. The mountain gains its
prominence from the Messianic prophecy in Habakkuk 3.3, which says:
"God came from Teman, and the Holy One from Mount Paran," and the
associated hymns of the Christian liturgy, which extol Mary as the
"Holy Mountain."[24]

Later medieval Nativity paintings tend to minimize the cave and
naturalize the "Mary-mountain" in a rugged landscape. Nevertheless, even at the beginning of the fourteenth century, there were
conservative representations of a steep mountain of the Nativity,
sometimes with terraced sides forming a series of steps with angelic or other figures upon them.[25] Such iconographic and liturgi-
cal traditions may well have suggested the founding of secular literary *puys* dedicated to the celebration of Mary, such as the Puy
Notre-Dame of Le Puy. I suspect (but cannot yet prove) that the
Troilus illuminator did have a Northern French visual precedent
for representing a literary *puy* dedicated to the Virgin with a secular version of the religious emblem of the Mary-mountain: an idealized, "civilized" mountain, topped with fine buildings, with
courtly people climbing it and being welcomed.

   Even if we agree that the *Troilus* frontispiece depicts an idealized
dramatic presentation of Chaucer's *Troilus* before a *puy* (as an early-
fifteenth-century illuminator imagined such a performance), this
does not prove that *Troilus* had ever been so dramatized either in

Chaucer's lifetime or two decades afterward, nor does it prove that Chaucer intended his work to be enacted thus. Just as the Terence des Ducs illuminations are supposed to represent a contemporary Roman enactment of Terence's plays before "populus romanus," it may be that the *Troilus* frontispiece is meant to represent a late-fourteenth-century presentation of Chaucer's text before the original audience of lovers whom he addresses (and thereby fictionalizes) at the text's beginning. However, there is no way to prove that the frontispiece is supposed to represent a past performance, either fictive or real, of *Troilus and Criseyde*. It could just as well represent an eventual dramatizing performance of the text being copied or a performance that the reader was to imagine as he himself read and regarded the text. In either case, the image of the dramatization of *Troilus* before a *puy* is highly idealized. The pictured spectators are quite well dressed and include women. Most *puys,* on the other hand, admitted men (chiefly bourgeois, but sometimes including ecclesiastics, nobles, and even minstrels) but excluded women from membership, although not always from the enjoyment of festivities when these were performed in the open, as in the *Troilus* illumination.[26] All we can surely say from studying this frontispiece is that the early-fifteenth-century makers of the Cambridge Corpus Christi manuscript could *imagine* a dramatization of Chaucer's *Troilus* before a literary society or *puy*—and wanted the reader to do the same. Even this much is important.

Although there are modern recordings of the *Troilus* read in parts, and although Francis Utley has tried to analyze "scene division" and Robert Benson and Barry Windeatt have discussed expressive gesture in *Troilus,*[27] no modern interpreter that I know has gone so far as to imagine that the text might really have been acted out. The same nineteenth- and twentieth-century readers who called the *Canterbury Tales* dramatic have always denied the possibility of their performance as drama. In 1837, for example, John Hippisley cited Tyrwhitt's view that the *Canterbury Tales* and the *Decameron* might be classed as "comedies not intended for the stage." Hippisley elaborated: "As illustrating the vices and follies of the day, these works are, indeed, a substitute for (what did not in their age exist), the comic drama: but this chiefly when least dramatic, and when most purely descriptive. . . . in the general prologue we find an accurate and varied portraiture of all the stations of middle life in the poet's day. All this, however, is not the drama, but descriptive satire substituted for it."[28] Slightly earlier in the nineteenth century, an anonymous critic judged that Chaucer used a "dramatical form" of writing which allowed him to "indulge his imagination without responsibility for every sentiment he may amplify," and that he "first shewed the way how comedy should be constructed, and its characters grouped and diversified"; nevertheless, the same critic concluded that Chaucer's work had never been performed dramatically.[29]

In spite of the tradition of scholarly opinion to the contrary, for Chaucer's *Troilus* we have pictorial evidence that one manuscript illuminator, at least, was able to conceive of the dramatic presentation of the verbal text that he was engaged in preserving in the authoritative format of a book. This illuminator shows his awareness that he is helping to inscribe *play*. What the evidence of the *Troilus* frontispiece suggests is that perhaps we ought to consider in dramatic, rather than novelistic, terms a great deal of medieval literature that uses personae and dialogue, even mixed with third-person narrative. Paul Zumthor has made a slightly different, but analogous, suggestion: that it would be more appropriate to think of every [poetic] text earlier than the thirteenth century [and some later] as "dance" (involving a text, melody, and movements).[30] Even the "comedy" of the *Canterbury Tales* could have been enacted using some combination of medieval dramatic performance techniques. One speaker might perform the whole—"General Prologue," links, and tales—but with appropriate voice changes, dropping one persona to assume another, while mimes gestured the disputes of the linking interludes and/or key episodes of the tales. Even if the *Canterbury Tales*—or other works by Chaucer— were never actually presented in this way, the possibility of doing so, the conventions of medieval performance practice, might color a medieval reader's understanding of the "book" of *Troilus* or of the *Canterbury Tales,* might counter the authorizing voice of their inscription in an historicizing frame and enable the medieval reader to perceive the text as something more than an object for serious study and a repository of moral *sentence*. This is the objective of the *Troilus* frontispiece: to persuade the lone reader to imagine himself as part of the audience of the "tragedy" of *Troilus*.[31] The game of interpretation of the *Canterbury Tales,* or *Troilus,* begins with the recognition that they are *play* in bookish historical guise.

Notes

Introduction

1. Charles Baudelaire, "De l'essence du rire," in *Oeuvres complètes,* ed. Marcel Ruff (Paris, 1968), p. 372: "le comique est un des plus clairs signes sataniques de l'homme et un des nombreux pépins contenus dans la pomme symbolique." Baudelaire also very acutely observes that "laughter is the expression of a *double* or *contradictory sentiment,* and for that reason it is convulsive" (p. 374, my italics).

2. *The Riverside Chaucer,* 3d ed., general editor Larry D. Benson (Boston, 1987). All future citations from Chaucer's works will be from this edition, which revises F. N. Robinson, *The Works of Geoffrey Chaucer,* 2d rev. ed. (Boston, 1957). Capital letters preceding verse numbers in my citations refer to the groupings of tales or "fragments" as reordered by modern scholars and used by the Chaucer Society.

3. James Hastings, *A Dictionary of the Bible,* 4 vols. (Edinburgh, 1899), vol. 2, p. 44, summarizes the character of the fool as depicted in Proverbs: "While wisdom consists primarily in circumspect behavior, self-control, self-restraint, and teachableness, the fool is he who lets his undisciplined nature have free play—the self-reliant, self-pleased, arrogant, indocile, hasty with words, contentious, envious, quick to anger, intemperate, credulous, sluggish, given to pursuit of vain things, unable to conceal his own folly and shame."

4. Millard Meiss, *Painting in Florence and Siena after the Black Death* (Princeton, 1951), p. 159.

5. Johan Huizinga, *Homo Ludens: A Study of the Play Element in Culture* (London, 1944); Clifford Geertz, "Deep Play," in *The Interpretation of Cultures* (New York, 1973); Sigmund Freud, *The Standard Edition of the Complete Psychological Works of Sigmund Freud,* Vol. 10 (1909): *Two Case Histories* [for "Little Hans"] and Vol. 21 (1927–1931): *The Future of an Illusion, Civilization and Its Discontents, and Other Works,* trans. James

Strachey et al. (London, 1955, 1961); Melanie Klein, *The Psycho-analysis of Children,* trans. Alix Strachey, 5th ed. (London, 1954), and "La Personnification dans le jeu des enfants" and "Les Situations d'angoisse de l'enfant et leur reflet dans une oeuvre d'art et dans l'élan créateur," in *Essais de psychanalyse (1921–1945),* trans. M. Derrida (Paris, 1984); Jean Piaget, *Play, Dreams, and Imitation in Childhood,* trans. C. Gattegno and F. M. Hodgson (London, 1951).

6. Freud, *The Standard Edition.* Vol. 8 (1905): *Jokes and Their Relation to the Unconscious,* trans. James Strachey et al. (London, 1960), pp. 165–80.

Chapter One

1. Guillaume de Lorris and Jean de Meun, *Le Roman de la rose,* ed. Félix Lecoy, 3 vols. (Paris, 1965–1970), vol. 1, p. 169, verse 5507, "cui Jupiter coupa les couilles," and pp. 174–76, verses 5667–723 for the debate between Reason and the Lover over Reason's indiscretion.

2. The *Oxford English Dictionary* defines *trough* as a "narrow open box-like vessel, of V-shaped or curved section." In the ninth century a trough could designate a "small primitive boat . . . hollowed out of a solid block of wood." *Tub* was a general term, but it could also specify a round, flat-bottomed wooden vessel made with staves and hoops (OED). A *kim(e)lin* also seems to have been a round, shallow basin (from Medieval Latin *ciminile,* "hand-washing basin"). See the *Middle English Dictionary,* ed. H. Kurath and S. Kuhn (Ann Arbor, 1952–).

3. Joseph Baird, "The Devil's Privetee," *Neuphilologische Mitteilungen* 70 (1969): 104; Roy Peter Clark, "Christmas Games in Chaucer's *The Miller's Tale,*" *Studies in Short Fiction* 13 (1976): 285; Paula Neuss, "*Double-Entendre* in *The Miller's Tale,*" *Essays in Criticism* 24 (1974): 331. See also Thomas W. Ross's note on *pryvetee* in his edition of the "Miller's Tale" for *A Variorum Edition of the Works of Geoffrey Chaucer.* Vol. 2: *The Canterbury Tales,* part 3 (Norman, Okla., 1983), p. 126.

4. See Benson, *Riverside Chaucer,* p. 654 for "Gentilesse," and p. 120, D 1109–76, for the hag's lecture on gentility in the "Wife of Bath's Tale."

5. "Nun's Priest's Tale," B² 4630–33:

> Taketh the moralite, goode men.
> For Seint Paul seith that al that writen is,
> To oure doctrine it is ywrite, ywis;
> Taketh the fruyt, and lat the chaf be stille.

The author of the twelfth-century romance of *Partonopeu de Blois* (ed. Joseph Gildea, 2 vols. [Villanova, 1967–1968]) also quotes St. Paul to the effect that *everything* is morally instructive if interpreted the right way:

> Sains Pols, li maistre de la gent,
> Nos dist en son ensegnement

Que quanqu'est es livres escrit
Tot i est por nostre porfit
Et por nos en bien doctriner
Que saçons vices eschiver.
Il dist raison et bien et voir,
Et parfont et repus savoir,
Car nus escris n'est si frarins,
Nes des fables as Sarrasins,
Dont on ne puist exemple traire
De mal laissier et de bien faire.
                    (vol. 1, pp. 4–5,
                        verses 95–106)

St. Paul, the people's teacher, / tells us in his instruction / that everything written in books / is there for our profit / and to teach us about good, / so that we know how to avoid vices. / He states right reason, both good and true, / and profound and hidden wisdom; / for no writing is so worthless, / even the fictions of the Saracens, / that one cannot draw a lesson from it: / to abandon evil and to do good.

From this argument, it follows that bawdiness is in the eye of the beholder:

Fox hom ne puet nul sens trover
Fors le gros sens c'on puet taster;
Li sages de quanqu'a sos ciel
Trait sens, com ex trait d'erbe miel.
                    (vol. 1, p. 5, verses 117–20)

A foolish [sinful] man is able to find no sense / except the crude [sensual, material] sense that can be touched. / From everything under the heavens, the wise man / extracts [abstract or moral] sense, like [a bee] extracting honey from grasses.

Such reasoning can be a double-edged razor, as Jean de Meun, the Archpriest of Hita, Chaucer, and many other medieval writer-interpreters playfully demonstrated. For example, the late-thirteenth-century jongleur Gautier Le Leu, author of some of the most obscene and sacrilegious surviving fabliaux, teases his audience in the opening lines of his "conte" *Du Con* ("On Cunt") (ed. Charles H. Livingston, *Le Jongleur Gautier Le Leu* [Cambridge, Mass., 1951]) by repeating, through a foolish jongleuresque persona, a version of the old maxim concerning interpretation, that bawdiness is in the eye of the beholder, not in the text itself:

Guautiers Li Leus dit a devise
Que l'en ne doit en nule guise
En malvais leu mestre son oevre.
Cil est molt fox qui la descuevre
As orz vilains et as cuivers

. . . .

Ce dïent li auctor de Rome.

Mais ge n'en sai chanter ne lire
Ne les malvais des bons eslire.

. . . .

Se vos volez estre en silance
Et de parler en abstinence,
Ge vos dirai ençois la nuit,
Conment qu'il me griet ne ennuit,
Ce conte du plus halt estoire
Qui onques fust mis en memoire.
(pp. 238–39, verses 1–28)

Gautier Le Leu says it as a motto / that in no way should a man / show his work in an immoral place. / He is very foolish who discovers it / to gross peasants and to the vulgar-minded, / . . . / so say the Roman authorities. / But I know nothing about singing nor reciting / nor distinguishing the bad places from the good. / . . . / If you will be silent / and abstain from talking, / I will tell you tonight, / no matter how much it burdens and bores me, / this account of the most noble history / ever committed to memory.

6. B. J. Whiting, *Chaucer's Use of Proverbs* (Cambridge, Mass., 1934), p. 84.

7. On Chaucer's use of these words, see Edward Costigan, "'Privitee' in *The Canterbury Tales,*" *Studies in English Literature* 60 (1983): 217–30.

8. See George Boas, *Essays on Primitivism and Related Ideas in the Middle Ages* (1948; rpt. New York, 1966), pp. 123–24, for an English translation of St. Bernard's exegesis of Eve's sin as intellectual curiosity. Bernard makes much of the double meaning of the Latin word *sapere* as "to taste" and "to know." The passage is from his *De gradibus humilitatis et superbiae* (J. P. Migne, *Patrologiae cursus completus . . . . Series latina,* 221 vols. [Paris, 1844–1864], vol. 182, col. 958).

9. *A Book of Showings to the Anchoress Julian of Norwich,* ed. Edmund Colledge and James Walsh, 2 vols. (Toronto, 1978), vol. 2, p. 429.

10. On Joseph's depiction in Nativity scenes and the textual sources for changes in his image, see Gertrud Schiller, *Iconography of Christian Art,* trans. Janet Seligman, 2 vols. (Greenwich, Conn., 1971), vol. 1, pp. 72–73.

11. These burlesques are treated by Heiko Jürgens, *Pompa diaboli: Die lateinischen Kirchenväter und das antike Theater* (Stuttgart, 1972), p. 234.

12. Genesis 9:22, 24–25: "And Ham, the father of Canaan, saw the nakedness of his father, and told his two brethren without. . . . And Noah awoke from his wine, and knew what his younger son had done unto him. And he said, 'Cursed be Canaan, a servant of servants shall he be to his brethren.'"

13. Leo Steinberg, *The Sexuality of Christ in Renaissance Art and in Modern Oblivion* (New York, 1983).

14. See the section "Frontal and Profile as Symbolic Forms," in Meyer

Schapiro's *Words and Pictures: On the Literal and the Symbolic in the Illustration of a Text* (The Hague, 1973), pp. 37–49.

15. In "Wit and Mystery: A Revaluation in Mediaeval Latin Hymnody," *Speculum* 22 (1947): 316–18, Walter Ong notes similar examples of serious wordplay in medieval hymns and theological writings on the subject of the Incarnation of the Word.

16. Steinberg, *Sexuality of Christ*, p. 1.

17. Steinberg attributes the veil-as-improvised-loincloth motif to medieval artists' attempts to depict pious Franciscan texts such as the late-thirteenth-century *Meditations on the Life of Christ* attributed incorrectly to St. Bonaventure. According to the *Meditations,* after washing the new-born Christ in the milk of her breasts, Mary wrapped him in the veil from her head. (See the edition and translation of the *Meditations* by Isa Ragusa and Rosalie Green [Princeton, 1961], p. 33.) Mid-fourteenth-century artists invented a second veil for Mary, a diaphanous underveil, for didactic purposes that went far beyond the pseudo-Bonaventure's commonsensical imagining that the Madonna's head veil (hardly gossamer!) was the best cloth at hand for swaddling. Later contemplatives from more northern climates imagined an even more humble (and warmer) impromptu swaddling material—Joseph's woolen stockings. For this fifteenth-century motif in art, see Schiller, *Iconography,* vol. 1, p. 80.

18. On the symbolism of Christ's Circumcision, see Steinberg, *Sexuality of Christ*, pp. 50–65 and excursus 26, "The Blood Hyphen."

19. Ibid., pp. 96–108, and excursus 37, "The Un-dead Hand on the Groin."

20. Mikhail Bakhtin, *Rabelais and His World,* trans. Hélène Iswolsky (Bloomington, Ind., 1984).

21. Versions of the *Cena Cypriani* are discussed by Paul Lehmann in *Die Parodie im Mittelalter,* 2d ed. (Stuttgart, 1963), pp. 12–16, and by Bakhtin, *Rabelais,* pp. 286–89.

22. For aspects of biblical parody in the "Miller's Tale," see the following essays: Paul Beichner, "Absolon's Hair," *Medieval Studies* 12 (1951): 222–33; Kelsie Harder, "Chaucer's Use of the Mystery Plays in the *Miller's Tale*," *Modern Language Quarterly* 17 (1956): 193–98; Robert Kaske, "The Canticum Canticorum in the *Miller's Tale,*" *Studies in Philology* 59 (1962): 479–500; Edmund Reiss, "Daun Gerveys in the *Miller's Tale*," *Papers on Language and Literature* 6 (1970): 115–24; James Wimsatt, "Chaucer and the Canticle of Canticles," in *Chaucer the Love Poet,* ed. Jerome Mitchell and William Provost (Athens, Ga., 1973), pp. 66–90; Beryl Rowland, "The Play of the *Miller's Tale:* A Game within a Game," *Chaucer Review* 5 (1970–1971): 140–46, and "Chaucer's Blasphemous Churl: A New Interpretation of the *Miller's Tale*," in *Chaucer and Middle English Studies in Honour of Rossell Hope Robbins,* ed. Beryl Rowland

(Kent, Ohio, 1974), pp. 43–55; Clark, "Christmas Games in Chaucer's *The Miller's Tale.*"

23. On Joseph as Synagogue, see Schiller, *Iconography,* vol. 1, pp. 72–73 and accompanying figures.

24. Steinberg, *Sexuality of Christ,* p. 14.

25. Schiller, *Iconography,* vol. 1, p. 78; Henrik Cornell, *The Iconography of the Nativity of Christ* (Uppsala, 1924), p. 12.

26. Ragusa and Green, eds., *Meditations,* p. 32.

27. Alfred David, *The Strumpet Muse* (Bloomington, Ind., 1976), pp. 96, 99. See also Carl Lindahl, "The Festive Form of the *Canterbury Tales,*" *ELH* 52 (1985): 531–74. I disagree with Lindahl's otherwise excellent essay for its too easy equation of gentles' or churls' festivals with *actual* social status or origins.

28. See Johan Huizinga, *The Waning of the Middle Ages,* trans. F. Hopman (orig. pub. 1924; London, 1965), pp. 163–64, for analysis of the medieval comic rendition of St. Joseph. Rowland, in "The Play of the *Miller's Tale,*" lists English dramatic portrayals of St. Joseph.

Chapter Two

1. Johan Huizinga, *The Waning of the Middle Ages,* trans. F. Hopman (orig. pub. 1924; London, 1965), pp. 163, 151, 153, 154.

2. Mikhail Bakhtin, *Rabelais and His World,* trans. Hélène Iswolsky (Bloomington, Ind., 1984), p. 316, reminds us that the size and shape of the nose represented the size and shape of the penis in the medieval popular imagination. For literary and "scientific" treatments of this relationship, see Alfred David, "An Iconography of Noses: Directions in the History of a Physical Stereotype," in *Mapping the Cosmos,* ed. Jane Chance and R. O. Wells, Jr. (Houston, 1985), pp. 76–97.

3. The quotation from Byron is edited and anthologized by Derek Brewer, *Chaucer: The Critical Heritage,* 2 vols. (London, 1978), vol. 1, p. 249.

4. Ibid., p. 167.

5. This may help to explain why art historians, until Steinberg, have ignored the Christ Child's exposed phallus in late medieval and Renaissance paintings.

6. Lydgate in Brewer, *Chaucer,* vol. 1, p. 50. Hoccleve, ibid., p. 63. Caxton, ibid., p. 75. In the Harley manuscript (London, B.L. 4866, fol. 88r) of Hoccleve's *Regement of Princes,* Chaucer's famous half-length portrait functions as a *nota* sign. In medieval manuscripts, disembodied hands with pointing index fingers frequently gloss and mark sententious or proverbial passages. Chaucer's extended index finger points to Hoc-

cleve's lines about Chaucer's own "fructuous entendement," his capacity as a *serious* interpreter. The Harley illuminator cleverly presents an image of Chaucer doing precisely what Hoccleve praises him for: pointing out the pithy, noteworthy statement. This pointing finger and the *pointel* (writing tool) hanging around Chaucer's neck in the Harley portrait represent Chaucer's interpretive abilities as a writer.

7. See Paull Baum, "Chaucer's Puns," *Publications of the Modern Language Association* 71 (1956): 225, for a brief history of early discoveries of puns in Chaucer's work and for the first citation from Lounsbury; the second is from Brewer, *Chaucer,* vol. 2, p. 230.

8. F. N. Robinson, *The Works of Geoffrey Chaucer,* 2d rev. ed. (Boston, 1957), p. 658, n. 297.

9. Larry D. Benson, "The 'Queynte' Punnings of Chaucer's Critics," in *Studies in the Age of Chaucer, Proceedings, No. 1: Reconstructing Chaucer,* ed. Paul Strohm and Thomas J. Heffernan (Knoxville, 1985), pp. 23–47.

10. D. W. Robertson, Jr., *A Preface to Chaucer: Studies in Medieval Perspectives* (Princeton, 1962), pp. 20–22.

11. Leo Steinberg, *The Sexuality of Christ in Renaissance Art and in Modern Oblivion* (New York, 1983), pp. 147–54. By means of a false gesture, Carlo Crivelli burlesques this contemporary iconography of revelation as striptease: his Virgin very delicately lifts a diaphanous veil from the Christ's Child's *back.* Many other aspects of this painting, the late-fifteenth-century Demidoff altarpiece in the National Gallery of London, confirm Crivelli's burlesque intention.

12. In "The Body of Christ in the Later Middle Ages: A Reply to Leo Steinberg," *Renaissance Quarterly* 39 (1986): 399–439, Caroline Walker Bynum argues that "medieval people" would not think of sexuality in viewing the Christ Child's bare phallus or Mary's nude breast in religious art:

There is reason to think that medieval viewers saw bared breasts (at least in painting and sculpture) not primarily as sexual but as the food with which they were iconographically associated. . . . There is also reason to think that medieval people saw Christ's penis not primarily as a sexual organ but as the object of circumcision and therefore as the wounded, bleeding flesh with which it was associated in painting and in text. . . . I am not here denying that medieval people saw a penis when they saw Christ's penis. Moreover, as I shall demonstrate below, they sometimes saw a breast (or a womb) when they saw Christ's side. But they probably did not associate either penis or breast primarily with sexual activity.

(pp. 408–9)

But who, precisely, is "medieval people"? Is this not a persona? In the final paragraph of her essay Bynum drops "medieval people" to assume the first person, albeit plural:

If we want to express the significance of Jesus in both male and female images, if we want to turn from seeing body as sexual to seeing body as generative, if we want to find symbols that give dignity and meaning to the suffering we cannot eliminate and yet fear so acutely, we can find support for doing so in the art and theology of the later Middle Ages.

(p. 439)

13. English translation by Robertson (*Preface*, pp. 28–29), from J. P. Migne, *Patrologiae cursus completus. Series latina*, 221 vols. (Paris, 1844–1864), vol. 79, col. 473.

14. Michel Zink, *La Prédication en langue romane avant 1300* (Paris, 1976), pp. 374, 369.

15. Ibid., pp. 333–34. See also the analysis of the near-pun *vie/vit* toward the end of the concluding chapter of this book.

16. Ibid., p. 290; *PL*, 177, cols. 826–27.

17. See Steinberg, *Sexuality of Christ*, fig. 13.

18. Augustine, *On Christian Doctrine*, trans. D. W. Robertson, Jr. (Indianapolis, 1958), p. 37, my italics.

19. Robert Kaske, "The Canticum Canticorum in the *Miller's Tale*," *Studies in Philology* 59 (1962): 497–500; James Wimsatt, "Chaucer and the Canticle of Canticles," in *Chaucer the Love Poet*, ed. Jerome Mitchell and William Provost (Athens, Ga., 1973), p. 88; Beryl Rowland, "Chaucer's Blasphemous Churl: A New Interpretation of the *Miller's Tale*," in *Chaucer and Middle English Studies in Honour of Russell Hope Robbins*, ed. Beryl Rowland (Kent, Ohio, 1974), p. 51; Roy Peter Clark, "Christmas Games in Chaucer's *The Miller's Tale*," *Studies in Short Fiction* 13 (1976): 281.

20. Roland Barthes, *Critique et vérité* (Paris, 1966), especially pp. 40–42.

21. For further discussion of this manuscript, see Paul Strohm, "Jean of Angoulême: A Fifteenth-Century Reader of Chaucer," *Neuphilologische Mitteilungen* 72 (1971): 69–76.

22. *Les Facéties de Pogge . . . accompagnées des Moralitez de Guillaume Tardif*, ed. Pierre des Brandes (Paris, 1919).

23. Thus C. David Benson, in *Chaucer's Drama of Style* (Chapel Hill, 1986), demonstrates the deliberate stylistic variations and experimentation in Chaucer's collection of fabliaux, yet organizes his own exposition of these fabliaux into a moral hierarchy concluding with the "Merchant's Tale," which he reads as Chaucer's "most morally challenging work in the genre":

No other Canterbury tale exposes evil more relentlessly. And yet, at the same time, the fabliau repeatedly offers visions of faith and love, both human and divine, that promise hope to the reader. This disgusting and bitter tale is also a compelling advocate for the highest Christian values. . . . Not only does the *Merchant's Tale* differ radically from Chaucer's other fabliaux, but its unique artist is also one of the most difficult, though ultimately rewarding, Christian poets in Middle English literature.

(pp. 129–30)

Chapter Three

1. Ruth Hirsh Weir, *Language in the Crib* (The Hague, 1962), p. 121.
2. Ibid.
3. Ibid., p. 18.
4. Jean Piaget, *Play, Dreams, and Imitation in Childhood,* trans. C. Gattegno and F. M. Hodgson (London, 1951).
5. Boccaccio, *The Decameron,* trans. G. H. McWilliam (London, 1972). Subsequent citations refer to this edition.
6. Sigmund Freud, *The Standard Edition.* Vol. 8 (1905): *Jokes and Their Relation to the Unconscious,* trans. James Strachey et al. (London, 1960), pp. 165–80.
7. Rosemary Bolig, "Play in Hospital Settings," in *Child's Play: Developmental and Applied,* ed. Thomas Yawkey and Anthony Pellegrini (Hillsdale, N.J., 1984), p. 342.
8. Millard Meiss, *Painting in Florence and Siena after the Black Death* (Princeton, 1951); Johan Huizinga, *The Waning of the Middle Ages,* trans. F. Hopman (orig. pub. 1924; London, 1965).
9. Thus it was for the Antonine monastery of Isenheim, which specialized in the care of syphilitics, that Matthias Grünewald was commissioned to paint his famous sixteenth-century altarpiece depicting a crucified Christ whose body is covered with suppurating syphilitic-looking sores. Gruesome as it may seem to us, such an artistic fiction was surely intended to be consolatory: "When a sufferer was brought in he was first led to the altar and prayers for miraculous healing were said. It is in the light of these pathetic and repulsive scenes that this Crucifixion must be seen" (Nikolas Pevsner and Michael Meier, *Grünewald* [London, 1958], p. 61).
10. Glending Olson, *Literature as Recreation in the Later Middle Ages* (Ithaca, N.Y., 1982).
11. Cited in ibid., p. 198.
12. Cited in ibid., p. 81.
13. Ibid., p. 199.
14. For an overview of the difficulties of this period, see Charles Muscatine, *Poetry and Crisis in the Age of Chaucer* (Notre Dame, 1972), pp. 15–22.
15. The story of Griselda, for example, was dramatized by Philippe de Mezières for the French king, in order to reinforce the power and authority of the monarchy by teaching political submission. Through dramatic representation of a suffering heroine with whom his audience would identify, Philippe hoped to encourage the king's subjects to conform their will to their lord's, just as Griselda obeyed and identified with her husband and lord. For Philippe's play, see *L'Estoire de Griseldis,* ed. Barbara M. Craig (Lawrence, Kans., 1954).

Chapter Four

1. Quotations from Herbert Read, *Art and Alienation: The Role of the Artist in Society* (London, 1967), p. 64.

2. In his seminal *Homo Ludens: A Study of the Play Element in Culture* (London, 1944), p. 26, Johan Huizinga defines play as (1) "a voluntary activity" that involves (2) a "stepping out of 'real life' into a temporary sphere of activity with a disposition all its own"; furthermore, play is (3) "disinterested," (4) "secluded and limited in time and space"; it (5) "creates order," and (6) its outcome is "tense and uncertain." Huizinga adds (p. 41) that "play possesses . . . at least one further very essential feature, namely, the consciousness, however latent, of 'only pretending.'"

3. Sigmund Freud, "Die Verneinung," *Gesammelte Werke*. Vol. 14: *Werke aus den Jahren 1925–1931* (London, 1948), pp. 13–15.

4. For an account of the Russian formalists' explorations of "making strange," that is, of the artifices of poetry, see Victor Erlich, *Russian Formalism* (The Hague, 1955), especially pp. 150–51.

5. Of course, this displacement goes on even in writings that we do not generally term fictional. For example, in his 1985 Haskins Lecture for the American Council of Learned Societies, in which he was asked to put his own historical writings in perspective, Lawrence Stone pointed out that the subjects he has written about in history all have symbolic references in contemporary political and social crises or changes. In researching and writing about crises centuries ago, he was, in some respects, mastering (and helping his readers to master) anxieties about those of our own times, as Stone himself recognizes: "Although I was not aware of it at the time, I seem to have been constantly stimulated by current events into diving back into the past to discover whether similar trends and problems have occurred before, and if so how they were handled. Whether this makes for better or worse history, I do not know" ("A Life of Learning," *ACLS Newsletter* 36 [1985]: 21).

6. On comic mechanism, see Henri Bergson, *Le Rire: Essai sur la signification du comique* (orig. pub. 1924; Paris, 1981), pp. 22–28. A translation is available in *Comedy,* ed. Wylie Sypher (Baltimore, 1956).

7. Anatole de Montaiglon and Gaston Raynaud, *Recueil général . . . des fabliaux des XIIIe et XIVe siècles,* 6 vols. (Paris, 1872–1890), vol. 1, pp. 289–93. This edition will henceforth be referred to as MR.

8. In the French, the number, but not the gender, of the subject is indicated by the verb ending, and no pronoun is necessary. This allows the wife to conceal the sex of her "healer." I have tried to suggest this linguistic ambiguity in English translation by the composite pronoun *s/he.*

9. Gautier Le Leu's verse has also been edited by Charles H. Livingston in *Le Jongleur Gautier Le Leu* (Cambridge, Mass., 1951).

10. For a Latin edition and French translation of *Babio* by Henri Laye, see Gustave Cohen, *La "Comédie" latine en France au XIIe siècle,* 2 vols. (Paris, 1931), vol. 2, pp. 30–56. The argument that Latin comedies such as *Babio* ought to be considered fabliaux is made by Edmond Faral in "Le Fabliau latin au moyen âge," *Romania* 50 (1924): 321–85: "the medieval Latin tale derived from antique comic drama; abusively designated by the name of comedy, it presents, in its spirit and the nature of its subjects, the closest analogies with the fabliau, or, more precisely, is nothing else, under the deceptive cloak of academic style, but the fabliau" (p. 385). On occasions of festive reversal, both vernacular fabliaux and Latin ones such as *Babio* may well have been dramatized, using medieval performance methods, either in the setting of the school, with clerics playing all the roles, or in secular settings, with the likely participation of jongleurs.

11. The early part of *Babio* is devoted to a different kind of humiliation of the father and mockery of his authority. Babio loves his stepdaughter Viola (Petula's daughter) with a repressed passion—only to see Viola abducted by a richer and more powerful man (at the urging of everyone in the family except Babio). During the abduction, the cowardly priest stands powerlessly by, using nothing but his tongue to try to goad his wife and servant to do battle with the abductor (p. 38, lines 169–72). Later Babio laments the "violation" of Viola by another man, when he, Babio, had so carefully brought her up for his own delight (p. 39, lines 179–84).

12. On this burlesque, see Alan Levitan, "The Parody of Pentecost in Chaucer's *Summoner's Tale,*" *University of Toronto Quarterly* 40 (1971): 236–46.

13. In *The Scandal of the Fabliaux* (Chicago, 1986), pp. 111–13, R. Howard Bloch makes incisive comments on the closely related subject of how "the joke cuts short" and thus symbolically castrates "proper" verbal expression, which I call the "father" tongue:

If the joke depends entirely on verbal expression, is language not ultimately its proper object, or a certain assumption of verbal propriety which is displaced, lost, substituted for? . . . Like the humor of the medieval tale, the effectiveness of the joke seems always to imply an ill-tailoring of verbal expression, a violence done to words; and this right down to the level of the letter. The "joke-work" may, for instance, involve condensation with formation of a composite word. . . . The joke cuts words in unexpected places, as in the multiple use of the same word as a whole and in parts. . . . Alongside the usual cuts, condensations, and substitutions that jokes work at the level of the letter are the displacements of sense or breaks in reference which are synonymous with humor as word play.

14. MR, vol. 4, p. 46; also edited by Jean Rychner, *Contribution à l'étude des fabliaux,* 2 vols. (Neuchâtel, 1960), vol. 2, p. 27. Different versions of this fabliau moralize it in different ways. Whereas the version of

Paris, B.N. fr. 19152, fol. 62v–63r, concludes, as previously shown, with a humiliation of the king, the ending of the version of Berne, Bibliothèque de la Bourgeoisie, 354, fol. 45v, for example, turns the joke back on the peasants and away from the king:

> A itant li vilains s'en part,
> Toz liez s'en vint en son païs;
> Si a mendé toz ses amis
> E les vilains de la contree:
> Male honte lor a donee.
> Onques nus frans hom point n'en ot;
> N'i a vilain qui ne s'en lot,
> Trestuit en furent parçonier.
> Por ce dit an en reprovier,
> Qui fu trové par icest conte:
> Que vilain aient male honte!
> (Rychner, vol. 2, p. 27)

With this the rustic left; / rejoicing, he returned to his land / and sent for all of his friends / and the peasants of the area. / He gave them "Evil Shame." / No free man was without a part, / nor was there any rustic who had none of it; / all were co-proprietors. / For this reason they have a saying, / which is demonstrated by this story: / "May the rustic have evil shame!"

Chapter Five

1. On the subject of words that the "gentils" in Chaucer's audience would probably have considered unspeakable, see Thomas W. Ross, "Taboo-Words in Fifteenth-Century English," *Fifteenth-Century Studies,* ed. Robert F. Yeager (Hamden, Conn., 1984), pp. 137–60.

2. Sigmund Freud, *The Standard Edition.* Vol. 8 (1905): *Jokes and Their Relation to the Unconscious,* trans. James Strachey et al. (London, 1960), pp. 125–26.

3. Ellen Winner et al., "The Ontogenesis of Metaphor," in *Cognition and Figurative Language,* ed. R. P. Honeck and R. R. Hoffman (Hillsdale, N.J., 1980), p. 358. Moreover, some studies suggest that spontaneous production of figurative expressions, while decreasing at age six or with the child's entry into school, increases again in adolescence (a period of rebellion against authority). See Marilyn R. Pollio and James D. Pickens, "The Developmental Structure of Figurative Competence," in *Cognition and Figurative Language,* pp. 314–16. Other studies have shown that the humor of preschool children is largely based on playful violations—perpetrated by the child or by others in a nonserious mood—of the perceptual appearance of things, that is, on distortions of familiar sights and sounds (such as rhyming or nonsense words). This suggests that the laughter of preschool children at incongruities, at deviations from the

norm, may be a playful outlet for aggression and rebellion against the authority of norms, of "reality." See Paul McGhee, "Play, Incongruity, Humor," in *Child's Play: Developmental and Applied,* ed. Thomas Yawkey and Anthony Pellegrini (Hillsdale, N.J., 1984), pp. 229–30.

4. For descriptions of late medieval and early Renaissance festive rituals of regression (although they do not label them so), see Mikhail Bakhtin, *Rabelais and His World,* trans. Hélène Iswolsky (Bloomington, Ind., 1984), and E. K. Chambers, *The Mediaeval Stage,* 2 vols. (London, 1903), vol. 1, especially his chapters on the Feasts of Fools, of the Boy Bishop, of the Ass, and other New Year celebrations.

5. On these genres see W. Kellermann, "Über die altfranzösischen Gedichte des uneingeschränkten Unsinns," *Archiv für das Studium der neueren Sprachen* 205 (1968): 1–22; Paul Zumthor, *Langue, texte, énigme* (Paris, 1975), pp. 68–88; for examples, see Lambert C. Porter, *La Fatrasie et le fatras: Essai sur la poésie irrationnelle en France au moyen âge* (Paris, 1960), and *Le Recueil Trepperel: Les sotties,* ed. Eugénie Droz (Paris, 1935).

6. Charles Muscatine, in *The Old French Fabliaux* (New Haven, 1986), takes a similar view, that the fabliaux "seem to be responding to an outbreak of decency" (p. 133): "there is another palpable source of verbal taboo in the rapid spread, in the thirteenth century, of the courtly ethic. In showing sharply divergent responses to so-called obscene terms the fabliaux seem to be recording the impact of relatively new taboos, the mixed reception of these taboos in the fabliau period, and indeed, some opposition to them" (p. 109).

7. In *Jokes and Their Relation to the Unconscious,* pp. 148–58, Freud reasons that we laugh at obscene or aggressive ("tendentious") jokes because the psychic energy required to repress forbidden desires is suddenly rendered unnecessary by our encounter with these very desires expressed in the joke. The "economy" of psychic energy that would ordinarily be used to repress illicit desires gives us pleasure (rather like a good bargain), and we release this surplus energy ("discharge it," according to Freud's masculine orgasmic metaphors) in laughter.

8. Paul Zumthor, *Essai de poétique médiévale* (Paris, 1972), p. 73.

9. The Summoner shows himself to be a virtuoso at the excremental insult. Earlier, when the Friar interjected his opinion of the Wife of Bath's lengthy prologue, the Summoner ribbed the Friar by comparing him to a fly that gets into every "matter" (textual and fecal):

> "Lo," quod the Somonour, "Goddes armes two!
> A frere wol entremette hym everemo.
> Lo, goode men, a flye and eek a frere
> Wol falle in every dyssh and eek mateere."
> (D 833–36)

This is what starts the exchange of playful ripostes between the Summoner and the Friar in which each tells a fabliau aimed at making a laughingstock of his rival:

> "Ye, woltow so, sire Somonour?" quod the Frere;
> "Now, by my feith I shal, er that I go,
> Telle of a somonour swich a tale or two
> That alle the folk shal laughen in this place."
>   (D 840–43)

10. For example, in the fabliau of "Berengier of the Long Asshole" ("Berengier au lonc cul," MR, vol. 3, pp. 252–62), the cowardly husband's greatest humiliation consists not so much in his cuckolding, although this too happens, but in his agreeing to kiss the anus of his conqueror, "according to the law of a cowardly, lowborn man" (p. 260). What is worse, the strange knight who conquers him with threats alone is really his wife in knightly disguise. She calls herself "Berengier au long cul," for anatomical reasons, in a burlesque of epic epithets. In this fabliau, as in Chaucer's "Miller's Tale," a kiss bestowed on the lower orifice, instead of on the mouth, puts woman "on top" in a grotesque parody of the ceremony of vassalage.

11. Muscatine, *The Old French Fabliaux*, p. 115, also signals this punning play: "The author of one version of 'Les Quatre Sohais Saint Martin' is so pleased with the pun on *connue* (known/'cunt-ed') that within a few dozen verses he elaborately repeats it."

12. For an edition of and commentary on this text, see Omer Jodogne, "*Audigier* et la chanson de geste," *Le Moyen Age* 15 (1960): 495–526.

13. Muscatine, *The Old French Fabliaux*, p. 145, notes that "the author capitalizes on the fact that the word *vit* in Old French . . . has a number of common and harmless homonyms." *Vis* ("face") is another possible harmless interpretation of the same syllable, pronounced with emphasis on the first consonant and the vowel sounds.

14. For example, Gautier de Coinci, in his *Miracles de Nostre Dame* (ed. V. Frédéric Koenig, 4 vols. [Paris, 1955–1970]), uses the figure of the nut to signify the deeper meaning of the Scriptures, which many men boastful of their learning never penetrate, because they are content to gnaw the shell:

> Mout se vantent de letreüre,
> Mais n'entendent de l'Escriture
> Ne l'efficace ne la force.
> De la nois vont runjant l'escorce,
> Mais ne sevent qu'il a dedens.
>   (vol. 2, pp. 13–14,
>   verses 213–17)

They boast a great deal of their learning / but do not understand from Scripture / either the means or the meaning. / They gnaw the nutshell / but do not know what lies within.

15. In "Modes of Signification and the Humor of Obscene Diction in the Fabliaux," *The Humor of the Fabliaux,* ed. Thomas Cooke and Benjamin Honeycutt (Columbia, Miss., 1974), p. 183, Roy Pearcy discovers a sudden shift of linguistic registers in many fabliaux "at the moment of peripety, when the dupe suffers a sudden reversal of fortune and when the illusions he has trusted are dispelled in a sudden outburst of accumulated obscenities that are in contrast to earlier euphemisms."

16. *Le Roman de la Rose,* ed. Félix Lecoy, 3 vols. (Paris, 1965–1970), vol. 1, p. 217, verses 7076–85.

17. Pearcy, "Modes of Signification," pp. 190–91, rightly reads the ending of this fabliau, with its delivery of "bran" instead of "avainne" (chaff—or worse—instead of grain), as a deliberately mocking subversion of the procedure of allegorization, which is here closely connected to the courteous euphemism, "a means . . . of distancing the [lovers'] discussion of their sexual relationship from its true nature."

18. Larry D. Benson, "The 'Queynte' Punnings of Chaucer's Critics," in *Studies in the Age of Chaucer, Proceedings, No. 1: Reconstructing Chaucer,* ed. Paul Strohm and Thomas J. Heffernan (Knoxville, 1985), p. 30.

19. Berne, ms. 354, fol. 78; ed. Jean Rychner, in *Contribution à l'étude des fabliaux,* 2 vols. (Neuchâtel, 1960), vol. 2, p. 81.

20. Benson, "The 'Queynte' Punnings," p. 40.

21. Beryl Rowland, "The Play of the *Miller's Tale:* A Game within a Game," *Chaucer Review* 5 (1970–71):144.

22. Jill Mann, *Chaucer and Medieval Estates Satire* (Cambridge, Eng., 1973). Indeed, Mann goes much further, arguing that "all these ambiguities, together with the 'omission of the victim' and the confusion of moral and emotional reactions, add up to Chaucer's *consistent removal of the possibility of moral judgement*" (p. 197).

Chapter Six

1. Per Nykrog, *Les Fabliaux* (Copenhagen, 1957), p. 70, for example: "The difference between the fabliau and the courtly tale is that which separates a sublime genre from its burlesque caricature." Nykrog argues that the fabliaux are an aristocratic genre because no one else "could dare to make fun of an aristocratic genre [the courtly tale] by discussing vulgar problems courteously" (p. 95).

2. For Philippe de Beaumanoir's sequence of eleven *fatrasies,* see the

edition of Lambert C. Porter in *La Fatrasie et le fatras: Essai sur la poésie irrationnelle en France au moyen âge* (Paris, 1960), pp. 142–44.

3. Charles H. Livingston, *Le Jongleur Gautier Le Leu* (Cambridge, Mass., 1951), pp. 96–97.

4. For evidence of Rabanus Maurus's ninth-century version of the *Cena Cypriani*, see his letter of presentation to Lothar II in *Hrabani (Mauri) Epistolae*, no. 52 in *Monumenta Germania Historica, Epistolarum tomi V pars prior. Karolini Aevi III*, ed. E. Dümmler et al. (Berlin, 1899), p. 506; for an edition of Neckam's verses praising wine, see M. Esposito, "On Some Unpublished Poems Attributed to Alexander Neckam," *English Historical Review* 30 (1915): 450–71; for Philippe de Beaumanoir's *fatrasies* see Porter, *La Fatrasie;* for Eustache Deschamps's facetious verses see Le Marquis de Queux de Saint-Hilaire and Gaston Raynaud, *Oeuvres complètes de Eustache Deschamps,* 11 vols. (Paris, 1878–1903), vol. 7, pp. 155–92, 312–62; and on Molinet and the *rhétoriqueurs* see Paul Zumthor, "From Hi(story) to Poem, or the Paths of Pun: The Grands Rhétoriqueurs of Fifteenth-Century France," trans. A. and E. Tomarken, *New Literary History* 10 (1978–1979): 231–63.

5. Whether in the sense of rape, abduction, or forced marriage, *raptus* was a crime against the authority of the "fathers," first and foremost the woman's own father or the male protector who had the right to bestow her on another man, and second against the paternal authority of civic and ecclesiastical institutions that enforced law, order, and Christian morality. This is demonstrated in a case of *raptus* in Paris in 1405 for which there are full records. The nobleman Regnault d'Azincourt, with his male relatives and a priest, entered by night the house of a wealthy bourgeois grocer in the rue St. Denis. With the priest as witness, it was Regnault's intention to engage himself to the coquettish widow against the will of her father, who had previously vowed that he would prefer to pay the *taille* weekly than have his daughters taken from him by noblemen. Regnault's plan failed (because the lady fainted), but he still had to face the judgment and penalties of civil and ecclesiastical authorities. For the documents relating to this trial, see Antoine le Roux de Lincy, "Tentative de rapt commise par Regnault d'Azincourt sur une épicière de la rue Saint-Denis en 1405," *Bibliothèque de l'Ecole des Chartes,* 2d sér., 3 (1846): 316–33.

Although it is extremely risky to speculate about the personal motivation of Chaucer's fictions or the private purposes they may have served, it is nevertheless reasonable to assume that Chaucer, like other writers before and after him, used his fiction as therapy and also, in some cases, to persuade under cover of game. *The House of Fame* is particularly evocative in these respects. Chaucer's friends witnessed to his good "reputation" and Cecily Chaumpaigne released him from charges of *raptus* in 1380, during Chaucer's period as collector of customs, when he is believed to have written *The House of Fame,* partly because of his allusion therein to his "rekenynges" (book 2, verse 653). Chaucer's equivocating discussion of the different causes and meanings of dreams and his claim not to know the meaning or cause of this one clouds the waters so as not to be too obvious. Nevertheless, Chaucer's "dream" fiction will "turne . . . to goode" only if we understand it as a self-defense and are amused and persuaded by it. If we misunderstand it through willfully "malicious entencion," Chaucer prays that we will come to harm (book 1, verses 94–108). The first dream sequence of *The House of Fame* dwells on the story of Aeneas and Dido, who willingly gave her love to Aeneas and suffered from "wikke Fame" for her misjudgment, that is, for giving herself to a family man with another mission in life. Chaucer's sympathies in his narration of the love affair lie entirely with Dido, "that loved al to sone a gest" (book 1, verse 288); nevertheless, it is not difficult to see that she is carried away by Aeneas's stories of his adventures and his appearance (book 1, verses 253–64). With reference to Chaucer and Cecily, such a "dream" may be self-serving, for the lesson the classical story teaches is that men are not always faithful, especially when they are ambitious, and women are not always taken against their will.

In the second book of *The House of Fame,* Chaucer attacks the problem of absolving himself from another direction. He debunks the notion that he could possibly have carried any woman off by force. Here, it is the timorous, hermitlike Geoffrey who suffers *raptus* by an eagle that finds him, probably for his rotundity, "noyous for to carye" (book 2, verse 574). Chaucer is not, however, the object of Jove's desire, a second Ganymede, as he first imagines; instead, his *enlèvement* to the House of Fame is a reward for his diligence at poetry and reading, that is, for the reclusive life he has led for so long, oblivious even to his closest neighbors' doings (book 2, verses 614–60). The third book treats the issue of reputation, which, as Geoffrey discovers in the palace of Fame, is totally arbitrary and unstable, as is the report that issues from the whirling rumor mill. Where truth lies in the relationship between words and deeds is impossible to tell, and the vision breaks off before Geoffrey meets the person who "semed for to be / A man of gret auctorite" (book 3, verses 2157–58). The conclusion we may be meant to draw from *The House of Fame* is that we had better not believe any rumors defaming Geoffrey Chaucer and blackening his reputation for the *raptus* of Cecily Chaumpaigne.

6. If Harry Bailly is miming *politesse,* he may be using a French expression. In his *Dictionnaire de l'ancienne langue française* (10 vols. [Paris, 1880–1902]), Frédéric Godefroy gives examples before 1350 of *gentillesse*

used as a term of honorable address, more commonly in the plural to designate a group of gentlemen, but also in the singular to designate a ruler, as in the following instance (vol. 4, p. 262): "'Honneur a vostre gentillesse, / Roy renommé par dessus tous' (*Viel Testament,* 29190, A.T.)." On the courteous "youre," see Alfred David, *The Strumpet Muse* (Bloomington, Ind., 1976), p. 186.

7. Larry D. Benson, "The 'Queynte' Punnings of Chaucer's Critics," in *Studies in the Age of Chaucer, Proceedings, No. 1: Reconstructing Chaucer,* ed. Paul Strohm and Thomas J. Heffernan (Knoxville, 1985), pp. 23–47.

8. Alan Gaylord, "*Sentence* and *solaas* in Fragment VII of the *Canterbury Tales:* Harry Bailly as Horseback Editor," *PMLA* 82 (1967): 232.

9. On festive gender reversal and playful female dominance, see Natalie Zemon Davis, "Women on Top," in *Society and Culture in Early Modern France* (Stanford, 1975); for images of "Mère Folle," see Claude Gaignebet and J. Dominique Lajoux, *L'Art profane et religion populaire au moyen âge* (Paris, 1985), pp. 187–88.

10. On the use of garlands in popular medieval agricultural festivals, as well as offerings of cakes, see E. K. Chambers, *The Mediaeval Stage,* 2 vols. (Oxford, 1903), vol. 1, pp. 116–20, 142–43.

11. Benson, *Riverside Chaucer,* p. 863: "Of the thirty-five MSS in which the Epilogue to the Man of Law's Tale appears, six read 'Sommonour/Sompnour,' twenty-eight 'Squier,' and one (the late Selden) 'Shipman,' which most editors have taken as the most probable reading. All three readings, however, are most likely scribal inventions."

12. Carl Lindahl, "The Festive Form of the *Canterbury Tales,*" *ELH* 52 (1985): 548.

13. On the customs of charivari in the late Middle Ages and the Renaissance in England and France, see E. P. Thompson, "Rough Music: Le Charivari anglais," *Annales, Economies, Sociétés, Civilisations* 27 (1972): 285–312; the excellent collection of articles in *Actes de la table ronde organisée à Paris (25–27 avril 1977) par l'Ecole des Hautes Etudes en Sciences Sociales et le Centre National de la Recherche Scientifique,* ed. J. Le Goff and J. C. Schmitt (La Haye, 1981); and Henri Rey-Flaud, *Le Charivari: Les Rituels fondamentaux de la sexualité* (Paris, 1985).

14. Donald Howard, *The Idea of the Canterbury Tales* (Berkeley and Los Angeles, 1976), pp. 48–49.

15. See the chapter on Eustache Deschamps in my unpublished doctoral dissertation, "Criticism of the Ruler, 1100–1400, in Provençal, Old French, and Middle English Verse," Columbia, 1978.

Chapter Seven

1. Peter Weidkuhn, "Le Carnaval de Bâle ou l'histoire inversée," in *Les Grandes Traditions de la fête,* ed. G. S. Métraux (Paris, 1976), p. 40,

fig. 7. On the use of festive personae to express satire and criticism and to license rebellious political actions in the Renaissance, see Natalie Zemon Davis, "The Reasons of Misrule" and "Women on Top" in *Society and Culture in Early Modern France* (Stanford, 1975).

2. The discussion of taboo topics puts great pressure on scholarly writers to adopt comic masks in their prefaces and epilogues. An extreme example of this is Gustave Witkowski's *L'Art chrétien, ses licences* (Paris, 1912), which he frames with a self-mockingly philosophical preface beginning "The Ego is detestable" and ends with a facetious, black-bordered announcement of his own demise.

3. A version of the first chapter of this book was given as a talk for the Chaucer Division of the Modern Language Association, 29 December 1985, in Chicago.

4. Melanie Klein, "La Personnification dans le jeu des enfants," *Essais de psychanalyse (1921–1945), trans.* M. Derrida (Paris, 1984), pp. 243–51.

5. G. L. Kittredge, *Chaucer and His Poetry* (Cambridge, Mass., 1927), pp. 154–55. R. M. Lumiansky quotes this passage in the introduction to *Of Sondry Folk: The Dramatic Principle in the Canterbury Tales* (Austin, 1955), pp. 5–6, and proceeds on the same assumptions as Kittredge concerning the realism of Chaucer's use of dramatic conventions.

6. Donald Howard, in *The Idea of the Canterbury Tales* (Berkeley and Los Angeles, 1976), calls attention to this layering of voices:

[Chaucer] places over his mask of the fool the masks of the pilgrims which he has displayed before us in the General Prologue. Yet each of these pilgrims whose roles he plays is himself a performer who plays the roles of various figures in his own tale. (In some instances the figures in a tale are performers too: Chauntecleer performs two tales, complete with characters, plot, and dialogues.) We have therefore a performer playing the parts of performers.

(p. 195)

7. For some of the authenticating conventions of medieval historical narrative, see Jeanette Beer, *Narrative Conventions of Truth in the Middle Ages* (Geneva, 1981). Guido delle Colonne's Latin-prose *Historia destructionis Troiae* has been edited by Nathaniel Griffin (Cambridge, Mass., 1936) and translated by Mary Elizabeth Meek (Bloomington, Ind., 1974). See Leopold Constans's edition of Benoît de Sainte-Maure, *Le Roman de Troie,* 6 vols. (Paris, 1904–1912).

8. Guido, *Historia,* trans. Meek, book 9, p. 86: "It was the time when winter had already shed its frost, and its cold was dispelled on account of the season. . . . The sun was running in the last stages of Pisces . . . and the month of March which was to follow was already near. At this time the whole Greek army, well supplied with a large fleet, had assembled in the port of the city of Athens."

9. V. L. Dedeck-Héry, "Boethius' *De Consolatione* by Jean de Meun,"

Mediaeval Studies 14 (1952): 168, lines 10–18. In *Chaucer's Narrators* (London, 1985), p. 102, David Lawton argues that Chaucer is presenting himself in the apology of his "General Prologue" as a transcriber; Lawton then, rather too hastily, equates transcription with translation: "the narrator as poet presents his transcription of the pilgrim's pretended experience as an act of *translation* (730–6), a task no different from that of *Troilus*. All writing, so apprehended, is indeed a matter of 'translating an invisible text.' The author's apology centres primarily on style. . . . The true reporter, in seeking to translate 'pleynly,' must reproduce others' words 'proprely': the theory is conventional and it is one of stylistic decorum." No sources of this "conventional" theory are cited.

10. Constans, ed., *Roman de Troie*, vol. 1, p. 9, verses 135–40.

11. On the practice of late medieval historians, see Bernard Guenée, "L'historien par les mots," in his *Politique et histoire au moyen âge* (Paris, 1981), pp. 221–37.

12. Howard, *The Idea*, p. 143, has called attention to "this fictional tour de force of memory."

13. Jean Froissart, *Chroniques,* ed. J. A. Buchon, 16 vols. (Paris, 1824–1829), vol. 9, p. 299 (from book 3). Froissart's compositional process, from the rapidly recorded building block of the *mémoire* to the embellished or historiated chronicle, seems to foreshadow the division of labor described by fifteenth-century historical writers. In the prologue to his work, which is known as a chronicle, Jean Le Fèvre describes his office in the Burgundian chivalric order of the Golden Fleece as that of a recorder of written *mémoires* of events. Le Fèvre then sends these *mémoires* to the court orator, Georges Chastelain, who, "according to his pleasure and discretion, would employ them in the noble histories and chronicles he made" (*Chronique de Jean le Fèvre,* ed. François Morand, 2 vols. [Paris, 1876], vol. 1, p. 1). Whereas Jean writes his "little book" (really a long chronicle) in his "gros" and "rude langaige" of Picard "after the manner of a record or *mémoire,*" Chastelain's duty is to turn this "crude" historical matter into an elegantly laudatory Latin work.

14. Constans, ed., *Roman de Troie*, vol. 1, pp. 7–8, verses 113–33.

15. Guillaume de Lorris and Jean de Meun, *Le Roman de la rose,* ed. Félix Lecoy, 3 vols. (Paris, 1965–1970), vol. 2, p. 175, verses 5683–89.

16. John Fleming, *Reason and the Lover* (Princeton, 1984), p. 102.

17. See Glending Olson, "Making and Poetry in the Age of Chaucer," *Comparative Literature* 31 (1979): 272–90.

18. For more detailed discussion, see my book *The Game of Love: Troubadour Wordplay* (Berkeley and Los Angeles, 1988), especially the chapter "Jonglerie and the Missing Signs."

19. Alain de Lille, for instance, in his *De Arte praedicatoria* (J. P. Migne,

Patrologiae cursus completus. Series latina, 221 vols. [Paris, 1844–1864], vol. 210, col. 112), considered leonine (heavily or internally rhymed) verse theatrical, typical of actors and mimes, hence to be avoided in preaching; and in his early-thirteenth-century *Ars versificatoria,* Matthew of Vendôme reiterated that the empty formalism of leonine verse was the province of jongleurs and mimes (ed. Edmond Faral, *Les Arts poétiques du XII*e *et du XIII*e *siècles* [Paris, 1958], p. 166). Nicholas of Senlis in 1202 went so far as to pronounce that "No story set to rhyme is true," as Paul Zumthor reminds us in *La Lettre et la voix* (Paris, 1987), p. 203.

20. Charles H. Livingston, *Le Jongleur Gautier Le Leu* (Cambridge, Mass., 1951), "De Deus vilains," p. 206, verses 169–76. The name of the storyteller in this fabliau, Goulius (Glutton), is reminiscent of the Golias persona of much medieval Latin goliard play.

21. Constans, ed., *Roman de Troie,* vol. 1, p. 1, verses 1–39.

22. For Dares' brief and very rudimentary descriptions of physical features and temperaments, see Daretis Phrygii, *De excidio Troiae Historia,* ed. Ferdinand Meister (Leipzig, 1873), pp. 14–17. Benoît de Sainte-Maure emphasizes the reliability of Dares' eyewitness accounts. He tells us that the Trojan Dares, who was "marvellously" learned in all the seven arts and who realized the magnitude and import of the war, nightly wrote down the events of the preceding day (Constans, ed., *Roman de Troie,* vol. 1, pp. 6–7, verses 91–116). Benoît greatly amplifies the details of Dares' "objective" portraits of Greek and Trojan heros and heroines (ibid., pp. 263–92, verses 5073–562), as does Guido delle Colonne in his Latin prose version (Griffin, ed., *Historia,* pp. 83–87). Furthermore, Guido follows his portrait series with an elaborate spring topos opening (quoted in n. 8 above) not found in Dares, who merely lists the Greek leaders and ships that gathered to sail for Troy. For detailed comparisons of Benoît's with Chaucer's portraits, see R. M. Lumiansky, "Benoît's Portraits and Chaucer's General Prologue," *Journal of English and Germanic Philology* 55 (1956): 431–38.

23. Brunetto Latini, *Li Livres dou trésor,* ed. Francis J. Carmody (Berkeley and Los Angeles, 1948), p. 204. The self-ridicule that distinguished the medieval jongleur remains a basic technique of modern stand-up comedians. By creating regressively infantile, foolish personae and thus deauthorizing or negating the seriousness of their words and gestures, modern comedians' self-mockery enables them to make extremely aggressive attacks on those in power. A master of such techniques was the French comedian Michel Coluche, the "buffoon of the French Republic," a comedian whose very name recollected the "coqueluche" (cock's comb) of the medieval fool's hood and whose persona was that of the plump *enfant terrible* from the suburbs (the margins), who

would be restricted by none of the rules of adult life, neither of polite behavior and manners nor of polite speech (his was filled with vulgar, slangy references to the body, sex, and excrement). Dressed in the bibbed overalls of a modern two-year-old or a manual laborer, he ran in the 1981 French presidential election in order, so he later said, to mock the grotesqueness of it, and his burlesque commentaries on political events and men in power were always cutting, truthful, and foolish. Because of Coluche's ability not only to express Everyman's hostility and frustration but to deny and control it through laughter, politicians may miss him most.

24. Howard, *The Idea,* p. 231.

25. On the ambiguity of this passage and of Chaucer's version of it, see P. B. Taylor, "Chaucer's 'Cosyn to the Dede,'" *Speculum* 57 (1982): especially p. 324: "Chaucer's epigram, as well as Jean de Meun's, plays on the word *cousin.* Besides 'blood-relative,' *cousin* denotes a 'dupe.' The word belies the thing it identifies or the idea it expresses. The pun dislodges Plato's point by affirming the ability of words to misconstrue the deeds they render while posing as the 'natural' expression of them."

26. *Le Roman de la rose,* ed. Lecoy, vol. 2, p. 211, verses 15,161–62, for the maxim; Jean's equivocal discussion of the relationship between words and *choses* ("things") begins several lines earlier.

27. Howard, *The Idea,* p. 302.

28. W. Beare, *The Roman Stage* (London, 1950), p. 150.

29. Florence Ridley, *The Prioress and the Critics* (Berkeley and Los Angeles, 1965), pp. 16–18.

30. Jill Mann, *Chaucer and Medieval Estates Satire* (Cambridge, Eng., 1973); Terry Jones, *Chaucer's Knight: The Portrait of a Medieval Mercenary* (London, 1980), p. 4.

31. John B. Friedman, "The Prioress's Beads 'of smal corel,'" *Medium Aevum* 39 (1970): 301–5. The Prioress's rosary beads "gauded al with grene" (A 150) may be loaded with more equivocal meanings than have already been discovered in the medieval symbolism and uses of coral and the "Amor vincit omnia" motto of the pendant brooch. In "Chaucer's Puns: A Supplementary List" (*PMLA* 73 [1958]: 168), Paull Baum did not mention the possible pun on sexual desire in "grene" nor the joyful connotations of the English word "gauded," which recollects the Latin *gaudium* and the French *gauder,* a verb of rejoicing that might be used in both sacred and secular contexts. From the same root, listed by Frédéric Godefroy in his *Dictionnaire de l'ancienne langue française* (10 vols. [Paris, 1880–1902]), vol. 4, pp. 244–45, are the Old French nouns *gaudete* and *gaudine* (a fun-loving woman or a pleasing woman) and *gaudee* (a "prayer said in haste and without paying attention" [perhaps because the thoughts

of the one who prays are distracted by worldly enjoyment]). Chaucer's phrase "gauded with grene" may describe not only the Prioress's beads themselves but also the spirit in which she tells, or plays with, them—with thoughts distracted by amorous pleasures. According to the *Middle English Dictionary,* ed. Hans Kurath and S. Kuhn (Ann Arbor, 1952–), the noun *grēne* means sexual desire, as in the example given from *Havelok* (vol. G1, p. 336):

> Of bodi was he mayden clene,
> Neuere yete in game ne in grene
> Wit hire ne wolde leyke ne lye,
> No more than it were a strie.

For Chaucer, *grēne* must have been a Northernism, a dialectal word. He may be playing the old goliardic and jongleuresque game of using a vulgar or dialectal pronunciation or meaning to subvert a more pious, proper one.

32. *Pamphile et Galatée,* ed. Joseph Morawski (Paris, 1917), p. 5, verse 48. For a complete list of appearances of the name Eglantine in Old French narrative sources, see Louis-Fernand Flutre, *Table des noms propres avec toutes leurs variantes figurant dans les romans du moyen âge* (Poitiers, 1962), p. 7.

33. To verify *pastourelle* conventions, one has but to leaf through a collection such as Karl Bartsch's *Romances et pastourelles françaises des XIIe et XIIIe siècles* (Leipzig, 1870). Curiously, the fruit of the eglantine, a sort of large rose hip, also appears in medieval verse. Peire Cardenal uses this fruit as a symbol for deception in two thirteenth-century Provençal lyrics. In "Un sirventes si en cor que comens," Peire compares a traitor to this fruit, "fleshy and round, full of evil humours" (no. 27, p. 156, verses 25–26), and in "Pos ma boca parla sens" (no. 64, p. 416, verses 37–45), he explicates the comparison (*Poésies complètes du troubadour Peire Cardenal,* ed. René Lavaud [Toulouse, 1957]):

> Semblans es als aguolens
> Crois homps can gen si garnis
> Que de foras resplendis
> E dins val mais que niens.
> Ez es majers fenhemens
> Que si us escaravais
> Si fenhia papagais
> Can si fenh que pros hom sia
> Uns fals messongiers savais.

Similar to the eglantine's fruit / is the vulgar man when he dresses like a gentleman / so that he is splendid on the outside / and worth less than nothing on the inside. / And it is a greater deception / than if a dung beetle / pretended to be a parrot / when a false, low-down liar / pretends to be a worthy man.

If the worthlessness of the handsome fruit of the eglantine was proverbial, or if it was part of any medical or natural lore that Chaucer may have
known, I have found no evidence of this.

34. J. L. Lowes, "Simple and Coy: A Note on Fourteenth-Century
Poetic Diction," *Anglia* 33 (1910): 446.

35. Gustave Servois, ed., *Le Roman de la rose ou de Guillaume de Dole*
(Paris, 1893), pp. 68–69. Lines missing in the manuscript are denoted by
centered ellipses in the following full citation and translation of "Bele
Aiglentine":

> Bele Aiglentine, en roial chamberine,
> Devant sa dame cousoit une chemise.
> · · ·
> Ainc n'en sot mot quant bone amor l'atise.
>   Or orrez ja
> Comment la bele Aiglentine esploita.
>
> Devant sa dame cousoit et si tailloit;
> Mès ne coust mie si com coudre soloit:
> El s'entroublie, si se point en son doit.
> La soe mere mout tost s'en aperçoit.
>   Or orrez ja
> Comment la bele Aiglentine esploita.
>
> "Bele Aiglentine, deffublez vo surcot,
>   · · ·
> "Je voil veoir desoz vostre gent cors.
> —Non ferai, dame, la froidure est la morz."
>   Or orrez ja
> Comment la bele Aiglentine esploita.
>
> "Bele Aiglentine, q'avez a empirier?
> "Que si vos voi palir et engroissier."
>   · · ·
>   · · ·
>   Or orrez ja
> Comment la bele Aiglentine esploita.
>
> "Ma douce dame, ne le vos puis noier:
> "Je ai amé .i. cortois soudoier,
> "Le preu Henri, qui tant fet a proisier.
> "S'onqes m'amastes, aiez de moi pitié."
>   Or orrez ja
> Comment la bele Aiglentine esploita.
>
> "Bele Aiglentine, vos prendra il Henris?
> —Ne sai voir, dame, car onqes ne li quis.
>   · · ·
>   · · ·
>   Or orrez ja
> Comment la bele Aiglentine esploita.

"Bele Aiglentine, or vos tornez de ci.
"Tot ce li dites que ge li mant Henri,
"S'il vos prendra ou vos lera ainsi.
—Volontiers, dame," la bele respondi.
 Or orrez ja
Comment la bele Aiglentine esploita.

Bele Aiglentine s'est tornee de ci,
Et est venue droit a l'ostel Henri.
Li quens Henri se gisoit en son lit.
Or orrez ja que la bele li dit.
 Or orrez ja
Comment la bele Aiglentine esploita.

"Sire Henri, velliez vos o dormez?
"Ja vos requiert Aiglentine au vis cler
"Se la prendrez a mouillier et a per?
—Oil," dit il, "onc joie n'oi mes tel."
 Or orrez ja
Comment la bele Aiglentine esploita.

Oit le Henris, mout joianz en devint.
Il fet monter chevaliers trusqu'a .xx.,
Si enporta la bele en son païs
Et espousa, riche contesse en fist.
 Grant joie en a
Li quens Henris, quant bele Aiglentine a.

Beautiful Eglantine, in a royal chamber, / was sewing a shirt in front of her mother. / . . . / Not a word did she catch while love inflamed her. / Now hear / how the beautiful Eglantine performed.

Before her mother she stitched and clipped, / but she was not sewing at all as she ought to. / She was troubled, and so she pricked her finger. / Her mother noticed this right away. / Now hear / how the beautiful Eglantine performed.

"Beautiful Eglantine, take off your outer robe / . . . / I want to see your lovely body underneath." / "I will not, milady; the cold will kill me." / Now hear / how the beautiful Eglantine performed.

"Beautiful Eglantine, what is harming you / that I see you growing so pale and big?" / . . . / . . . / Now hear / how the beautiful Eglantine performed.

"My sweet lady, I cannot deny it. / I made love with a courtly soldier, / the worthy Henry, who won such praise. / If you ever loved me, have pity on me." / Now hear / how the beautiful Eglantine performed.

"Beautiful Eglantine, will Henry take you?" / "Truly, I don't know, milady, for I never asked him." / . . . / . . . / Now hear / how the beautiful Eglantine performed.

"Beautiful Eglantine, now depart from here. / Say to Henry everything I ask, / whether he will take you or leave you this way." / "Gladly, milady," the beauty replied. / Now hear / how the beautiful Eglantine performed.

Beautiful Eglantine departed from there / and went straight to Henry's lodging. / Count Henry was lying in bed. / Now listen to what the beauty said to him. / Now hear / how the beautiful Eglantine performed.

"Sir Henry, are you awake or asleep? / Eglantine with the pretty face asks you now / if you will take her for wife and companion." / "Yes," he said, "I've never had such joy." / Now hear / how the beautiful Eglantine performed.

When Henry heard this, he became joyful. / He ordered twenty knights to mount / and carried the beauty off to his land / and married her, made her a rich countess. / Great joy has / Count Henry when he *has* beautiful Eglantine.

36. Georges Duby discusses the historical situation behind such literary fantasies in *Le Chevalier, la femme, et le prêtre* (Paris, 1981), p. 166, for example.

37. For the short version, "Bele Eglentine," see Gaston Raynaud, *Recueil de motets français des XIIe et XIIIe siècles,* 2 vols. (Paris, 1881), vol. 1, pp. 175–76. The context of this motet is the more common one of a manuscript collection of lyrics with no framing narrative. Paul Zumthor analyzes the "Bele Aiglentine" lyrics and uses them as an example of *mouvance* in "La Chanson de Bele Aiglentine," *Travaux de Linguistique et de Littérature* 8 (1970): 325–37, and again in his *Essai de poétique médiévale* (Paris, 1972), pp. 290–98. Zumthor argues in "La Chanson," pp. 328–30, against the modern editorial assumption that all of the stanzas of the *Roman*'s version of "Bele Aiglentine" must originally have been of equal length, an assumption that leads to the conclusion that any irregularities and "missing lines" in the sole surviving manuscript version must be due to unintentional errors of transmission. Zumthor's argument for deliberate change is supported by my interpretation of the Aiglentine lyrics as deliberately debasing parodies of courtly love situations, deliberately errant transmissions of an authoritative courtly text.

38. Dictionary compilers have traditionally turned a censoring or blind eye to subversive puns, near-puns, innuendos, images. Even if they list erotic or scatological meanings, "serious" dictionaries do not list veiled puns or innuendos or metaphors that seem in any way conjectural. In short, we should not expect to be able to authorize and validate subversive goliardic or jongleuresque linguistic play by turning to the conventionally censorious authority of dictionaries.

39. For the "Miracle de l'abbeesse grosse," see *Miracles de Nostre Dame par personnages,* ed. Gaston Paris and Ulysse Robert, 8 vols. (Paris, 1876–1893), vol. 1, pp. 58–100. When it has no metrical purpose, the scribal doubling of vowels in some words, such as "abbeesse" here (or Chaucer's "solaas"), may sometimes signal wordplay by exaggerating and dwelling on the letter (rather than the spirit). This particular play, from a cycle of miracles of the Virgin written for performance before or by members of a

late-fourteenth-century northern French *puy,* is full of erotic innuendos. A precursor of Molière's *femmes savantes,* Sister Ysabel protests that the priest seems to be trying to incite the nuns with his vulgar sermonizing interlarded with "foolish" (or sinful) words (or syllables understood as words):

> Il semblera ja qu'il nous tence,
> Tant sermonnera lourdement:
> Car de soz moz dit largement
> En son preschier.
> (p. 60, verses 38–41)

Indeed it would seem that he is inciting us / by preaching so laboriously; / for he uses foolish words freely / in his preaching.

The abbess responds to this complaint with a reprimand: Sister Ysabel would evidently rather be dancing than listening to sermons and ought not to have her mind on such "solace." ("Dancing" could be a metaphor for love play or sexual intercourse, the "old dance"; and "solace" could suggest the same, as well as wordplay, often involving vulgar innuendos.) Sister Ysabel's protest prepares us to perceive the erotic innuendos in the text of the priest's sermon, which is a biblical-sounding pastiche of Matthew 11:28 ("Come unto me all ye . . .") and of the language of the Pauline epistles. The priest's text is "Transite ad me, omnes qui concupiscitis me, / Et generacionibus meis implemini" (p. 61, verses 52–53). Instead of covering up, the priest's vernacular gloss tends to point possible erotic innuendos in the text:

> . . . car je vous puis nuncier
> Que ceulx qui ce desir entier
> Ont en eulz par devocion,
> Sanz vaine similacion,
> La doulce vierge les appelle
> Par une escripture moult belle,
> Laquelle je vous proposay,
> Quant je mon sermon conmençay,
> Et dit: Venez a moy, venez,
> Vous trestouz qui me desirez,
> Et je vous vouldray acomplir
> Touz voz desirs et raemplir
> Vous de mes generacions.
> (p. 62, verses 106–14)

. . . for I announce to you / that those who have this desire wholly / within themselves through devotion, / without vain pretense, / the sweet Virgin calls them / with a very beautiful passage of Scripture / that I proposed to you / when I began my sermon / by saying: Come to me, come, / all you who desire me / and I would like to fulfill / all your desires and fill / you with my generations.

The priest presents the speaker of the text he repeats as the "sweet Virgin," perhaps punningly pronounced *verge* (slang for penis) or easily misunderstood as such. Such a pun completely subverts any spiritual understanding of the pastiched scriptural text: "I would like to fulfill / all your desires and fill / you with my generations."

How are we to take such wordplay? For one thing, it is temporary; few plays in the miracle cycle are on such potentially comic subjects as a pregnant prioress. Once we recognize the signs of a temporary ritual reversal, of game overturning earnest, we are supposed to participate actively in the subversion of authority. We are not supposed to think that the characters of this miracle play are real people who intend erotic puns in addressing one another; rather, these characters are masking personae that allow their author and audience to play with the deauthorized words voiced through them. We enjoy the erotic puns and innuendos because of their incongruity and subversive effect in the mouths of religious personae. The erotic subtext is also perfectly appropriate to the burlesque plot of this miracle play in which the abbess will seduce and become pregnant by her clerk and then be rescued from the investigation of the bishop by a miraculous "Virgin delivery."

Conclusion

1. Le Marquis de Queux de Saint-Hilaire and Gaston Raynaud, eds., *Oeuvres complètes de Eustache Deschamps,* 11 vols. (Paris, 1878–1903), vol. 11, p. 14.

2. Philippe de Navarre, *Les Quatre Ages de l'homme,* ed. Marcel de Fréville (Paris, 1888; rpt. 1968), pp. 52–53. For an analysis of Matthew Arnold's criticism that Chaucer "lacked high seriousness," see Richard Lanham, "Game, Play, and High Seriousness in Chaucer's Poetry," *English Studies* 48 (1967): 1–7.

3. Benson, *Riverside Chaucer,* p. 584.

4. This English translation of St. Bernard's letter is by E. G. Holt, *Literary Sources of Art History* (Princeton, 1947), p. 19.

5. For visual confirmation, see the collection of exhibitionistic images in Claude Gaignebet and J. Dominique Lajoux, *L'Art profane et religion populaire au moyen âge* (Paris, 1985), for example, the section entitled "The Siren" (pp. 142–43). See also the images collected by Karl Wentersdorf, "The Symbolic Significance of *Figurae scatologicae* in Gothic Manuscripts," in *Word, Picture, and Spectacle,* ed. Clifford Davidson (Kalamazoo, 1984), pp. 1–19, figs. 1–27; and by H. W. Janson, *Apes and Ape-Lore in the Middle Ages and the Renaissance* (London, 1952).

6. Gaignebet and Lajoux, *L'Art profane,* pp. 192–201.

7. Ibid., pp. 210–15.

8. Charles Muscatine, *Chaucer and the French Tradition* (Berkeley and Los Angeles, 1957), p. 180.

9. This is the subject of Thomas Cooke's *The Old French and Chaucerian Fabliaux: A Study of Their Comic Climax* (Columbia, Mo., 1978).

10. R. Howard Bloch, *The Scandal of the Fabliaux* (Chicago, 1986), p. 127.

11. On ritual *communitas* and its functions, see Victor Turner, *The Ritual Process: Structure and Anti-Structure* (London, 1969).

Appendix

1. There is a beautiful color reproduction of this frontispiece in the facsimile edition of Cambridge, Corpus Christi College ms. 61 of *Troilus and Criseyde,* with introductions by M. B. Parkes and Elizabeth Salter (Cambridge, Eng., 1978).

2. See Margaret Galway, "The 'Troilus' Frontispiece," *Modern Language Review* 44 (1949): 161–77; and George Williams, "The 'Troilus and Criseyde' Frontispiece Again," *Modern Language Review* 57 (1962): 173–78.

3. James H. McGregor, "The Iconography of Chaucer in Hoccleve's *De Regimine Principum* and in the *Troilus* Frontispiece," *Chaucer Review* 11 (1977): 346.

4. Derek Pearsall, "The *Troilus* Frontispiece and Chaucer's Audience," *Yearbook of English Studies* 7 (1977): 68–74, with three plates of pulpit preaching scenes; Elizabeth Salter, "The '*Troilus* Frontispiece,'" in Parkes and Salter, eds., *Troilus,* pp. 15–23, with several reproductions of preaching scenes, especially from the *Pèlerinage de vie humaine.*

5. Salter, "'*Troilus* Frontispiece,'" p. 17.

6. Of these preaching scenes Salter writes (ibid., pp. 17–19), "in direct response to the wording of the opening lines of the poem in which Deguileville, a Cistercian monk of the Royal Abbey of Chaalis, near Senlis, addressed himself to 'riche, povre, sage et fol / soient roys, soient roynes / pelerins et pelerines . . . ,' we can trace the development of a lively 'recital' scene, with poet-monk addressing an appropriately mixed audience from his pulpit."

7. *Lydgate's Troy Book,* ed. Henry Bergen, 2 vols. (London, 1906–1935), vol. 1, pt. 1, p. 169, verses 863–67. In this and subsequent citations from this edition, I have replaced the thorn symbol by *th,* the yogh by *gh,* and modernized the usage of *u* and *v.*

8. This definition is cited by Henri Rey-Flaud, *Le Cercle magique: Essai sur le théâtre en rond à la fin du moyen âge* (Paris, 1973), p. 33. In the early

printed edition of the *Aequivoca* I examined (Andreas Myllar Scotus, 1505), this explanation of a theater appeared at the beginning of quire *c* as part of the entry explaining the equivocal senses of Latin *cena*. It is interesting that *cena* and *scena* should be associated, not only by the sounds of the two words, but also in practice, banquets being the context for many plays. I do not want to get into the issue of whether or not there were permanent public theater buildings in the Middle Ages after the Roman ones had been put to other uses or fallen to ruin. See "Were There Theatres in the Twelfth and Thirteenth Centuries?" by Roger S. Loomis, with commentary by Gustave Cohen, *Speculum* 20 (1945): 92–98; and Dino Bigongiari's essay by the same title, *Romanic Review* 37 (1946): 201–24. There is good sense in Bigongiari's suggestion, p. 222, that *theatrum* in writings of the eleventh through early thirteenth centuries may mean no more than "scaffolding" or "platform."

9. See Mary H. Marshall, "Theater in the Middle Ages," *Symposium* 4 (1950): 22–23.

10. In a chapter on "Sermon and Drama" in *Literature and Pulpit in Medieval England,* 2d rev. ed. (New York, 1961), pp. 471–547, G. R. Owst explored relationships between medieval sermons (some heavily dialogued and versified) and medieval religious drama.

11. The similar Terence illuminations of Paris, B.N. lat. 7907A, fol. 2v, and Paris, Arsenal lat. 664, fol. 1v, are reproduced in color by Millard Meiss in *French Painting in the Time of Jean de Berry: The Limbourgs and Their Contemporaries (1400–1425),* 2 vols. (New York, 1974), vol. 2, figs. 209, 210.

12. See Nicolai Treveti, *Expositio Hercules Furentis,* ed. V. Ussani, Jr. (Rome, 1959), p. 5; the passage is cited by Mary Marshall in "Theater in the Middle Ages," p. 27; and by Beryl Rowland in *"Pronuntiatio* and its Effect on Chaucer's Audience," *Studies in the Age of Chaucer* 4 (1982): 33–51. In "Isidore and the Theater," *Comparative Drama* 16 (1982): 47n. 25, Joseph R. Jones cites a commentary by Raoul de Praelles from 1375 in which Raoul gives contemporary analogies for Isidore's definition of drama: "est une petite maison ou milieu du theatre en laquelle avoit ung letrin ou len lisoit les tragedies et comedies des poetes et y avoit gens desguisez qui faisoient les contenances de ceulx pour lesquelz len chantoit et faisoit ces jeux ainsi comme tu vois que len fait encores au jour duy les jeux de personnaiges et charivalis. Et y avoit joueurs de divers instrumens et autres qui se desguisoient et contrefaisoient les personnes de qui la tragedie ou comedie parloit" ("there is a little house in the middle of the theater in which there was a lectern where they read the tragedies and comedies of the poets, and there were disguised men who imitated the facial expressions of those for whom they sang and held these games, *just*

as you see people doing still today in plays involving characters and in charivaris, and there were players of various instruments and others who disguised themselves and played the characters of whom the tragedy or comedy spoke").

13. See, for instance, Meiss's reproduction in *French Painting,* fig. 208, of an early-fifteenth-century illumination of a Roman theater production, with three sets of lovers embracing in the audience (Paris, Arsenal 5060, fol. 27).

14. On the London *puy* and its regulations in the reign of Edward I, see Henry Riley, ed., *Liber Albus, Liber Custumarum et Liber Horn,* in *Munimenta Gildhallae Londoniensis.* Vol. 2, Part 1: *Liber Custumarum* (London, 1860), pp. 216–28 (the quotations are taken from page 219); John H. Fisher, *John Gower* (New York, 1964), pp. 78–83; and Martin Stevens, "The Royal Stanza in Early English Literature," *Publications of the Modern Language Association* 94 (1979): 62–76.

15. On the *puy*'s sponsorship of plays, see the ordinances of the Puy Nostre-Dame of Amiens edited by Victor de Beauvillé in *Recueil de documents inédits concernant la Picardie,* 2 vols. (Paris, 1860, 1867), vol. 1, p. 141: "Lequel disner il fera apointier à gracieuse et courtoise despence sans excès, et durant iceluy disner fera le maistre jouer ung jeu de mistère, et donra à chascun des assistans ung chapel vert et ung mès dudit mistère, avec une couronne d'argent que gaignera celuy qui fera le meilleur chant royal selon le reffrain du tablel" ("He will organize this dinner according to gracious, courteous liberality, without excess; and during the dinner the master will see that a 'mystery' play is performed, and he will give to each of the seated banqueters a green cap and a course at dinner of [in some way representing] the said 'mystery,' along with a silver crown, which will be won by the man who makes the best *chanson royale* according to the refrain on the painted tableau"). The ordinance goes on to state that everyone from Amiens, even if he has composed a *chanson royale,* must pay his share of the dinner, at the discretion of the master; the only exceptions to this rule are invited foreign poets or religious mendicants. This wording suggests that the *chansons royales* made by local members were somehow integrated into the performance of the play (which was perhaps an enactment of the allegorical tableau); on the other hand, "foreign" poets' lyrics (probably not composed upon that year's chosen refrain) "serve" or enhance the festivities and the reputation of the Puy of Amiens in a more general way.

The occasional nature of this verse, which "serves" the visual representation of the painted tableau or the festivities and reputation of the *puy* in general, may explain the name *serventois* frequently applied to lyrics praising the Virgin in French manuscripts pre-dating these Amiens ordinances, which were drawn up in 1471, in "renewal of the ordinances introduced in the past for the maintenance of the feast of the Puy Nostre-Dame founded and established by the rhetoricians of the town of Amiens in the year of grace 1388" (Beauvillé, *Recueil,* pp. 139–40). For some speculations on the *puy* of Arras's dramatic productions, see Edmond Faral, *Les Jongleurs en France au moyen-âge* (Paris, 1910), pp. 141–42. The practical issue of who paid for the dinner seems to loom large in the rules of medieval literary societies (even fictive ones): the London *puy* encouraged poetic composition by accepting a *chanson royale* (set to music) as payment; Chaucer's Canterbury pilgrims agreed that they would all chip in to pay for the dinner of the best storyteller; the Amiens *puy* excused only invited guests from paying for their dinners. It got progressively more difficult to win a free dinner by means of poetic prowess.

16. The rules of the London *puy* are the first to prescribe modesty in the decoration of the hall: no silken or golden draperies or curtains, but only an "honest" beautification of fresh leaves and a "cloth of gold" (such as we see in the *Troilus* frontispiece) upon the raised *puy* or podium, here termed a seat or "siege," from which the singers perform the lyrics: "Endroit de la sale ou la festu du Pui serra serve, est assentu qe desore ne soit drap de or ne de saye pendu, ne la sale cortinee; sauve qe ele soit honestement florie des foillez, enjunchee, apparile des banquers, ausi come il appent a tele feste roiale; sauve qe li siege ou li chantour chaunterount les chauncouns reals, soit covert de un drap de or" (Riley, *Liber custumarum,* p. 226). See also A.-G. Ballin, *Notice historique sur l'Académie des Palinods* (Rouen, 1834), p. 9, on the rules of 1486 for the tribune or podium that the Palinods called the "Puy de la Conception" (for performing verses especially conceived to celebrate the Conception of the Virgin).

17. Peire d'Alvernha, *Liriche,* ed. Alberto Del Monte (Turin, 1955), no. 12, p. 127, verses 85–86.

18. Fisher also counters Riley's view that the London *puy* no longer existed in the fourteenth century (*John Gower,* p. 80): "the Puy was a cultural organization and . . . the period of the Hundred Years' War marks the high point of French influence in England, on language, literature, dress, and manners. There is no reason to suppose that an organization so thoroughly naturalized that by 1299 it could be endowed with income from London real estate, and whose third Prince—indeed the only individual named in the regulations—was evidently an Englishman, Johan de Chesthounte (John Cheshunt), should not have survived into the middle of the century."

19. For an explication of this wordplay, see Auguste Breuil, *La Confrérie de Notre-Dame du Puy d'Amiens* (Amiens, 1854), pp. 56–59.

20. A beautiful facsimile edition of B.N. fr. 145 has been edited by

Georges Durand, *Tableaux et chants royaux de la confrérie du Puy Notre-Dame d'Amiens* (Paris, 1911).

21. Breuil, *La Confrérie,* p. 7: "The frequent translation of the word 'Puy' by 'well' in the documents concerning this society; the well accompanying the great silver image carried in processions; the wells embroidered on church ornaments—give us no difficulty. Picardy, as we know, was the acknowledged home of the *rebus.*"

22. See Salter, "'*Troilus* Frontispiece,'" p. 17 and fig. 1; and Meiss, *French Painting,* figs. 403–5. In the Limbourg illumination that is iconographically closest to the *Troilus* frontispiece, a courtly retinue is emerging from a castle doorway in the left foreground and heading on *down* the road. Although there is a conical mountain topped by a castle in the distant background, there is no sign that the group will change direction, turn left, and climb the mountain.

23. See, for example, the early-fifteenth-century Boucicaut Hours (Paris, Jacquemart André Museum ms. 2, 18v, 20v), where such cone-shaped mountains rise behind the pilgrim St. James and the roasting of St. Lawrence; these, and a number of similar peaks in the exotic landscapes of medieval travel and pilgrimage narratives, are reproduced by Millard Meiss in *French Painting in the Time of Jean de Berry: The Boucicaut Master* (London, 1968), figs. 6, 8, 81, 86, 87.

24. Gertrud Schiller, *Iconography of Christian Art,* trans. Janet Seligman, 2 vols. (Greenwich, Conn., 1971), vol. 1, p. 65; cf. figures.

25. Two such fourteenth-century Nativity images of scalable Mary-mountains appear in American collections: one in the Gallery of the University of Miami at Coral Gables, the other in the Detroit Institute of Arts. For reproductions of these paintings, see Fern Shapley, *Paintings from the Samuel H. Kress Collection: Italy, XIII–XV* (London, 1966), fig. 187; and Walter Heil, *Catalogue of Paintings in the Permanent Collection of the Detroit Institute of Arts,* 2 vols. (Detroit, 1930), vol. 1, fig. 208. My references come from Princeton's Index of Early Christian Art.

26. The thirteenth-century regulations of the London *puy* completely shut out women's participation and justified this as a lesson that men could and should honor women "as much in their absence as in their presence": "nule dame ne autre femme ne doit estre a la graunt [siege] du Pui, par la resoun ke om doit de ceo ensample prendre, e droit aveyement, de honurer, cheir, et loer trestotes dames, totes houres en touz lieus, au taunt en lour absence come en lour presence" (Riley, *Liber custumarum,* p. 225). The Amiens *puy's* fifteenth-century renewal of its regulations shows a certain softening of earlier policy. If wives of former members leave gifts to the *puy* in their wills, the wives are entitled to special funeral services with all the masters and their wives in obligatory atten-

dance. This additional item is dated 18 March 1493 (Beauvillé, *Recueil,* p. 145). Moreover, the great manuscript of paintings and poems, Paris, B.N. fr. 145, was executed by the members of the *puy* of Amiens for a curious female.

27. Francis Lee Utley, "Scene-Division in Chaucer's Troilus and Criseyde," in *Studies in Medieval Literature in Honor of Albert C. Baugh,* ed. MacEdward Leach (Philadelphia, 1961), pp. 109–138; Robert G. Benson, *Medieval Body Language: A Study of the Use of Gesture in Chaucer's Poetry* (Copenhagen, 1980), pp. 82–100; Barry Windeatt, "Gesture in Chaucer," *Medievalia et Humanistica* 9 (1979): 143–61.

28. Anthologized in Derek Brewer, *Chaucer: The Critical Heritage,* 2 vols. (London, 1978), vol. 1, p. 326.

29. Ibid., p. 301.

30. Paul Zumthor, "The Text and the Voice," trans. Marilyn Engelhardt, *New Literary History* 16 (1984): 89.

31. See Walter J. Ong, "The Writer's Audience Is Always a Fiction," *Publications of the Modern Language Association* 90 (1975): 13–17, for an overview of authorial techniques of getting readers to assume roles, to fictionalize themselves.

Index

Accommodation: in *Canterbury Tales,* 48, 50, 115, 156, 162; Chaucer's early fictions of, 154; defined with respect to fiction, 52–53; in *Troilus,* 154–56

Aggression, playful denials of, 58–59. *See also* Castration; Cuckoldry; Jokes, tendentious

Alain de Lille, 194–95 n.19

Allegorization: and euphemism, 88; as sublimation, 28

Ambiguity, 184 n.8

"Anelida and Arcite," 154

Arnold, Matthew, 154

Art, game of, 3–4, 55

Assimilation: defined with respect to fiction, 52–53; through play, 36

Audience, *Canterbury Tales'* fictionalized, 101

Augustine, Saint, 27–28, 182 n.18

Authority: derision of in fabliau, 61, 68, 71, 98–99; effect of Chaucer's on us, 78–79; and foolishness, 160–61; identification with through role-playing, 39, 50–51; playful attacks against, 130–31; and *raptus,* 190–91 n.5; setting up and dethronement of in *Canterbury Tales,* 97, 100–101, 111–12. *See also* Father tongue

Babio, 66–67, 160, 185 n.11

Baird, Joseph, 6, 176 n.3

Bakhtin, Mikhail, 15–16, 21, 127–28, 179 n.20

Ballin, A.-G., 206 n.16

Barthes, Roland, 30, 182 n.20

Bartsch, Karl, 197 n.33

Baudelaire, Charles, 1, 175 n.1

Baum, Paull, 181 n.7, 196 n.31

Beare, W., 196 n.28

Beauvillé, Victor de, 205 n.15

Beer, Jeanette, 193 n.7

Beichner, Paul, 179 n.22

"Bele Aiglentine," versions of, 149–51, 198–200 n.35

Benoît de Sainte-Maure, 134, 137, 142–43

Benson, C. David, 182 n.23

Benson, Larry D.: Chaucer edition by, 175 n.2; on puns and euphemism, 23, 30, 92, 95, 107, 181 n.9

Benson, Robert G., 173, 208 n.27

Bergen, Henry, 203 n.7

Bergson, Henri, 184 n.6

Bernard, Saint, 157

Bigongiari, Dino, 204 n.8

Bloch, R. Howard, 159, 185 n.13

Boas, George, 178 n.8

Boccaccio, Giovanni. See *Decameron*

"Boece," 154

Bolig, Rosemary, 183 n.7

Book of the Duchess, 43, 50, 154

Bracciolini, Poggio, *Facetiae* of, 32, 182 n.22

Breuil, Auguste, 206 n.19, 207 n.21

Brewer, Derek, 180 n.3

Bridget, Saint, 17

Burlesque: Chaucer's uses of, 16, 80, 118, 146; of high literary genres in fabliau, 84–85, 98–99, 188 n.10; through performance, 150

Bynum, Caroline Walker, 181–82 n.12

Byron, George Gordon, Lord, 21

209

Compositor: G & S Typesetters, Inc.
Text: 11/13 Bembo
Display: Bembo
Printer: Braun-Brumfield, Inc.
Binder: Braun-Brumfield, Inc.